Exquisite Mixture

EXQUISITE MIXTURE

The Virtues of Impurity
in Early Modern England

Wolfram Schmidgen

PENN

UNIVERSITY OF PENNSYLVANIA PRESS

PHILADELPHIA

A volume in the Haney Foundation Series, established in 1961 with the generous support of Dr. John Louis Haney.

Published by
University of Pennsylvania Press
Philadelphia, Pennsylvania 19104-4112
www.upenn.edu/pennpress

Printed in the United States of America on acid-free paper
10 9 8 7 6 5 4 3 2 1

Library of Congress Cataloging-in-Publication Data
Schmidgen, Wolfram.
    Exquisite mixture : the virtues of impurity in early modern England / Wolfram Schmidgen.—1st ed.
        p. cm.—(Haney Foundation series)
    Includes bibliographical references and index.
    ISBN 978-0-8122-4442-7 (hardcover : alk. paper)
    1. England—Civilization—17th century.   2. Cultural fusion—England—History—17th century.   3. Cultural pluralism—England—History—17th century.   I. Title.
II. Series: Haney Foundation series.
    DA380.S45 2013
    942.06—dc23
                                                            2012014282

For Beth, with love

Deploy instead of unveiling, add instead of
subtracting, fraternize instead of denouncing,
sort out instead of debunking.
—Bruno Latour, *We Have Never Been Modern*

CONTENTS

Anglo-American readers may not be terribly surprised to hear that Hector St. John de Crèvecoeur answered the question "What is an American?" in *Letters from an American Farmer* (1782) by pointing to the racial and religious "mixtures" made possible by a free country.[1] But most of us would not expect that many early eighteenth-century Englishmen gave the same answer to the question "What is an Englishman?" *Exquisite Mixture* examines that surprising response.

It begins with the observation that early eighteenth-century culture prized the mixture of different kinds: linguistic, literary, religious, racial, and political. The mixture of the Roman, Saxon, Danish, and Norman kinds that composed the English breed and language was as much a sign of English superiority as the blending of the different species of government (monarchy, aristocracy, and democracy) that made the body politic. What made a good poem? If you asked the author of *The Rape of the Lock* (1714), one of the greatest poems of the period, it was the exhilarating mixture of tragedy, comedy, farce, and epic. Across different fields of inquiry and political persuasions, early eighteenth-century Englishmen were increasingly assertive about mixture as the source of their nation's perfections, as the cause of its unity, power, and civility.

My book asks: what were the cultural and historical forces that sponsored such unprecedented awareness among the English that their culture reproduced itself through mixture? How was it possible that mixture, whose products had been distrusted or vilified for centuries, could be considered the engine of English civilization? I argue that seventeenth-century science and politics are largely responsible for the value the English were finding in mixture. The scientific and political revolutions of the seventeenth century meet in the search for a new answer to the classic question of the proper relationship between the many and the one. Because it reflected on the relative powers of subjects and sovereign, this question had roused intense political passions. The

Aristotelian and the much more recent absolutist traditions asserted that one had primacy over many. But that was not acceptable to those natural and political philosophers who worried about absolutism. This group developed a different answer. By appropriating a metaphysical framework that belonged to the Catholic tradition, they promoted mixture to the status of a fully legitimate cause that leveled the relationship between many and one. Equipped with causal powers, mixture could explain how the many generated the one and how the one depended on the active and continuous involvement of the many. In science and in politics, mixture was deployed to topple the primacy of one over many, of whole over parts, and of form over matter. It was hailed as a creative force, capable of producing new poems, superior breeds, and civil societies whose union and power were heightened by multiplicity.

Exquisite Mixture contributes to current research in the social sciences and humanities that reexamines phenomena previous generations of scholars considered contaminated, promiscuous, or impure—phenomena best explained as the temporary transgression of a dominant order. In part because of the accelerating speed of globalization and technological innovation, we are today more likely to consider such phenomena not as transgressing, but as producing order. We have become more aware of the real transformations that can be triggered when political, geographic, aesthetic, ethnic, or species boundaries are crossed. If that awareness has made us realize that concepts such as hybridity, mixture, or multitude could be descriptive of order rather than being a threat to it, my book shows that we are not the first to experience this realization. It can already be found in the joint scientific and political struggles of the seventeenth century to displace ideas of order that privileged strong boundaries, clear forms, and sovereign essences.

The early modern struggle for the legitimation of mixture challenges the basic narrative we have relied on to explain the development of modern societies in Europe. As I show at the end of the book, in that narrative differentiation, not mixture, is the driving force. But that is not the only challenge early modern writers present to us. By making mixture a modernizing force, seventeenth- and eighteenth-century writers also raise questions about the conceptual resources we have mobilized to capture the historical and political difference of the postcolonial world order. Our current attraction to concepts such as hybridity or mixture to describe new modes of identity and agency in a globalizing world has to confront the fact that these concepts also helped early enlightenment thinkers to imagine and promote the modernization of their culture. I will try to sort out the significance of these connected challenges in my conclusion.

*   *   *

This study would not have been possible without the electronic databases that have transformed research in the humanities and social sciences over the past twenty years or so. *Exquisite Mixture* combines a *Begriffsgeschichte* (history of concepts) that is powered by these electronic tools with some of the more traditional procedures of intellectual history. Electronic databases play a key role in early modern studies, where old-fashioned bibliographic enterprises such as Donald Wing's *Short-Title Catalogue of Books Printed in England, Scotland, Ireland, Wales, and British America* (1945–1951) have successfully merged with the digital world of the twenty-first century. My study began by taking advantage of these mergers.

Once I recognized the importance of mixture in early eighteenth-century culture and became curious about the history of this concept, I used electronic databases to draw a semantic map of mixture in seventeenth-century culture. This map involved about thirty authors. It allowed me to see the uses mixture was put to, the contexts and fields in which it occurred, and the oppositions that seemed to structure the debate about mixture in several fields of inquiry (these included, among others, generation/corruption; quantity/quality; perfect/imperfect; natural/artificial; heterogeneous/homogeneous). This was a promising start, but considering that the database I was using made only 25 percent of its texts available for the content searches on which I had relied, my semantic map was fairly rough. Still, this was a precious first step. It opened the semantic field in which mixture signified.

My second step was more traditional: a close study of those texts that occupied the most prominent places on my semantic map (indicated by number of references to the various grammatical forms of mixture and sustained engagement with the issue of mixture: chapters or sections devoted to the topic). This study showed that confusion, conflation, and ambiguity played an important role in the revaluation of mixture and its migrations across different fields of inquiry. I realized that the life of concepts is not always controlled by human actors, that it can be influenced by human actors we consider unimportant, and that it can take surprising turns into seemingly distant fields. I decided to respect these insights. My study brings minor and major intellectuals into conversation, it follows the migrations of mixture across fields of inquiry that we do not consider close neighbors (from geography to embryology, from chemistry to politics), and it describes the problematics that these fields share and that make them hospitable to the revaluation of mixture.

This second step also yielded more practical results. In addition to giving me more detailed knowledge of the debates about mixture, it gave me an additional set of concepts that were closely related to mixture and made prominent appearances in these debates. Of these, the most significant was probably *decompound,* a term that in seventeenth-century England meant pretty much the opposite of what it signifies today. First used by grammarians to designate highly compounded words (typically in treatises on Latin, but also in comments about the composite nature of English), *decompounded* was adopted by chemist Robert Boyle to describe physical realities (highly compounded/highly mixed bodies). From here, *decompound* traveled through the networks of the newly founded Royal Society to a number of other scientists (William Petty, Isaac Newton, Nehemiah Grew) and was eventually redeployed by John Locke. Locke used the materialist connotations the concept had gained under Boyle and others to describe the workings of complex ideas (which he called "mixed modes"). Conducting open-ended and less-open-ended content searches for *decompound* and its variants thus revealed some of the migratory patterns of the language of mixture. *Decompound* also turned out to be a highly symptomatic word: its appearance in fields other than linguistics pointed to thinkers who were clearly aware of the revaluation of mixture.

Meanwhile, the synonymic forms of *decompound* that I stumbled over along the way (*demixed* or *decomposite,* for example) revealed further patterns. Coined in the first half of the seventeenth century, *demixed* made me realize that Boyle had been anticipated in his adoption and use of *decompound* by the Catholic philosopher Thomas White in a work devoted to explicating the natural philosophy of Kenelm Digby (another Catholic, whose works I had already studied in detail because of their prominent use of mixture). This turned out to be a crucial discovery. It opened up the possibility that the revaluation of mixture owed a debt to Catholic thought, a possibility that I was later able to confirm with some of the more traditional means of intellectual history. In these ways and others, my research tried to nurture close relationships between the traditional procedures of intellectual history and my electronic searches in databases.

The migrations of *decompound* serve to illustrate another basic insight that guides this study: the fruitlessness of distinguishing rigorously between the literal and figurative uses of the language of mixture. It is not impossible, for example, that grammarians saw *decompound* and *mixture* as at least partially metaphorical: no literal blending takes place, after all, in the combination of several simpler semantic or grammatical units. Things get more complicated, however, when authors use this vocabulary to talk about the mixed nature of the English language (again, not necessarily a literal mixture) and then go on to compare the linguistic fact of mixture to the mixed nature of English blood (likely a literal meaning for them, though not for us) or conduct arguments about foreign words by describing them as naturalized denizens of English. In such transactions, the literal shifts into the figurative and back without much gear noise. Whenever Boyle uses mixture to talk about chemical processes, he would seem to invoke a literal meaning. But he also uses these literal meanings to devise metaphors that describe other phenomena (the composition of scripture from a variety of sources, for example). Locke often uses the more literal meanings of *decompound* or *mixture* he borrowed from Boyle to think through problems of complex identity, but holds back on contending that the decompounding of ideas in the mind, for example, is driven by a literal mixture of mental atoms.

Mixture's ability to claim and evade conceptual rigor, to be sometimes metaphorical and sometimes not, I would argue, does not indicate the concept's insignificance or weakness. On the contrary: I contend that mixture's varied uses and appearances evidence that this concept had a significant career in seventeenth-century culture. Mixture connected a wide array of thinkers and fields, and its attractions were apparent even to those who did not quite know how to manage its established and emergent, literal and figurative meanings.

Such wide connectivity helps to make a more general point about knowledge in seventeenth-century England. It indicates that the building of analogies between different fields of inquiry was not just a rhetorical maneuver, but a vital strategy in the generation of new knowledge. Just as the *Begriffsgeschichte* in this book is not raised on distinctions between concept and metaphor, it also does not divide substance and rhetoric.[2] In refusing to reduce its organizing term, *Exquisite Mixture* cultivates a repressed dimension of *Begriffsgeschichte* that Ulrich Schneider has recently pointed to when he observed that "the starting point of *Begriffsgeschichte* is the excess of meaning."[3] That excess is part of my story. We should not strive, I believe, for purity of concepts or disregard the generative powers of analogy, metaphor, and ambiguity. If we do so, we are likely to miss the extent, the channels, and the modes of the semantic traffic between different fields of inquiry and between obscure and canonical texts. The intellectual history I offer is for this reason literary. It pays attention to words in a way that only the discipline of close reading practiced in literature departments can cultivate. This book is thus also an experiment about what happens when such close reading collaborates with more distant, digital modes of reading.

As my emphasis on mixture's synonyms and associates has already intimated, I also modify the tendency of *Begriffsgeschichte* to focus on a single concept. Mixture anchors this study, but its revaluation in seventeenth-century England has consequences for a wider conceptual horizon that includes concepts such as multitude, heterogeneity, deformity, and mutation. Once mixture begins to be widely recognized as a legitimate cause and as the irreducible reality of all bodies, these concepts can be viewed with different eyes. Wittingly and unwittingly, religious, scientific, political, and philosophical writers engage in a shared project when they reinterpret mixture's conceptual horizon. My book tries to reconstitute this project by acknowledging that semantic shifts are not isolated events, but typically affect a cluster of related concepts.

The currencies of the word *decompound* and its synonyms in seventeenth-century England are one convenient indicator for an increasing belief in the complexity of bodies and a corresponding need for an expanded lexicon of mixture among the learned. The fate of this word in the later eighteenth century might suggest a decrease in such beliefs and needs. Samuel Johnson observed in 1775 that the verb "to decompound" had come to mean to "resolve into simple parts," noting that "this is a sense that has of late crept irregularly into chymical books."[4] In line with this tendency, the adjective "decompounded" begins to signify in the 1790s a body that is separated into its constituent parts.[5] But whether these shifts add up to a larger semantic history will not concern me here. In the following pages, I focus on the emergence of a conceptual horizon that promoted natural and political bodies whose existence and virtues rested on mixture.

Introduction

England's Mixed Genius

Identities—national, ethnic, cultural—are never simple. They dwell, uneasily, between the competing narrative lines of purity and impurity, homogeneity and heterogeneity, continuity and discontinuity. Over the past thirty years or so, this truth has been brought home to us by a global capitalism that has expanded the mobility of persons and things and deepened the relationships between them. The objects that today we are willing to host in our bodies; the electronic mediation of intimacy, sociability, and political action; the restless circulation of commodities and capital around the globe; the splicing of corporations across multiple nations; and the increasing contact among people from different cultural and ethnic backgrounds—we surely live in a period of weakening boundaries and increasing mobilities.

These very material changes have prompted some thinkers to stress the political value of impurity, heterogeneity, and discontinuity. Homi Bhabha's and Donna Haraway's portrayals of hybridity come to mind, as does Antonio Negri and Michael Hardt's diagnosis of a new, territorially unbounded political force, the multitude.[1] In each of these cases, we are dealing with an attempt to grasp the increasing boundlessness of our world-historical moment as an enabling condition. Yet these attempts have found a striking counterpoint in the different calls from environmentalists, ethnic nationalists, and antiglobalization activists for a return to greater purity, homogeneity, and continuity. On both practical and theoretical levels, then, the weakening boundaries that characterize our historical moment have dramatically increased our awareness of the competing narratives that tell us who we are.

All of this strikes us as fairly new, a sign of our postmodern, postcolonial, and even post-human existence. "The universe of the postmodern," as Perry Anderson put it in 1998, "is not one of delimitation, but intermixture—celebrating the cross-over, the hybrid, the pot-pourri."[2] But are we really the first to celebrate (and fear) the transformative promise of ethnic and cultural mixtures? The first to experience highly visible tensions between boundary-crossing and boundary-drawing visions of regional, national, ethnic, and cultural identity? Behind these questions, I would like to suggest, lurks the deeper truth that our current situation brings home to us. This truth points beyond our own moment to the modes by which cultures in different historical periods respond to weak boundaries and increased mobilities.[3]

I have felt the force of these questions and this truth, curiously enough, in studying early eighteenth-century England, a period that has long been recognized—one way or another—as the cradle of modern nationalism and colonialism, of enlightenment and rationalization, as the moment when the English disciplined the revolutionary impulses of the preceding century and settled down to the business of building a powerful civilization. The early eighteenth century has long been viewed, in other words, as the time when cultural order, national unity, commercial success, and international influence began to align and reinforce each other.

This view of early eighteenth-century England has found significant support in the galvanizing influence that the myth of the Saxon origins of English culture was beginning to exert. The political, religious, linguistic, and racial motifs that coalesced in this period around the peculiar idea of an essentially Anglo-Saxon culture formed one of the crucial foundations for the projection of English superiority in the next two hundred years. Or so the story goes. When I examined the early eighteenth-century print record more closely, this homogeneous vision of English civilization did not seem that dominant. The time when the Anglo-Saxon myth comes into its own as a resonant ideology, I realized, is also the time when a counternarrative asserts itself. According to this narrative, English culture is superior not because of its Saxon foundations, but because of its extensive and irreducible mixtures with various foreign nations. The process of English civilization is fueled by sexual, linguistic, social, and political mixtures. Let me explain this in a little more detail.

Many historians have shown how, in the sixteenth and seventeenth centuries, Englishmen became increasingly invested in their Saxon ancestors. They turned to their German past to reform and legitimize the present. In politics, Saxon origins began to dominate stories about the long roots of English liberty.

Attempting to resist Stuart encroachments on parliamentary privilege, many political writers in seventeenth-century England resorted to the Saxon myth. It was from the forests of Germany and the fierce independence of its inhabitants, these writers argued, that England received its parliamentary institutions. However problematic historically, the story about the Saxon origins of parliament and its continuous existence became a powerful force in the political battles over sovereignty and succession in seventeenth-century England.[4] David Hume's popular *The History of England* (1762) canonized this view and reinforced the complementary story—cherished by radicals in the previous century—of the Norman Yoke by which William I reduced the freedom-loving Anglo-Saxons to the "most abject slavery."[5]

In religion, significant similarities can be seen. Despite the difficulties posed by Saxon paganism and the introduction of Roman doctrines during Saxon times, ecclesiastical writers in the sixteenth century found ways to reclaim Saxon institutions for the reformed Church of England.[6] To strengthen the Protestant turn, writers such as John Bale and John Foxe drew on documents from the Saxon period to support their case for a primitive church that had protected itself from the Roman influences that would triumph under William I. This helped them construe the reformation as a "restoration of primitive purity and . . . continuity with the early church."[7] Foxe saw a linguistic connection as well. He assisted the efforts of Matthew Parker, Archbishop of Canterbury, to recover the Saxon language, whose excellence and purity soon became a common standard against which contemporary English was measured.[8] The call for a return to the linguistic purity of Saxon dominated the seventeenth century and reverberated far into the eighteenth century.[9] When Samuel Johnson published *A Dictionary of the English Language* (1755), he wished to reclaim the "original Teutonick character" of English from "Gallick structure and phraseology."[10]

Along with its political, religious, and linguistic meanings, the Saxon myth developed its most disturbing legacy around the question of race. Tacitus had already claimed "that the peoples of Germany have never been tainted by intermarriage with other peoples, and stand out as a nation peculiar, pure and unique of its kind."[11] English historians such as William Camden and Richard Verstegan picked up on this description in the late sixteenth and early seventeenth centuries. Verstegan was especially vehement in defending the purity of English blood. He rejected the notion that England's subjection to repeated conquests suggested a mixed ancestry. England's Saxon blood was German and remained German, he insisted, because the invading Danes and Normans were originally German themselves. They brought nothing foreign or strange to the English breed.[12]

Camden and Verstegan also began to emphasize the links between the racial, political, and linguistic dimensions of England's Saxon ancestry. In the mid-seventeenth century, John Hare and Francis Whyte joined them. "Our Progenitors that transplanted themselves from Germany hither," Hare wrote, "did not commixe themselves with the ancient inhabitants of the Countrey." Rather, they expelled the natives, "thereby preserving their blood, lawes, and language incorrupted."[13] It was this unmixed racial, political, and linguistic heritage that sourced the strength of the English nation, Hare and Whyte claimed. Not everyone who subscribed to one aspect of the Saxon myth subscribed to all others. But to understand the sway of the myth—which unraveled only in the late nineteenth century—all its strands need to be considered together. Camden, Verstegan, Hare, and Whyte understood the power that lay in connecting the different strands. The broad resonances the myth acquired in this way were instrumental in amplifying and diffusing the idea of an Anglo-Saxon culture.

Even historians who have tried to identify alternative ideologies for the formation of national and cultural identity in early modern England concede that this idea, with its powerful appeal to purity, continuity, and homogeneity, rapidly gained traction in seventeenth-century England.[14] But while the repeated invasions and conquests that England had suffered over hundreds of years added a powerful motive to the divining of Saxon foundations, the rubble left by this violent history also suggested alternative stories about English culture. The Anglo-Saxon myth may establish itself in the seventeenth century as a powerful paradigm, yet in the late seventeenth century a very different narrative begins to assert itself. This narrative makes clear that we are not the first to celebrate cultural and ethnic mixtures, not the first to witness intense contact between homogeneous and heterogeneous, essentializing and anti-essentialist visions of nation, race, and culture. The period between 1670 and 1730 is full of writers and texts that recognize the virtues that could be found in the impurity, heterogeneity, and discontinuity of English civilization.[15]

Take Nathan Bailey and Paul de Rapin-Thoyras. Both dominated their respective fields—lexicography and history—in the first half of the eighteenth century.[16] Both praised the English language for its mixed character. English was "the most Copious and Significant Language in Europe, if not in the World," Bailey argued, because it was a "Mixture of Saxon, Teutonic, Dutch, Danish, Norman and Modern French, imbellish'd with Greek and

Latin."[17] For Bailey as for de Rapin, the history of the English language was discontinuous and unfolded through repeated "Mutation[s]" brought about by successive waves of foreign invasion and conquest.[18] Yet these invasions, conquests, and the mutations they triggered were nothing to be ashamed of. Rather, the extensive mixture of the English with foreigners explained the superiority of the English language. Mutation equaled improvement.

Bailey's and de Rapin's claims raise the question Verstegan had tried to put down. If the refinement of the English tongue happened through the blending with foreign ones, what did that suggest about English blood? Was English blood mixed as well, and was that also a sign of superiority? Bailey nodded at these questions from afar; de Rapin conceded the fact of mixed blood but did not evaluate it.[19] Others were less circumspect. Edward Chamberlayne's popular *Angliae Notitia: or, the Present State of England* (first published 1669) and its successor, Guy Miege's *The New State of England Under Their Majesties K. William and Q. Mary* (first published 1691), popularized the link between linguistic and racial mixture in the numerous editions they enjoyed. After noting that "the English blood at this day is a *mixture* chiefly of *Norman* and *Saxon*, not without a *tincture* of *Danish*, *Romish*, and *British* Blood," Chamberlayne turned to the English language. He believed that English is "at present much refined, exceedingly copious, expressive, and significant," and he attributed such qualities to the "liberty taken by the Natives of borrowing out of all other Languages." "As their blood," the English people's language is "a *mixture* chiefly of the Old *Saxon* . . . and the Old *Norman* . . . the *Britains*, *Romans*, and *Danes* Languages." The mixed state of English blood and language, Chamberlayne suggested in language Miege would borrow, was an index of superiority.[20]

Others were more explicit. The German Herman Moll became the most distinguished English cartographer of the first half of the eighteenth century.[21] In *A System of Geography* (1701), he argued that the intermarriage between different races allowed them to "incorporate themselves into one People." "The great Ingredients of our Inhabitants at this day," Moll explained, are the Saxons, Danes, and Normans. "As we are a mixture of the Northern Nations and of the French or Norman," he noted, "so we seem to retain something of the HUMOUR and TEMPER of both, keeping a mean between the two."[22] Moll connected the traditional Galenic emphasis on virtuous middles with the idea that this temperament was created by the physical mixture of Saxon, Danish, and Norman ingredients.[23] English civility, along with the suppleness of the English language (which Moll praised in the same place), derived from the mixture with foreign nations.

Tory historian Thomas Salmon worked with Moll on the maps for his twenty-six-volume *Modern History: The Present State of All Nations* (1727–1735).[24] Like Moll, Salmon did not flinch from the destructions and discontinuities England had suffered.[25] Yet he was more concerned than Moll about what this might mean for England. At the end of *Historical Collections* (1706), he asked the crucial question: how could England "defend the Honour of her People, who now derive their Original from a Mixture of so many Nations"?[26] His answer was that the repeated incursions of foreign nations brought excellent breeds to the nation. While England's sons "were slain in the Wars, her Strength spent in defending either Empire or her self, she had the greatest Heroes of the neighbouring Nations to supply the Loss. Such a Mixture must be much more Generous and Powerful than Nature left to it self in a Solitary Retirement. That Britain has been so much courted, and so often forc'd by her Foreign Lovers, is a Demonstration of the Excellency of that Prize which so many have fought for."[27] The sexual mixture of the English with foreign conquerors multiplies nature's powers and explains why the English are a superior people. Fittingly, the well-traveled Salmon saw himself as a "Citizen of the World" who looked "upon all men as my Brethren" and criticized claims of essential differences between savage and civilized, commoners and aristocrats.[28]

The most aggressive and visible contender for England's discontinuous national history and its mixed racial heritage in the early eighteenth century was probably Daniel Defoe.[29] He, too, collaborated with Moll, who drew maps for *Robinson Crusoe* (1719) and *A Tour Through the Whole Island of Great Britain* (1724–1726).[30] Defoe's *The True-Born Englishman* (1700) charged that England's inglorious subjection to foreign nations proved that the English race, English manners, and English language derived from elsewhere. The poem became instantly infamous and an "unprecedented best-seller" that still influences public debate today.[31] The following lines show Defoe's sardonic vision of English history:

> By sev'ral Crowds of Wandring Thieves o're-run,
> Often unpeopl'd, and as oft undone.
> While ev'ry Nation that her Pow'rs reduc'd,
> Their Languages and Manners soon Infus'd.
> From whose mixt Relicks our compounded Breed,
> By spurious Generation does succeed;
> Making a Race uncertain and unev'n,
> Deriv'd from all the Nations under Heav'n.[32]

Defoe's satire summarizes historical vicissitudes that repeatedly ruptured whatever there might have been of continuity, identity, purity, legitimacy, and homogeneity. English culture was thoroughly mixed, Defoe argues, and it contained nothing that could nourish a vision of nationhood organized around concepts like these. An island that lay open "to ev'ry Nation" (l. 153), England was so frequently overrun, undone, unpeopled, and infused by others that it could not define itself by pointing to even a shred of sameness. Englishness did not exist. The races, languages, and manners introduced by foreigners were the "mixt Relicks" from which the "compounded Breed" of Englishmen had been generated, and the mixture was too deep to be analyzed and reduced.[33] Nothing was native, pure, or homogeneous in England: just like the Romans, who were actually composed of "*Gauls, Greeks,* and *Lombards*" as well as "Auxiliaries or Slaves of ev'ry Nation" (ll. 177–178) when they conquered England, and just like the Jews who were joined in their escape from Egypt by several nations and tribes, the English were—in the oft-cited phrase of the King James Bible—a mixed multitude.[34] Triggered by mixtures with others, England's repeated mutations made it "modern to the last degree" (l. 404). England was liberated in this way from the tyranny of pedigree and descent, continuity and resemblance, and it was therefore more modern than nations such as Ireland, Wales, or Scotland, which Defoe claimed were relatively "clear from Mixtures of Blood."[35]

These statements appeared in the medium of satire, yet Defoe soon explained what his critics had already surmised: the medium was the message. Satiric distortion was truth.[36] Responding to the public outrage caused by his poem, Defoe expressed surprise over the accusation that he had abused the English nation. He denied that it was a "Satyr upon the English Nation, to tell them, they are Deriv'd from all the Nations under Heaven." It was simply a fact. More than that: the mixed origins of the English were a blessing. "Had we been an unmix'd Nation," Defoe argued, "I am of Opinion it had been to Our Disadvantage." And he explained: "if I were to write a Reverse to the Satyr, I wou'd examine all the Nations of Europe, and prove, That those Nations which are most mix'd, are the best, and have least of Barbarism and Brutality among them."[37] The repeated incursions throughout England's history into its political, racial, and linguistic fabric certainly had destructive effects, but they also enabled England to become the freest and most advanced civilization in Europe. England's humiliatingly extensive history of foreign invasions could be redeemed. Yes, England had passively received "all the Gleanings of the World" (l. 381). But it was better off as a result.[38]

Defoe's aggressiveness is as remarkable as the breadth of his vision of England's mixed character, but these traits are not unrepresentative. They are related to the confidence with which a Bailey, Moll, or Salmon articulated the discontinuities of English history and seized on the improving effects of mixture. Some of these writers may have wished that England had a different history, but they all squarely faced what the Saxonists so implausibly repressed or downplayed: the fact that England had frequently been subject to colonization and had been defined, over and over in its long history, by foreigners. They claimed that a national history marked by impurity, discontinuity, and heterogeneity did not have to be a record of shame. The mixture with the foreign, they argued, was not just a defect. It was also the source of English perfections.

These arguments for the civilizing effects of foreign mixtures are intriguing because they seem to turn on their head our assumptions about early English nationalism and its increasingly virulent Saxonism. Historian Colin Kidd concedes that there were some who disagreed with the Saxon story, but for him Defoe's claim that England is a mongrel nation is pure satire—politically useful but unreflective of broader cultural trends.[39] Yet broader cultural trends were involved in Moll's, Salmon's, and Defoe's assertions about the value of mixture. These writers understood that the issue of mixture's role in England's distant past had direct bearings on the debates over the unity, power, and civility of the English body politic after the Glorious Revolution of 1688. Two related issues, immigration and toleration, helped shape these debates.

*   *   *

Almost as soon as they were saved from popery and absolutism by a Dutch prince's decisive military intervention, the English became concerned about the influence of foreigners on their new king and about the "wave of fortune-seeking Dutchmen, Huguenots, and Jews" that entered England in the 1690s.[40] John Tutchin's *The Foreigners* (1700), which occasioned Defoe's satire, expressed this concern stridently. Defoe responded by arguing that the influx of foreigners into England was not only nothing new, but that it was also the key to English prosperity and power. He thought that "the Multitudes of Foreign Nations who have took Sanctuary here, have been the greatest Addition to the Wealth and Strength of the Nation." The populousness of nations, he believed with many others (including Bailey), caused their prosperity.[41] Foreign words and foreign people were good for England, even after the era of conquests. Instead of priding themselves on their "Antiquity," Defoe recommended that the English should "boast among our Neighbours, that we are a part of themselves, the same Original as they, but better'd by our Climate, and like our Language and Manufactures, deriv'd from them, and improv'd by us to a Perfection greater than they can pretend to."[42] Whatever the English had accomplished that distinguished them was derived from foreign blood, languages, manners, and technologies. Perfectibility thrived on mixture. For these reasons, Defoe drew a conclusion that Salmon resisted.[43] Defoe supported the naturalization of foreigners. He wished for more rather than fewer immigrants.[44]

Such an argument could draw on a powerful and—for an England now joined with Holland—pertinent example. Holland was the great European showcase for the success of an active policy of attracting foreigners. The prosperity of this commercial republic had preoccupied the imagination of English economic writers to a remarkable degree even before William landed on England's southern shore.[45] The causes of Holland's success were diagnosed, for example, in William Temple's influential *Observations upon the United Provinces of the Netherlands* (1673).[46] Temple argued that Holland's liberal policies on immigration and toleration had attracted foreigners in droves. They had produced a density of population that, by occasioning scarcity and high prices, naturally fostered meritocracy, the expansion of economic activity beyond Holland's narrow boundaries, and a rapid transformation of the countryside "forced . . . by the Improvements of Industry in spight of Nature." Beyond these material and social benefits, the same density, combined with a highly diverse population possessed of different "Faces, or Customs, or Ceremonies," improved civility and knowledge. Because Holland's diversity "left nothing strange or new," curiosity, envy, and hatred could find no footing among its inhabitants. The collection of differences by "so vast a Confluence of People" in such a small space rapidly produced unusually broad cultural knowledge. Contacts multiplied fast. This led to a wisdom, Temple claimed, that the inhabitants of other countries gained only in old age, after the gradual acquisition of painfully learned life lessons. "The Multitude of the People" in Holland, he concluded, had unleashed the forces of civilization and commerce in a manner that made Holland unique among European nations.[47]

Temple wished to apply Holland's lessons to England, but the English were not quick to embrace Dutch policies on immigration and toleration after William and Mary were crowned.[48] William supported making immigration easier, but parliament rejected six bills to this purpose between 1688 and 1698. When a comprehensive naturalization bill finally passed in 1709, the argument that it would be good for the nation to attract more foreigners was undermined by the sudden immigration in the same year of thousands of starving Germans.[49] The act was repealed after the Tories took over government in 1710. Similarly, William's initial vision for a broad-based act of toleration that would have included Catholics was curtailed by the bill that passed in 1689 with support from Tories and Whigs.[50] Though an improvement over past practices, the so-called Toleration Act was narrow and did not confer full civil rights on dissenters. It merely exempted them from "penalties contained in the Clarendon code and earlier penal laws."[51]

Still, the act made high-flying churchmen and Tories nervous because it raised the prospect of increased religious mixture.[52] These churchmen and politicians used the connection between toleration and naturalization to sound the alarm about the dangers the nation faced under the new religious settlement. Henry Sacheverell—"Dr. Firebrand" for Defoe—worried in 1702 that the civil power was weakened because the dissenter's occasional conformity with the ceremonies of the Church of England had undercut the "True Worship of God, and the Exercise of His genuine and Unmixt Religion."[53] This was dangerous because, for Sacheverell, a strict union between church and state was the only means of securing a stable body politic. Occasional conformity had allowed dissenters to occupy the ambiguous position of simultaneously conforming and not conforming to the Church of England. The boundary between the established church and "That Confus'd Swarm of Sectarists, that Gather about its Body" was becoming murky. Sacheverell warned that the complete disappearance of this boundary would produce "the same Consequence in the Church, as that of a General Naturalization in the State: It would introduce an Heterogeneous Breed of Foreigners into Both, that in Time would corrupt our Laws, Break down Our Ancient Constitution, and drive the Good Old Natives out of All."[54] In the year that saw passage of the immigration bill, Sacheverell castigated such a "Heterogeneous Mixture of all Persons" as the hopeless "Model of an Universal Liberty, and Coalition." He preferred purity and the "Uniform, and Well-Compacted Body."[55] Mixture could not promote unity.

Sacheverell was not alone in seeing affinities between the naturalization of foreigners and a more expansively conceived toleration. Among the critics, Francis Atterbury and Jonathan Swift saw this as well.[56] For Swift, who had received Temple's patronage in the 1690s, the twinned demands for a general toleration and naturalization were symptomatic of what he called "Republican Politicks." He criticized such a politics in 1710, saying that the men who professed it "take it into their Imagination, that Trade can never flourish unless the Country becomes a common Receptacle for all Nations, Religions, and Languages." Swift was thinking of men such as John Toland, who had been a special target of his animosity in the pages of *The Examiner* and later in his satire on the Calves Head Club, which supposedly met annually to toast the beheading of Charles I.[57]

Toland was one of the more prominent advocates of the benefits of mixture in early eighteenth-century Britain. He exemplifies the more aggressive advocacy of the virtues of impurity that became possible in the aftermath of the Glorious Revolution. Toland had understood Temple's lesson about Holland well.[58] Toleration and naturalization were for him the central ingredients of a flourishing body politic. In 1717, Toland rejected Atterbury's rant against foreigners. Atterbury had compared naturalization to grafting on England's tree "so many exotick Scions, of quite different and of base Species, as entirely to alter the Property of the old honest English Stock."[59] Toland saw virtue in such mixture. The Dutch enjoyed an unusually high degree of civility and union, he had already argued in 1711, because their diverse population was "so intermixt and intermarry'd."[60] Recommending the naturalization of the Jews in England, Toland dismissed all talk that character was determined by blood. One of the most regrettable "vulgar errors" was the "notion of a certain genius, or bent of mind, reigning in a certain Family or Nation." Such talk was nonsense. "The Romans," he pointed out, "were not less esteem'd for being descended from Shepherds and Fugitives (which original they had in common with the Jews) than are the English for being the Progeny of barbarous pyrates, and a repeated mixture of several nations."[61] Like Defoe, Toland saw mixture as the law of history. It was not only senseless, but damaging to resist its imperatives. Calls for racial, religious, or linguistic purity were detrimental to the well-being of the nation. Though Toland's major statements on mixture came after Defoe published *The True-Born Englishman*, at least one critic intuited a similarity of thought and suggested that Toland had penned Defoe's anonymous satire.[62]

When Tories and High Churchmen succeeded in their quest for religious purification by outlawing occasional conformity in 1711, Toland cited William III, who had exhorted parliament in 1688 that a broad-based toleration was vital for the "Strength and Unity" of the nation. For such an expanded toleration Toland now pled, arguing that the admission of dissenters "to all offices in the state" would produce "perfect Unity." Because such an expansion gave a greater diversity of people a stake in the body politic, "a stricter Unity in the nature of things cannot be obtain'd." "To unite therefore and to strengthen, to inrich and to inlarge the Kingdom, to make it more Humane and Christian," Toland demanded that the first step be the repeal of the Act against Occasional Conformity. "Occasional Communion," he explained, is not despicable: it "is the noblest practice in the world . . . as it shows an approbation of each others way at least in part."[63] As one might imagine, Sacheverell abhorred such "Scandalous Fluctuation, and Trimming betwixt the Church, and Dissenters." Toland commended the practice of trimming, in matters of church and in matters of state.[64]

To conservative churchmen, Toland's stance on occasional conformity looked like a calculated strategy to undermine the authority of the Church of England (Toland's deism was well known). This perception was probably justified, but Toland's position was also part of what he described, with another nod toward mixture, as his principle of "promiscuous communication"—the free exchange between men of different origins, ranks, professions, and religions.[65] To him, the fact that "our People of all sorts drive their Traffick and Commerce, set up their Stocks and Companies, and keep their Feasts and Clubs *promiscuously*" (emphasis in original) was the clearest sign imaginable that England was strong and united. The benefits of such social mixture, as the "Plenty, Riches, Power, and Populousness of Holland" showed, were incalculable.[66]

* * *

The revolution of 1688 helped Toland to assert the virtues of impurity. The succession of a Dutch prince (whose name prompted historians to discover civilizing effects in William I's Norman Yoke), the debates about the naturalization of foreigners, and the limited toleration that was passed in 1689 combined to create conditions in which anxieties about religious and ethnic mixtures thrived—and could be met by a more aggressive advocacy of the value of mixture.[67] The heightened public concern over the mingling of ethnic and religious kinds was roused by the implications such mixtures had for the unity, power, and civility of the body politic. Thus, when Bailey, Salmon, or Defoe pointed to the beneficial effects of England's long history of mixture with foreigners, they did not kick up antiquarian dust but intervened in a vital debate about the fate of the English nation.

In the late seventeenth and early eighteenth centuries, that fate seemed increasingly to depend on promiscuous exchanges not only within England, but also between England and the rest of the world. The example of Holland was powerful because it bore on debates over naturalization and toleration, and because these debates were directly linked to a national vision that saw increased international trade as a vital source of English strength and prosperity. Historians have recognized for some time that the late seventeenth century saw the emergence of commerce as a matter of state. Politics was no longer viewed as dealing only with the structures and relationships within a single sovereign community or the military projection of that community beyond its borders. Tory Charles Davenant, for example, clearly recognized that England's power and strength depended on the "more extended Traffick" in goods that had been at the root of Holland's admirable success.[68] As David Armitage has noted, "the political economists of the 1690s agreed that European states, whether republics or monarchies, could no longer afford to choose whether they would be self-sufficient or expansive. . . . They were all now interdependent."[69] The expansive and integrative effects of mixture, the value it found in porous borders and in the combination of different kinds, thus harmonized with the way in which political economists theorized the power and prosperity of the English body politic, which seemed to depend more and more on exchanges with other bodies.

Indeed, even the internal workings of England's body politic were increasingly viewed in these more relational, more interdependent terms. A powerful reason why mixture became a prominent term in the national conversation about the life of the body politic lay in the fact that political power itself was now broadly seen to derive from mixture. After 1688, the view that the English constitution was made up of a mixture of different political kinds went mainstream. In the seventeenth century, the theory of so-called mixed government had resurfaced as a major means of resisting Stuart claims for royal supremacy. But what was once the tool of political opposition turned into a national consensus about the nature of England's constitution in the early eighteenth century. The mixture of the different "species" or "kinds" of government—monarchy, aristocracy, and democracy—united Whigs, Tories, republicans, deists, and high-church Anglicans in the belief that political power did belong to more than one.[70] We can count among the defenders of mixed government John Toland, John Locke, Jonathan Swift, Francis Atterbury, Lord Bolingbroke, Robert Walpole, Joseph Addison, Francis

Hutcheson, Bernard Mandeville, Alexander Pope, and Daniel Defoe. While their visions of political mixture differed in important respects, all of these figures agreed that the blending of political kinds produced a superior body politic and guaranteed English liberty.[71]

Of course, insofar as the Saxons had brought democratic institutions with them, the idea of mixed government could be part of the narrative about the Saxon origins of English liberties. But these democratic institutions merged historically with aristocracy and monarchy and were only one aspect of a more comprehensive political and legal reality. Mixed government, as Swift stressed, was not a "*Gothick* invention."[72] That honor belonged to ancient Greece and Rome. While many writers tried to see 1688 as fresh proof that England's ancient constitution always survived despite significant change, straightforward claims for its continuity and integrity had become less believable. By the end of the seventeenth century, as J. G. A. Pocock has shown, Sir Edward Coke's insistence on immemorial sameness—degeneration constantly balanced by restoration—had lost credibility. Matthew Hale's more dynamic notion of the ancient constitution as "society's response to the vicissitudes of its history" was gaining influence.[73] Hale, too, had made England's racial mixture his point of departure.

Hale began his discussion of the "Original of the Common Law" by pointing out that England's history of repeated conquests and foreign invasions had "mingled" and "incorporated together" so many foreigners that it was impossible to identify national origins. This had consequences for England's constitution. The "various Ingredients and Mixtures of Laws" that various foreigners had introduced made it "an impossible Piece of Chymistry to reduce every *Caput Legis* to its true original." Like the English people, English law was the product of mixtures so transformative that they had erased any trace of an original. Both were best compared to the ship of the Argonauts that "was the same when it returned home, as it was when it went out, tho' in that long Voyage it had successive Amendments, and scarce came back with any of its former Materials." In a culture that had developed through mixture, Hale suggested, identity could not be explained by the persistence of the same substance. "Titius," he noted, "is the same Man he was 40 years since, tho' physicians tell us, That in a Tract of Seven years, the Body has scarce any of the same Material Substance it had before."[74] The English people and constitution could not be defined substantively. Analytic reductions were as pointless as distillations of essences.[75]

At a time when toleration, naturalization, commerce, and mixed government were reordering the body politic or threatened to do so, the recognition that the English nation reproduced itself through mixture was thus remarkably broad. It cut across religious and political lines and often featured interlinked arguments about language, race, religion, and politics. If Hale saw a logical line extending from racial to constitutional mixture, so did Defoe (a vociferous critic of common law) when he claimed that "the Crown was like the People, always mixt."[76] If Atterbury and Swift were worried about the mixtures that a broad toleration and naturalization promised, Temple and Toland celebrated such a promise. And while Whig historian de Rapin wished to hang on to the idea of ancient English liberty persisting since Saxon times (something the Tory Salmon took him to task for), he also argued that parliament had been discontinued under William I, a king he otherwise credited with laying the foundations for England's ascendance to "the Height of Grandeur and Glory we behold it in at present."[77]

De Rapin seemed to acknowledge, indeed, that mixture was something of a key to understanding English culture. In relating an episode of linguistic mixture, he denied that the English learned French or the Normans English, but that the two languages instead "form'd a Third, which was neither one nor the other, but partook of both."[78] In describing William I's title, he suggested that it might have been a "strange mixture" of election, inheritance, conquest, and usurpation.[79] And in characterizing England's "mixt Government"—"the only one of the Sort in the World"—he argued that it was neither monarchy, aristocracy, or democracy, "but a Composition of all the Three."[80] The appeal to purity, continuity, and homogeneity in the construction of English culture was thus as unhelpful to the Tory Salmon as it was for the Whig de Rapin. They both recognized that England was the product of irreducible mixtures.

I have to go one irresistible step further and add that even the production of English culture in this period seems to have fallen under the spell of mixture. Swift provides a helpful starting point. While he criticized the culture industry of his time by mocking the "mixed multitude of Ballad-Writers, Ode-Makers, Translators, Farce-Compounders, Opera-Mongers, Biographers, Pamphleteers, Journalists," Swift realized that mixture was to some extent inescapable and even positive.[81] He warned against the unlimited entry of foreign words, for instance, but praised the refinements that the English language had received by its "mixture with French."[82] Like many writers who credited mixture with at least some benefits, Swift had a healthy respect for the discontinuities and mutations that affected nations. He thought it a "great Error to count upon the Genius of a Nation . . . since there is hardly a Spot of Ground in Europe, where the Inhabitants have not frequently and entirely changed their Temper and Genius." Government, morals, religion, and learning were all changeable from one age to the next. On this issue, Swift agreed with Toland.[83]

Swift's poetic practice relied on mixture as well, and it is here that we can observe mixture's culture-making potential. At first blush, Swift's famous "A Description of a City Shower" (1710) looks like an exercise in satiric disintegration: a violent rainfall jumbles the multifarious ingredients of dense urban living, exposing London's dirt and corruption.[84] Yet the poem is interestingly nuanced about its program of disintegration. While this program seems fulfilled in the gruesome concluding triplet, in which "Sweepings from Butchers Stalls, Dung, Guts, and Blood,/ Drown'd Puppies, stinking Sprats, all drench'd in Mud,/ Dead Cats, and Turnip-Tops, come tumbling down the Flood" (ll. 61–63), earlier effects of the storm are less obviously negative. To be sure, there is the "mingled Stain" (l. 30) of water and dust that mars the poet's coat, but there is also the rain-induced gathering of "various Kinds" of politicians who "commence Acquaintance underneath a Shed" (ll. 39–40), suggesting a political union that seemed hard to come by at the time Swift was writing. The poet's apparent disgust over the mixed multitude of dung, guts, puppies, sprats, and cats should not mislead us. The flood causes chaos and exposes rot, but it also promotes a gathering of different kinds that may be objectionable only in its most extreme and disorderly manifestations.

Such gathering, indeed, is the condition of Swift's poetic practice—the poet's appropriately mingled strain. "A Description of a City Shower" is made from what eighteenth-century observers regarded as different literary kinds. Its opening lines, for example, apply georgic poetry's agricultural lessons to an urban landscape, instructing us how to predict and avoid violent rain. And the scene immediately following the reunited party politicians depicts a young beau in a coach who is so frightened by the water splashing on his roof that Swift is prompted to construct an ingenious simile to the siege of Troy. This simile jumbles together, in mutually qualifying ways, the water-shy socialite and the heroic exertions of the Greeks, the quotidian and the epic (ll. 43–52). In these ways, the poem accepts that the realities of modern life are best captured by the blending of different poetic kinds (and that modern life can change our perception of ancient kinds). "A Description of a City Shower" displays what Margaret Ann Doody has called the "extreme generic self-consciousness" of early eighteenth-century poetry, which led to a concerted "search for new and mixed genres."[85]

We can see related patterns in Alexander Pope, Swift's friend and partner in cultural critique. Pope's crowning satiric achievement, *The Dunciad* (1728), presented a stinging attack on modern culture that condemned its literary products as "Monsters," "Miscellanies," and "Medleys." These products relied on a "Mob of Metaphors" and promoted the unnatural "embrace[s]" of "Tragedy and Comedy," "Farce and Epic." "Prose swell[s] to verse" and "Prologues [decay] into Prefaces."[86] The illegitimacy of modern culture shows in its heterogeneous products, which derive from an increasing willingness to violate and cross literary kinds and species. And yet like Swift, Pope practiced the mixture of forms, genres, and modes, merging tragedy and comedy, farce and epic into the shimmering hybrid of *The Rape of the Lock* (1714). Swift, Pope, and the practices of their poetic colleagues—from Lady Mary Wortley Montagu to James Thomson, from John Gay to Richard Savage—indicate that the literary culture of the first half of the eighteenth century was indebted to mixture in fairly dramatic fashion. It may very well be possible, in fact, to extend this insight to that "quintessentially modern" genre, the novel, which was so often seen as the illegitimate offspring of more established genres boasting purer pedigrees.[87]

These tendencies in literary culture probably also owed something to the changed historical and cultural circumstances after 1688. Lord Shaftesbury's remarks on the popularity of "miscellaneous writing" in this period—a kind of writing that he sees proceeding by patchwork and mixture—point us in this direction. Miscellaneous writing, he claimed, was symptomatic of an age in which "the distinctions of bastardy and legitimacy" had been removed and in which literary merit was judged "without examination of the kind or censure of the form." Though he could be sanguine about the prospects of the arts in a country that had so recently regained its political liberty, Shaftesbury criticized literary culture in terms that resonated politically because they alluded to the continuing struggle in British politics to quell the idea that rulers inherit the crown through continuous and long-established bloodlines.[88] That idea had taken a significant hit in 1688, a circumstance that pleased Shaftesbury, whose republican sympathies led him to collaborate with Toland.[89] Yet despite some irony, Shaftesbury still used what was essentially a Tory complaint—the erosion of essential differences between

legitimate and illegitimate rulers—to criticize the form-defying literary mixtures of his time.

*   *   *

I could go on with this portrait of a period characterized by what I believe is
an extraordinary, highly public awareness that English culture reproduced
itself through mixture. I could mention the false etymology that still linked
satire, the dominant literary mode of the period, with the hybrid satyr, depicted as half-beast, half-man.[90] I could invoke the revival of georgic poetry in
the period, a genre with significant formal and topical investments in mixture
as a cultivating action.[91] I could talk about the advantages Defoe saw in the
sexual mixture of different classes.[92] I could take a hint from Temple, who
linked densely mixed Dutch populations to expanding international trade, or
from Robert Beverley, who wished that English settlers had intermarried more
with native Americans, and investigate the projection of mixture abroad, as a
strategy of empire.[93] Completing this portrait, however, would contribute little
to understanding the deeper cultural and historical forces that legitimized mixture as a cause of unity, power, and civility in the first place. From a more
schematic historical perspective, indeed, the very public elevation of mixture to
such a causal role in early eighteenth-century England remains startling, even
after many of the pertinent features of the period following the Glorious
Revolution have been accounted for.

     For centuries, the causal capacities of mixture were confined to pretty
tight quarters in the world of ideas. Mixture's products seemed threatening or,
at best, strangely alluring—born of secrecy, deformed, seductive, and doomed
to wither prematurely. While theologians, doctors, and scientists believed that
all bodies were made up of a mixture of four basic elements, they successfully
rejected, for much of Western history, the claim that mixture could be a
cause and generate new bodies or new qualities. Mixture could ameliorate or
temper the ingredients it combined or render them more effective, but more
substantive transformations were the stuff of alchemy, magic, or radical ma-
terialism. In the broad daylight of officially sanctioned knowledge, nothing
real or durable could come out of mixing things together. Some higher spiritual agent, such as a soul or a form, had to shape the parts, guide the generation of bodies, and maintain their unity. At least since Plato and Aristotle, the
offspring of mixture was prominently associated with impurity, degeneration,
instability, and formlessness. Order and identity, the learned commentators as-

serted again and again, could not come out of mixture. It came out of actions that resolved the murkiness of mixture, actions of purification, differentiation, specification, and classification. Above and below, male and female, inside and outside, form and matter, one and many: without clear boundaries between spheres like these, order collapses and carnival commences. Having little respect for these borders, mixture could not contribute to the civilizing process.

The broad strokes of this picture sharply expose the different status mixture began to acquire in the later seventeenth century. How did mixture emerge from its confinement and become a fully legitimate cause in its own right? How did it ascend to its widely visible function as a maker of forms, an agent of improvement, a guarantor of liberty and unity? These are the questions I am most curious about. They direct us to the intellectual resources that rendered plausible the challenges mixture delivered to the Anglo-Saxon paradigm in the late seventeenth and early eighteenth centuries. I will try to answer them by showing that mixture began to be redefined in the first half of the seventeenth century. This happened in reaction to powerful religious, scientific, and political movements: Calvinism, which reached the zenith of its influence in the early seventeenth century; Aristotelian philosophy, which dominated the world of learning; and absolutism, which emerged as the theoretical foundation of the unusual claims for royal power made by Charles I. These three movements did not form a united front. Calvinists associated mixture with the fall and corruption; Aristotelians with imperfection and formlessness; absolutists and royalists with a shapeless, egalitarian body politic. Yet they agreed that nothing truly formed, virtuous, or durable could come from a mixture of parts. Out of this agreement tactical alliances were born (Aristotelian and royalist formalism, for example) that helped crystallize the need to revaluate mixture and prompted the recognition that such revaluation could sponsor powerful counteralliances in which scientific, political, and religious truths converged.

I argue that this need and this recognition became palpable in the 1630s and 1640s. The remarkable religious and political conflicts of these decades reopened the question of national unity and promoted quite principled theorizing on the fundamentals of such unity. Because political writers relied on the more tangible realities of the body to argue about political structures, these fundamentals were recognized as applying to natural as well as political bodies. Numerous natural and political philosophers were concerned in this period with reexamining how a unified body comes about and how it maintains unity. To that end, they scrutinized the relationships between many and one, parts and wholes, matter and form. The causal elevation of mixture,

I argue, changed the way these relationships could be theorized and transformed the imagination of natural and political bodies. I make this transformation visible by tracing three related developments that expanded the material and symbolic usefulness of mixture.

The first development (described in Chapter 1) is the scientific revaluation of mixture, which is closely tied to the revival of ancient atomism in seventeenth-century England. Numerous atomists rejected the strictures Aristotle had placed on the causal functions of mixture. They turned mixture into an agent that opened up causal pathways from parts to wholes, matter to form, many to one. The old hierarchies that secured the primacy of whole, form, and one did not apply in atomism. Unity here had to be grasped not as the effect of a dominant form, but as the result of a mixture of parts. Such mixture, in fact, could produce new qualities and new bodies. Chemists were eager to show that higher forms of unity or greater durability could be achieved through a mere mixture of parts—even as the new body that possessed these qualities remained heterogeneous or deformed. The belief that mixture could transform and even generate bodies began to take hold in the first half of the seventeenth century, but it became genuinely influential in the second half when Robert Boyle emerged as a prominent promoter of mixture's experimental and theoretical value. In a culture that was accustomed to using natural bodies to imagine political ones, such a basic reorientation had political consequences.

I show next how, in a second development (described in Chapter 2), the scientific revaluation of mixture assisted the fight against absolutist and royalist norms of political order. One significant form this fight took was the appropriation and radicalization of classical ideas of mixed government, which went through two revivals (in the 1640s and 1680s) before it became the canonical theory of English government in the early eighteenth century. The theorists of mixed sovereignty heard from the scientists about the constitutive role played by parts, matter, and many in natural bodies. This helped them legitimize a body politic that was not unified under one sovereign but through the mixture of the powers possessed by People, Commons, Lords, and King. It allowed them to reject the absolutist and royalist charge that the deformities of mixed political bodies were the sign of a degenerating political order, and it helped them make plausible that political forms originated in the cooperative action of political matter—the people. By authorizing mixture, political and natural philosophers strove to undo the hierarchies and even the boundaries that structured the relationships between matter and form, many and one, parts and whole.

To promote this basic change in the way Englishmen imagined the body, natural and political philosophers had to displace the restrictive Calvinist metaphysics that dominated the early seventeenth century. They did so by drawing on the highly mediatory metaphysics promoted by Catholic counter-reformers and Arminian theologians. This metaphysics granted God's sovereignty as the first cause of all living things but accorded these living things liberty to order their own affairs. It is only through this departure from Calvinist orthodoxy, I show, that mixture could become a fully legitimate cause, in nature and in politics. The departure first manifests itself in the 1620s and 1630s, but it gains broad acceptance in the years following the Restoration, at the very time when the political clock seems to be moving backward.

The third development I describe is the increasing popularity of the argument for scientific and political mixture in the second half of the seventeenth century. In Chapter 4, I show how this increase affected England's foremost enlightenment philosopher, John Locke. Under the pressure of the political crisis that ignited in the late 1670s and renewed the threat of absolutism along with arguments for mixed government, Locke acknowledged that the relationships between many and one, matter and form, parts and whole were simultaneously political and philosophical. To solve the problems posed by these relationships, Locke drew on the new value mixture had acquired. His long-standing anti-Aristotelianism, he realized, was clearly aligned with a politics of liberty that banked on mixture. In *Two Treatises of Government* (1689) and *An Essay Concerning Human Understanding* (1690), Locke developed a connected argument that defined the realization of human liberty in terms of our ability to generate ideas, things, and political relations—including those that justified the colonizing of territories abroad—through mixture. These works offer a prominent expression of the revaluation of mixture I trace throughout this book. Because Locke has been so central to our histories about the development of modern society, his appearance as an advocate of mixture—a concept fundamentally at odds, as we shall see, with our narratives of modernization—is crucial to my diagnosis of a countermodernity that is articulated not only on the radical fringe but also in what we tend to consider elite culture.[94]

Taken together, these three developments show how mixture surfaced across several fields of inquiry in seventeenth-century culture as a process that could overcome the determinations of the past, the hold of pedigree and descent, the superiority of preexisting forms and species. For Englishmen, mixture assumed positive functions in this period because it allowed multiple

actors to cooperate in an open-ended manner to produce and reproduce superior bodies. This revaluation normalized the threatening forces of multiplicity
and heterogeneity, deformity and mutation, and laid the foundations for the
broad recognition of mixture as a source of perfectibility in early eighteenth-
century England. I contend that such normalization is not engineered by a
rationalizing modernity that disciplines the heterogeneous, the multitudinous,
and the deformed, all the while developing more subtle and more comprehensive modes of domination. Instead, this book stresses the revolutionary aspects
of integrating order and disorder, form and deformity, one and many.[95] Mind-
ful of the varied consequences such revolutionary integration fostered, I argue
that the reinterpretation of mixture in science, politics, and philosophy expanded the faith in human liberties and powers in early modern England. That
faith did not rely on distance, detachment, and differentiation—the classic
sources of increased liberty and power in our stories about the emergence of
modern societies and liberal subjects. It relied on blending *with* the world and
of the world's ingredients. In this way, mixture could become a vital agent in
the expansion, integration, and improvement of nature, societies, and peoples.
It could become a cause of order and identity that challenged the Anglo-
Saxon vision of English civilization.

Exquisite Mixture is indebted to historians such as Margaret Jacob, Steven
Shapin, and John Rogers, who have shown that we need to connect political
and scientific developments to understand seventeenth-century culture.[96] But
while these historians tend to view the scientific, religious, and political drift
of the period as narrowing toward a conservative desire for stability and order
that represses the more radical democratic possibilities of the commonwealth,
I show that there are important continuities between the radical political fer-
ment of the 1640s and influential thinkers such as Boyle and Locke who made
their mark after the restoration. Along with others—including many in the
scientific club of the establishment, the Royal Society—Boyle and Locke were
not interested in repressing instability and disorder, but in bringing them into
nature and society. In this way, my book builds on Barbara Shapiro's and
Richard Kroll's insight that seventeenth-century culture was concerned with
finding ways to justify greater complexity, cooperation, and uncertainty.[97] It
argues that the revaluation of mixture across several areas of inquiry in this
period is a crucial and unacknowledged expression of such justification.

The shifting meanings of mixture, I contend, also shape the revival of
the classical idea of mixed government in seventeenth-century England, an
important event in the history of mixture that I will approach through Shap-

iro's and Kroll's insight. Political historians are familiar with the idea that this revival was built on a vision of political order that replaced hierarchy by the equalizing coordination of Commons, Lords, and King.[98] Virtually all of the histories of mixed government, however, do not discuss mixture as a concept that changes much in seventeenth-century England. In fact, they hardly discuss mixture at all. As a result, political historians tend to have a fairly rarefied notion of mixed government, which they treat as a constitutional idea that does not interact with the shifting meanings of mixture in seventeenth-century culture.[99] I hope to change that. The more comprehensive vision of the politics of mixture I offer in this book will situate the revival of mixed government in a wider intellectual context. Tending to the shifting meanings of mixture allows me to show how mixed government—an idea that easily emits the air of political compromise—was radicalized by its advocates in the seventeenth century.

One of the central intellectual puzzles *Exquisite Mixture* tries to solve is how difference and discontinuity could be claimed to *produce* identity and virtue in early modern England. In approaching such unusual productivity, a statement attributed to the ancient naturalist Pliny may be helpful. Pliny compares personal development to the grafting of trees, a process that was often described in terms of mixture in seventeenth-century England. He writes: "A tree of her own nature doth bring forth but one onely fruit, but by grafting it becomes loaden with fruits of diuers kinds: so hee that followeth his owne nature, is alwayes the same; but hee that is guided by Art, is like himselfe."[100] Adding scions of different kinds is here not destructive of some native stock— nor is difference subordinated to a dominant sameness. Rather, Pliny presents identity as the art of cultivating difference and discontinuity, excellence as the result of combining diverse kinds. The same and the different, the one and the many, go hand in hand. It is this paradoxical logic that my book traces in the increasingly public and powerful uses that mixture finds in seventeenth-century science, politics, and philosophy.

CHAPTER I

The Science of Mixture

For centuries, mixture was a basic concept in science. From Aristotle's and Galen's influential writings to the Islamic reception of Greek learning by Avicenna and Averroes, through Duns Scotus, Thomas Aquinas, and Renaissance thinkers such as Julius Scaliger and Giacomo Zabarella, mixture was indispensable if you wanted to explain what a body was and how it behaved.[1] Minerals, plants, animals, and humans were all characterized by different mixtures of four basic elements. These bodies could be understood only if you had a theory of mixture—of its variations, its locations, its balances and imbalances. But despite this broad acceptance of mixture, one critical limitation was upheld for much of the early history of this concept. While it was central to understanding the character and state of bodies, a mixture of the four basic elements—fire, air, water, and earth—could not generate new things. Mixture was sterile. Generation depended on the guidance of a higher agent like a form or a soul. This limitation fell apart in seventeenth-century science, liberating mixture to become a fully legitimate cause capable of generating new bodies and qualities. In the following pages, I seek to explain how this happened.

I have three goals. First, I would like to give an idea of how and why mixture was constrained from becoming a fully legitimate cause. My discussion will begin with Galen and Aristotle, two thinkers who are central to the history of mixture. They will help us understand the philosophical stakes involved in the removal of mixture's limitations, not only in seventeenth-century science but also, as we will eventually see, in late twentieth-century thinkers such as Bruno Latour and Homi Bhabha. My reading of Galen and Aristotle does not aim to historicize their influence on seventeenth-century culture. I take such influence for granted. Instead, I foreground their theoretical value—their ability to help us understand what seventeenth-century thinkers were up against and what they could work with as they tried to promote mixture.

My second goal is to begin to explain how the constraints under which mixture operated were loosened. One part of my explanation will be an ambiguity in the Aristotelian theory of mixture and the productive confusion it fostered among its interpreters. Another part will be the resistance developing in the 1620s to the widespread belief in the irreversible decay of nature, which found significant support in the Calvinist critique of mixture.

Third, I would like to position the revival of classical atomism in seventeenth-century England—and Robert Boyle's atomist chemistry specifically—as a central force in the broadening recognition of mixture's causal legitimacy and its acceptance as the irreducible reality of all bodies.[2] I will repeatedly refer to the political implications of this shift, but the emphasis in this chapter falls primarily on science. A fuller treatment of the connection between the science and the politics of mixture can be found in the next chapter.

*   *   *

One of Galen's basic beliefs—for him already associated with "ancient times"—is that bodies are "a mixture of hot, cold, wet, and dry."[3] These qualities are associated with the elements of fire, air, water, and earth, the four ultimate building blocks of bodies also central to Aristotle's philosophy. For Galen, determining the character or state of a human body—its temperament—means establishing which of the nine existing kinds of mixture are present. Subject to the distribution and balance of blood, phlegm, choler, and melancholia (which physically embody the four qualities), the state of the body and its parts become legible as the mixture of these humors.[4] For Galen, healthful and diseased states are associated with balanced and unbalanced mixtures.[5]

But mixture is not confined to the interior workings of the body. For Galen, the human body is fluid and permeable and exists in complex relationship to dietary and climatic environments that are themselves structured by different kinds of mixture.[6] The world inside and outside the body is made up of various mixtures of the four qualities. Mapping the interactions between the body's overall humoral mixture, the specific mixtures in different body parts, and the mixtures of neighboring bodies is a highly complex undertaking that produces extreme particularity. Even within a single species, Galen points out, "each body possesses some particularity of mixture which

belongs to its own specific nature but differs from any other specific nature."[7]
Such complexity and particularity also applies to the relationship between
disease and cure. "Many drugs which are taken internally," Galen believes,
"do good only at a certain time, in a certain quantity, and in a certain mixture, and are actually harmful if taken at the wrong time, in excess, and unmixed."[8] The consideration of the circumstances, contexts, and interactions
among several bodies always has to inform the analysis. For Galen, *mixture* is
the term that best captures such profound interdependence and particularity.

The centrality of mixture in Galen's theory of the body tempted some
doctors to use the term to describe processes of generation. Such an extension
struck Galen as problematic in an area where "even Aristotle was in some
doubt." He argued that the mixture of elements could not explain generation
because it lacked a "craftsmanlike power" that arranged and ordered the different parts that make up humans or animals.[9] Some more spiritual principle
like a soul or a form was required for the generation of complex bodies.[10]
While he promoted mixture as a basic framework to analyze the body, Galen
wanted to keep mixture out of generation. In this, he followed Aristotle.

In *De Generatione et Corruptione*, the single most commented-upon text
in the mixture debates, Aristotle is careful to establish the difference between
generation and mixture. His argument unfolds as an exercise in distinction.
Aristotle's goal is to draw clear boundaries between generation, growth, alteration, association, and mixture. His occasion is the, in his view, common
argument that "coming-to-be" is caused by "a process of mixing," the simple
association of particles.[11] Promoted by Leucippus and Democritus, this argument presupposes an atomist worldview in which all changes are caused by
the various motions and combinations of atoms. This view is problematic,
Aristotle believes, because it sees all change—including generation—as alteration and thus fails to distinguish between different kinds of change, a
failure he wants to remedy (185). This seemingly modest program receives its
charge from Aristotle's desire to preserve the superior agency of form against
a complete takeover by the physics of elemental mixture.

Aristotle establishes clear distinctions between generation, alteration,
and growth. He points out that, "in alteration and growth, that which grows
or alters persists in its identity, but, in the case of alteration the quality, and
in the case of growth, the magnitude does not remain the same" (213). A shift
in quality and size does not change the identity of the thing. Generation, by
contrast, involves a transformation in kind, for it "takes place when something as a whole changes from 'this' to 'that'" (185). Such substantial change

requires contrariety. In generation, Aristotle suggests, "the agent and patient are contrary to one another, and coming-to-be is a process into the contrary, so that the patient must change into the agent" (231–233). This transformation is precisely what he wishes to exclude mixture from.

Aristotle begins his discussion of mixture by denying it the cosmological primacy it had in philosophers such as Anaxagoras, who had argued that "all things were together and mixed" in the beginning of the world (255).[12] Aristotle believes instead that, logically and historically, separation has to precede mixture. If everything was mixed together in the beginning, he reasons, all things should still partake of each other. But since experiments show that "everything cannot be mixed with everything" (257), mixture cannot be primary. Only certain things, Aristotle believes, can be mixed: "Those agents are capable of admixture which show contrariety, for these can be acted upon by one another; and they mix all the better if small particles of the one ingredient are set side by side with small particles of the other, for then they more easily and more quickly cause change in one another" (261). No genuine mixture takes place, however, when one ingredient dominates too much. A drop of wine flicked into "ten thousand measures of water" simply turns into water (261). The mixture of copper and tin, though it looks genuine, is in fact an imperfect mixture because these two substances are only "slightly 'mixable'." Perfect mixture, by contrast, happens when the resulting substance is "uniform throughout" so that "any part of what is blended should be the same as the whole" (259). Mixture is thus an actual blending, not a loose or partial association of small particles. In Aristotle's view, a heap composed of barley and wheat is not a mixture because it is possible to isolate a part (a grain of wheat or barley) that does not represent the whole (257–259).

By accepting as genuine only those mixtures that are the uniform result of contrary bodies mingling in equal proportion, Aristotle has effectively distinguished mixture from association, alteration, and growth, but he still has to introduce a compelling distinction between mixture and generation. The emphasis on mixture as a close and uniform blending of two ingredients, indeed, raises the question whether such a blending might not be transformative. In addressing it, Aristotle introduces a number of qualifications that leave mixture divided against itself. He describes, for example, the two ingredients in a mixture as "each chang[ing] from its own nature . . . , without, however, becoming the other but something between the two with common properties" (261). Such "in-between-ness" keeps mixture from generating anything. Mixtures produce a kind of middle between their ingredients, but this does not make the ingredients disappear into the mixture. They may be altered, but such alteration is not substantial. In a further attempt at articulating the in-between-ness of mixture, Aristotle suggests that the compound resulting from a mixture is "actually something different but each ingredient [is] still potentially what it was before they were mixed" (257). In other words, Aristotle argues that the ingredients of a successful mixture produce an in-between thing that has some of the properties of both ingredients. This in-between thing is an actual body, but it is not generated because it still contains in latent form the ingredients in their state before mixture. The in-between thing produced by mixture is not a "that" that has been generated from a "this."

Even though the blending of two ingredients, in the perfect mixture Aristotle accepts, can produce a body that is actually different, such a body never escapes its association with the inferior states of potentiality and formlessness. The ontological ambiguity at the heart of mixture—"it is possible for things which combine in a mixture to 'be' in one sense and 'not-be' in another" (257)—maintains the prospect of a return to the state that preceded the act of mixing. While a different body may be produced by a perfect mixture, such a body can never claim a clear identity. Its ingredients glance backward, to their existence before mixture, and can always be reduced to their original state. Such a body is excluded from the noble striving for perfection that Aristotle reserves for all truly generated bodies. His denial of mixture's cosmological primacy matches his assertion of mixture's ontological limits: the state of separation that has to precede mixture is also the ground to which it can always be reduced and never fully depart from (257). Nothing is generated by mixture. The superiority of form, which generates by bringing spiritual action to bear on passive, inchoate matter, is secured.

Aristotle's attempt to keep mixture out of generation and preserve the metaphysics of form was sophisticated. Such sophistication is one of the sources of the extensive (and often confusing) debates about the meaning of *De Generatione et Corruptione*. Another was Aristotle's seeming inconsistency. Confirming Galen's point that he had doubts about formal agency in generation, Aristotle himself suggested a physical origin of form in book four of *Meteorologica*. In this text, he claimed that the mutual interactions between the four qualities hot, cold, moist, and dry cause "simple generation and natural change . . . as well as the corresponding natural destruction: and these processes occur both in plants and in animals and their constituent parts."[13] Not surprisingly, this led some interpreters—most influentially, the twelfth-century philosopher Averroes—to argue that elemental mixture could be generative and thus constitutive of form. Playing Aristotle against Averroes's Leucippus, Thomas Aquinas tried to remove form from such a low pedigree by tying it directly to divine agency. The Thomistic theory of generation confirmed mixture's ontological limits. It rescued, once again, the metaphysics of form and was widely accepted in the fourteenth and fifteenth centuries.[14]

Yet by the seventeenth century the tide seemed to be turning in favor of mixture's generative abilities. In 1618, the German doctor Daniel Sennert regretted that Zabarella—prime representative of Italian Aristotelianism in the sixteenth century—"ever and anon . . . fals back into the common Opinion, and endeavors to reduce the Generation of living things . . . unto the Concourse and simple mixture of the Elements."[15] Sennert tried to refute this opinion with a lucid account of the mixture debates that played a steady drumbeat on the superiority of form. Nonetheless, he also undercut these efforts by giving mixture a prominent place. "The Doctrine of Mixture," he pointed out, "is exceeding necessary rightly to understand the Generation of al Natural Things, and the Foundation wel-neer of al Natural Philosophy."[16] Perhaps not surprisingly, Sennert's call for a clearer distinction between mixture and generation was not widely heeded. The common opinion that related them spread in seventeenth-century England, even among those who professed to defend Aristotle's strict distinction between alteration and generation.[17] The influential Flemish scientist Jan Baptista van Helmont responded by observing that "the reason of mixtures waxeth lean," but the usefulness of a generative mixture had been articulated quite clearly in the 1620s by two Anglican clergymen with shared backgrounds and philosophical interests.[18] George Hakewill and Nathanael Carpenter did so when they began to resist the popular belief that nature was in irreversible decay.[19]

*   *   *

The argument that Hakewill and Carpenter opposed found prominent articulation in Godfrey Goodman's *The Fall of Man* (1616). Goodman's natural theology blamed mixture for the progressive decay of nature after the fall.[20] Invoking motifs and dispositions that permeated Calvin's teachings, Goodman combined the story of the fall with the notion that a mixture of four simple elements characterized all bodies.[21] Man's fall, he contended, had infected all of nature, all the way down to the elemental level. If relative purity and harmony had reigned in paradise, mixture and conflict succeeded man's transgression of God's command. For Goodman, mixture was a dynamic process that corrupted things. Galen's balanced mixtures were no longer achievable. Disease was spreading everywhere.

When God created the world, Goodman explained, He protected the four elements from disarray, but when these elements turned "rebellious" he withdrew that protection. Man's fallen state therefore expressed itself in the "combate . . . of the elements" that daily took place inside our "mixt and compound bodies."[22] In Goodman's view, "the very constitution of man" was over time so affected by the undue agency mixture had gained in the wake of rebellion, so weakened by the absence of "subordination or subiec-tion," that "the vnitie of one person" could barely be sustained.[23] And since such disorder resulted from "mixed and impure" elements, all of nature's bodies were teetering on the brink of disunion.[24]

One symptom of nature's brinkmanship were the "mixt imperfect crea-tures" it produced. That some worms or flies were generated from rotting meat or cheese was for Goodman a sign of postlapsarian degeneration. "If nature were sound and entire," he pointed out, "shee would not busie her selfe, to beget such base and contemptible wormes." The imperfection of these "ephem-era" was obvious because "many of them are bred in an instant, and die in a moment."[25] Goodman extended this argument to "monsters"—those creatures "either defectiue or superabounding in parts, or differing from the ordinarie kinde"—and urged against the inclination to see these births simply as part of the way nature works. For him, "deformities" were not evidence of nature's delight in variety, but of the ungoverned elemental mixture that set in after the fall.[26] "O the abominable filth and uncleannesse of nature!" Goodman squealed.[27]

When Hakewill published his response to Goodman in 1627, he lamented that this "Opinion of the Worlds decay is so generally receiued, not onely among the Vulgar, but of the Learned, both Diuines and others, that the very commonnes of it, makes it currant with many, without any further examina-tion."[28] An effective critique, Hakewill knew, had to present an account of elemental mixture that did not make it the equivalent of unruly rebellion. If Goodman's story made corruption the most powerful force in the universe, Hakewill's featured generation.[29] Both thought they were acting as good Aris-totelians, but both ignored Aristotle's point that mixture could not cause corruption or generation. Though fierce opponents, Goodman and Hakewill thus joined the growing group of thinkers who described mixture as a transfor-mative cause from within the Aristotelian framework.

When Hakewill addressed the idea that the element's "continuall blending and mixing together now for the space of so many thousand yeares, [had]
altered their *inbred vigour* and originall constitution," he invoked an analogy.
He noted that this theory is often supported by a comparison with people
living on islands:

> *Islanders*, and in them specially their maritine parts are thought by
> *Aristotle*, and commonly by experience are found to be most tainted
> in their manners, by reason that lying open to trade, they draw on
> the commerce & intercourse of sundry forraine Nations, who by
> long conversation, debauch them in regard of their *Customes*, their
> *language*, their *habite* and naturall *disposition*. (115)

If Hakewill sounds ready to agree with the analogy, think again. "This allega-
tion," he follows up, "is in truth a bare and naked supposition." There is indeed
continual traffic and interchange between the elements, he continues, but it
does "not therefore follow that their *qualities* should thereby degenerate, or become more impure."[30] Hakewill explores two counterarguments in turn.

He notes, for one, that purity is overrated. "If the *earth* were pure," for
example, "it would be altogether Barren, and fruitlesse" (115). More dramatically, Hakewill suggests that "there is nothing lost but much gained to the
whole, by the losse of [the elements'] purity, nay the restitution and recovery
thereof . . . would vndoubtedly proue the vtter vndoing of the whole, as the
vntainted virginity of either sexe would of the race of the mankinde" (115–
116). We would be foolish to view purity as an ideal: impurity is essential to
the reproduction of the natural order.

This argument leads to a second, more decisive defense of mixture.
Hakewill makes clear that mixture and intercourse do not automatically lead
to decay. They can help the elements to "returne to their former estate and purity" (115). When Goodman invokes the "mixture of seedes" in human generation as an engine of disease, Hakewill responds by arguing that such mixture
often cures diseases.[31] This is possible because elemental life is naturally a life of
"continuall transmutation, or transelementation" by which one element can
turn into another (113), a position soundly within Aristotelian parameters.[32]
Naturalizing the mixture and transformation of elements in this way, Hakewill
insists that mutation does not equal corruption.[33] At one point, he even suggests that "transmutation" might secure "incorruptibility."[34]

Hakewill's ability to reclaim mixture as a positive force rested on his argument that nature was not subject to God's punishment after the fall. Only man was. Goodman's notion of universal decay, he argued, was too broad. Elemental mixture had to be interpreted not only as necessary and natural, as ancient learning already suggested, but as positively transformative. For Hakewill, mixture was not punishment. It was part of the way God had taught nature to preserve and renew itself. This attribution of positive agency to the mixture of elements also allowed Hakewill to oppose Goodman's claim that deformity and monstrosity were caused by elemental discord set off by divine displeasure. Responding to Goodman's complaint that nature's degeneration had made her "the mother and midwife of base and contemptible wormes," Hakewill turned to another popular example of natural deformity. While people of Goodman's persuasion saw mountains as monstrous excrescences that popped up after man's expulsion from smooth and level Eden, Hakewill begged to differ:

> I ever conceived that varietie, and disparitie in that varietie, serving for ornament, use, and delight, might likewise thereby serve to set forth the wisdome, power, and goodnesse of the Creator, no less then his greatest and most glorious workes. . . . Wee have no lesse reason to blesse God for the lesse fruitfull mountaines, then for the fat and fruitfull vallies. It is observed that [people who live in the] mountaines by reason of the clearnesse of the aire, the drynesse of the soile, and more temperate diet thereby occasioned, are for the most part stronger of limbe, healthier of body, quicker of sence, longer of life, stouter of courage, and of wit sharper then the inhabitants of the valley: As they dwell nearer heaven, so commonly have they more generous spirits and sublime thoughts, specially in preserving their libertie, and vindicating themselves from thralldome.[35]

Hakewill gestures toward the political and aesthetic implications of his turn on mixture. He associates phenomena Goodman would have considered excessively various and deformed with sublime feelings and tenacious ideals of liberty. This is not an isolated political moment. Against Goodman's frankly absolutist politics, Hakewill criticized the superiority of the oldest son and the institution of primogeniture, pointed to the often superior abilities of women, and rejected "Custome [and] inbred notions and preconceptions."[36] Goodman, meanwhile, was keen to display the political consequences of

Hakewill's claim that decay is reversible. The idea that "all things may bee improved," Goodman charged, might easily lead to a "mutinee" in which the "country boares . . . rise in sedition." While Hakewill brushed this off by suggesting that the country boars were unlikely to read his book, the accusation that a politics of liberation looms when mixture is a source of improvement was not just an exaggeration that bloomed in the hothouse of Goodman's obsession with a constantly degenerating universe. Despite his curt treatment of country boars, Hakewill endorsed such a politics.[37] We will see in the next chapter that Hakewill's intuition about the political meanings of a philosophy that attaches positive values to mixture, mutation, and deformity was prescient.

Hakewill had found encouragement for such a revaluation in his friend Carpenter's *Geographie Delineated* (1625). Two years before the initial appearance of Hakewill's book, Carpenter had already argued against the thesis of natural decay and offered an even more startling revaluation of mixture.[38] Hakewill's point that we could revise the old argument about islanders once mixture was dissociated from degeneration had been anticipated by Carpenter. The admixture of foreign elements in regions that border the sea, he had argued, should be seen as a motor of civilization. Carpenter began with the observation that "Arts, Civility, and many Inventions" were "propagated by traffic, and commerce with forraine nations: Whence it comes to passe many times that Sea borderers by conference with out-landish people, have gotten that knowledge and experience of things, for which others have with great cost and danger adventured on long and tedious travails" (274). As William Temple would do in the case of Holland some fifty years later, Carpenter argued that sustained exchange and contact with various foreigners did not taint but refine culture, producing a higher state of civility and knowledge.[39]

This argument about the propagation of arts and civility by traffic with foreigners prompted Carpenter to explore the civilizing functions of sexual mixture. It is here that he made a remarkable case for mixture's causal and transformative capacities through materials he culled from Jean Bodin's *Methodus ad facilem Historiarum Cognitionem* (1566), a book that was widely noticed in England.[40] Of particular interest to Carpenter was a chapter in Bodin's *Methodus* that mapped temperamental differences on a global scale. Reviving ancient climate theories by Hippocratus, Aristotle, and Galen, Bodin had divided the world into geographic and climatic zones that explained the temperamental mixtures of different nations. He followed Galen's principle that "the midpoint between the extremes in any kind of object is the same as the point of good proportion and of good mixture," and argued that the climatic and geographic expression of this truth privileged nations such as Greece, Italy, and France.[41] France had not traditionally been part of this elite club, but Bodin suggested that, like the others, it reaped the benefits of the middle position. All of these countries possessed the evenly mixed temper that fostered arts and civility.

This was not to Carpenter's taste. "Monsieur Bodin," he complained, "dreames of a golden mediocrity to magnifie his own Contrey, which hee finds in his middle region" (248). In Bodin and the ancient climate theories he referenced, England belonged to the northern extreme, which bred a beastly and fickle temper that obstructed civility.[42] Carpenter wanted to change this. His first impulse was to charge that Bodin underestimated the productive powers of nature. "Nature," he suggested, "triumphes in nothing more then variety" (249). To present the English as such a triumph, Carpenter did not so much argue against Bodin than undermine him by gleaning ideas and reframing passages he found in *Methodus*.

Carpenter made good on his charge that Bodin underestimated the powers of natural variation in a passage that significantly extended the latter's claims about the effects of mixture. Carpenter theorizes that the sexual "*Mixture*" of different kinds of people produces infinite racial diversity:

> The promiscuous *mixture* of these kindes being vnaequally tempered, must according to their seuerall combinations produce people, as unlike one to the other, as to the former. Hence a reason may be giuen, why the Inhabitants of the *extreame* regions, either *North* or *South* are found to be amongst themselves aswell in *temper*, as in externall *face* & habite more like one to the other: whereas the *middle* partake of more variety. . . . The *French*, *Germans*, and the *English*, admit of all varietie, hauing some *white-haired*, some *black*, some *yellow*, some *tawny*, some *smooth* and some *curled pates*. . . . This infinite diversity in the middle region, we cannot well ascribe to any other reason, then the manifold *intermixtion* and *combination* of both the *extreames*. (278–279)

There is no nation, Carpenter believes with Bodin, that in the course of its history has not undergone some mixture with other nations.[43] It is the middle that has had most of this. But by emphasizing that the "promiscuous mixture" and "manifold intermixtion" of extremes produces an "infinite diversity" in this middle, Carpenter begins to stretch Bodin's framework to a point at which climate and geography no longer pose defining limits for civility. Bodin had indeed argued that the middle was a region of extensive mixture, but not to a point at which such mixture transcended climatic and geographic limits.[44] Carpenter does just that. By redefining the middle as the place where extensive sexual mixtures take place, Carpenter overcomes the geographical and climatic forces that Bodin had continued to rely on in his mappings of civility.[45]

Carpenter's argument for English civility thus unfolds on unusual ground (ground that would also be claimed, as we have seen, in late seventeenth- and early eighteenth-century England): not the purity of descent or pedigree makes a nation powerful, but its impurity, produced by a long history of territorial and bodily incursions. The idea of the nation is not tied to a particular kind of people, and sexual mixture produces no cumulative average, no blending of ingredients that over time congeals into a median identity shared by many. The historically wide and sustained sexual contacts Carpenter emphasizes produce irreducible differences within a single nation, and it is this infinitely various racial makeup that *explains* the superior status of countries such as Germany, France, and England. What exactly this means for Englishness does not seem to worry Carpenter. To him, it seems more important to suggest value in England's history of repeated conquests and foreign invasions. Because England has had a particularly rich history of such conquests and invasions, he implies, it had probably benefited significantly from mixture's civilizing effects.

To explain the argument that extensive sexual mixtures produce infinite diversity, Carpenter adapts a point Bodin made about animal generation. In the following passage, we can begin to grasp the full meaning of Carpenter's claim that the "promiscuous mixture" of different kinds "must according to their severall combinations produce people, as unlike one to the other, as to the former." Carpenter describes the production of a diverse people as follows:

We find by experience, that out of the mixture of diverse *kinds*, diverse *Formes* and *Natures* are ingendred: As of the *Mule, Leopard, Crocuta, Lycisca,* and *Camelopardus*; which being *mixt* Creatures are vnlike their Sires: So may we iudge of the various mixture of diuerse kinds of men. A *Mastiffe* or *Lycisca*, little differs from a *Wolfe*, because he was conceived of a *Wolfe* and a *Dogge*; So that a *Wolfe* is (as *Varro* noteth) nothing els then a *wilde Dogge*. But on the otherside, a *Mule* from an *Asse* and a *Horse*, As a *Camelopardus* from a *Panther* and a *Camell*, differ very much; so that if people very neere in *Nature* be

linckt together, they produce an of-spring very like themselves: But if
two very vnlike in nature; as an *AEthiopian* and a *Scythian* should
match together, they must needs bring forth a birth very vnlike to
themselves. (279–280)

This passage echoes Bodin closely, but Carpenter links the civilized middle
quite explicitly with the extreme mixtures that produce new species such as the
mule and the *camelopardus*.[46] By letting the civilizing mixtures of the middle
find their model in cross-species generations, Carpenter secures his argument
that the sexual mixture between very different people is radically transformative. Against the strictures Aristotle imposed in *De Generatione et Corruptione*,
but with those Aristotelians who ignored them, Carpenter doesn't present mixture as an effect forever tied to the past and barred from the future, but as a
cause that produces the new. This logic applies even when northern white
Scythians and southern black Ethiopians mix: they produce a third kind, not
reducible to either of them. It is these extreme transformations rather than the
mixture of wolf and dog that make possible Carpenter's "infinite diversity": the
generation of individuals as unlike to each other as they are to their parents.
The most highly valued mixtures for Carpenter are those that produce new
kinds, and the proliferation of such kinds is a sign of civilization, knowledge,
and power. By reframing Bodin's statement, Carpenter lets the dream of golden
mediocrity flourish into a more radical vision, the vision of a civilizing process
that transcends climate and geography through the metamorphic mixture of
different species.[47] With this, he made mixture truly generative and broke with
the cyclical model of history that insulated Hakewill's mixture from more
radical possibilities of transformation.

Though dominant, Bodin was probably not Carpenter's only resource.
The idea that mixture was linked to a cultured infinity, for example, could
already be found in early modern agricultural treatises that described the art
of grafting as a means of increasing national prosperity. One important early
seventeenth-century example is Gervase Markham. Widely available in the
first half of the century and beyond, Markham's books on husbandry explained that grafting could produce new species of fruit, make fruits grow at
different times of the year, make a single tree bear various kinds of fruit, or
multiply the varieties of a single species. "The tastes of Apples," Markham
pointed out in 1613, "are infinite, according to there composition and mixture
in grafting."[48] As a kind of mixture, grafting could improve the quality, avail-
ability, and variety of fruits significantly, and Markham presented related argu-

ments in his books about horses.[49] In *Cauelarice; or, The English Horseman* (1607), he offered not only a Galenic analysis of the nine horse temperaments, but also advocated the "mixture" of different "races" of horses to breed performers that excelled at certain tasks.[50] Such "bastard[s]," he thought, were easily superior to plain-bred kinds.[51] Markham's program of breeding, in fact, is at least implicitly directed against the destiny of climate and geography: it includes the mixture of English with African and Greek horses, two countries whose claims to superior climates Markham disputes and concedes at the same time.[52] As in Carpenter, the generative potency of mixture produces different temperaments that escape the predicaments of English weather.

European ideas about Africa provide a second important background to Carpenter's argument. By identifying species mixture as the cause of species variety, Carpenter not only picks up observations by Bodin, but alludes to comments about African fecundity made by Giambattista della Porta in the mid-sixteenth century that had been popularized by Aristotle and were later echoed by Francis Bacon.[53] Della Porta had argued that Aristotle already believed that "Africk alwayes brings forth some new thing," but then treated this observation as a general truth.[54] He explained that Africa sports an extraordinarily rich variety of species because of its waterholes. Few and far between in such a dry and hot area, rivers—like islands with extensive trading ties—become common gathering places for an astonishingly broad range of creatures. Their socializing around such water fountains, della Porta explained, led to frequent sexual encounters that crossed species lines, producing, among others, the *camelopardus* Carpenter mentions, a mixture between camel and panther that we have been taught to call giraffe (or *giraffa camelopardalis*, to use the proper scientific name). Della Porta insisted that we should not "let the opinions of some Philosophers stay us, which hold that of two kinds divers in nature, a third cannot be made, unlike to either of the parents."[55] A third that did not echo its origins was possible. Carpenter's liberation of England from its northern destiny was indebted to European theorizing about African fecundity.

*   *   *

Carpenter's use of cross-species breeding in an argument about national superiority anticipates those who contended for racial mixture as a civilizing force in the late seventeenth and early eighteenth centuries. Though he offers a more radical argument than Goodman and Hakewill, Carpenter agrees with their basic point that mixture was a transformative force. This view was soon brought to bear on sexual generation in a far more detailed way. Kenelm Digby, one of the most important scientific figures in the first half of the seventeenth century, had studied Hakewill's debate with Goodman closely.[56] In 1644, he published a theory of embryonic development in which mixture and mutation were central. Digby was the first to explain embryonic development by an epigenesis that seemed to do without a guiding force distinct from the dynamics of the actual process of generation.[57] He placed mixture and mutation at the heart of the mysterious creation of human life.

To break with the Aristotelian model of embryonic development (in which male form prompted and specified inchoate female matter), Digby adopted what some historians of science have seen as a "strange mélange" of Aristotelianism and atomism.[58] Digby argued what Zabarella had suggested and what many in seventeenth-century England came to believe: that Aristotle embraced mixture as a generative cause. Digby based this argument on his belief that Aristotle was an atomist. Aristotle's "Books of *Generation and Corruption*," he explained, "expresly teach, that *Mixtion* (which he delivers to be the generation or making of a mixt body) is done *per minima*, that is, in our language and in one word, by Atomes."[59] What are the implications of attributing generative functions to the mixture of small parts? Digby rejected the preformationist view that the seed "carr[ies] with it in little the complete nature" of the future offspring (275). He was sweepingly skeptical of all accounts of generation that featured singular agency. "One agent," he argued, simply cannot be responsible for all the "diversity of work" that goes into a living thing (268). Experience could not confirm such "univocal generation," as contemporaries called it. If univocal generation was the norm, Digby asked, "how could vermine breed out of living bodies or out of corruption? How could Rats come to fill ships; into which never any were brought? How could Frogs be ingendred in the air? Eels, of dewy turfs, or of mud? Toads, of Ducks? Fishs of Herns? And the like. To the same purpose, when one *species* or kind of Animal is changed into another; as when a Caterpillar or a Silkworm becomes a Flie, 'tis manifest, there can be no such precedent collection of parts" in the seed (268). These transgenerations, as I would like to call them, demonstrated that equivocal generation was at least as common as univocal generation, a point Digby underscored with the story of a stick that became an insect (274).

Drawn from various sources and traditions, Digby's transgenerations would have made Goodman quiver with revulsion. They may make us laugh, but such laughter is full of knowledge. For it was precisely Digby's acceptance of transgeneration that allowed him to develop his theory of epigenesis. Because they illustrated the way of nature, cases of spontaneous generation and transmuted species convinced Digby that generation was a complex process whose actors one might not even identify as male or female. Digby explained such complexity through the language of mixture.[60]

To understand the formation of new life correctly, he began, we have to "take the pains and afford the time that is necessary . . . to note diligently all the circumstances in every change of it. In every one of which the thing that was becoms absolutely a new thing; and is endew'd with new properties and qualities" (272). A "this" becomes a "that" at every turn of the development of the embryo. Instead of a single agent that guides the business of generation, Digby charged a lengthy transformative process and constantly shifting circumstances with the production of a living being. Because the development of a living thing did not depend on the guidance of some superior force or preexisting pattern, Digby argued that resemblance played no role in generation. Generation began with a "homogenial compounded substance," but the development of the living thing out of this substance was tied to mutation and increasing heterogeneity. Once "outward Agents" began to work on this "homogenial" substance, it changed "into another substance, quite different from the first, and . . . less homogenal then the first was. And other circumstances and agents change this second into a third; that third into a fourth; and so onwards, by successive mutations (that still make every new thing become less homogeneal then the former was, according to the nature of heat mingling more and more different bodies together) till that substance be produced, which we consider in the period of all these mutations" (272–273). The agents and circumstances of generation are multiple. They include but cannot be reduced or attributed to sexual differences, and they all contribute to an "orderly succession of mutations" (272) that unfold "by much mixstion and consequent alteration" (280).[61] Digby gave to mixture and mutation what Aristotelians, preformationists, and (later in the century, thanks to Antoni van Leeuwenhoek's probing microscope) animalculists wished to tie, in one way or another, to the formative agency of the male seed.

In this regard, Digby went further than his acquaintance William Harvey, who worked on problems of generation around the same time that Digby did.[62] Despite the fact that Harvey rejected preformation and dethroned the male as the principal agent of generation, he favored a model of generation in which immaterial principles are the ultimate cause of conception.[63] This modified

Aristotle's argument quite substantially, but it also perpetuated the hierarchy of form and matter in a manner that was unacceptable to Digby, who had turned Aristotle into an atomist.

Let me describe in more concentrated theoretical form where Digby takes us in this period's theorizing about mixture and generation. Digby extends Hakewill's dissociation of mutation from decline by contending that the development of living things depends on mutations that constantly eclipse their origin. For Digby, the changes wrought by mixture in the generation of bodies are so comprehensive that the body after mutation is substantively different from the body before mutation. A series of such mutations makes it difficult to establish causal connections. Even establishing the causes behind an initial mutation is a daunting task, and every subsequent mutation compounds the difficulty. Male agency loses its trace in such mutations. It can no longer serve as a form-giving origin.[64] Taking the evidence about transgeneration seriously, Digby makes circumstantial, repeated mixtures the cause of form and abandons the controls of species and sexual difference. Generation is a dynamic, material process that forms and specifies by itself, both within and across species.

Because he lets mixture produce mutations that lead to substantive difference, Digby's position on development is close to Carpenter's. Digby's account is more detailed than Carpenter's, but both present mixture as a cause whose effects can escape the bands of resemblance between past and present. They not only reject the idea that earlier states of development have a clear relationship to succeeding ones, but embrace the theory that growth and development depend on multiple mixtures and the increased heterogeneity resulting from them. Digby makes an ontogenic truth of Carpenter's phylogenic claim that increased heterogeneity signifies a more developed state. Both inhabit the logic governing the statement by Pliny I quoted in the introduction: "A tree of her own nature doth bring forth but one onely fruit, but by grafting it becomes loaden with fruits of diuers kinds: so hee that followeth his owne nature, is alwayes the same; but hee that is guided by Art, is like himselfe."[65] Difference and discontinuity are laws of development.

Hakewill, Carpenter, and Digby thus found striking ways to give mixture positive agency. Shifting the game from within Aristotelian knowledge, they began to free mixture from the impotency, imperfection, and impurity that had characterized it in the scholastic and Calvinist traditions. Carpenter and Digby presented especially forceful arguments for the generative capacity of mixture. In the following section, I pursue this revaluation of mixture into the second half of the seventeenth century. I turn to an early admirer and mentee of Digby's who became the most important theoretician of mixture in this later period: the chemist Robert Boyle.[66]

*   *   *

To understand the value Boyle found in mixture as a cause and basic reality, it is helpful to describe a brand of seventeenth-century chemistry that was driven by a different emphasis. Goodman's association of mixture with degeneration was amplified by a vocal group of medical reformers who aligned themselves with the teachings of Paracelsus and van Helmont. An important aspect of the challenge this group issued to the Galenic medical establishment in the mid-seventeenth century had to do with the production of more effective, chemically produced medicines.[67] Such an agenda was unacceptable to the conservative Goodman, who had criticized the Paracelsians for their belief that a "vassal and slave" of nature such as "the Chemicall Arte" could somehow correct nature's dejection, but Goodman shared with these reformers a Christian cosmology that grasped mixture as divine punishment for human transgression.[68]

Followers of Paracelsus and van Helmont championed chemistry as a "Separatory art" that could restore some degree of prelapsarian purity by extracting simple, spiritualized essences from bodies.[69] These spagyric chemists, as they were called, believed that medicines could be most effective when they were made from bodies that had been freed from "those scurvy raggs wherein they were wrapt up by a due separation from the impurities and corruptible and filthy mixture of superficiall and externall Elements [so] that that pure and Christiline matter may be administred to our bodies."[70] The effectiveness of medicines hinged on such purification, which resonated with utopian potential. Van Helmont even linked the call for purity in remedies to a program of epistemological purification through divine inspiration.[71]

While Boyle believed in the potential of such chemical medicines, his chemistry does not treat separation and purification as privileged paths.[72] His most famous work, *The Sceptical Chymist; or, Chymico-Physical Doubts & Paradoxes Touching the Spagyrist's Principles* (1661), reveals him as a critic of the idea that chemistry is a "separatory art." In this book (which contains his most extended engagement with the mixture debates) and in others, Boyle expresses his belief that a chemistry preoccupied with reducing bodies to some simpler or purer state fails to realize its scientific promise. Rather than making separation and purification central, Boyle elevates the ontological and experimental value of mixture and promotes its use in other fields of inquiry. Although his atomism hinges on a massive act of theoretical reduction—all natural phenomena, Boyle believes, can be explained by matter and motion—such reduction opens a level playing field and thus gives mixture sway. Once every action, quality, and body is reduced to the interactions of variously shaped atoms, the potential for transformative relationships between different bodies radically increases. Boyle's reduction produces a "cosmic egalitarianism," as J. E. McGuire has put it.[73] It brings the world closer together, promoting boundless contact and continuous transformation.

I emphasize this dialectic unity of reduction and expansion in Boyle's atomism in part because a program of reduction has recently been claimed to be central to Boyle's scientific endeavor. William Newman has argued that "the backbone of Boyle's mechanical philosophy" is tied to the demonstration that relatively stable atomic clusters can persist unchanged through various chemical processes.[74] Such demonstration, Newman contends, was influenced by experiments Daniel Sennert conducted in the early seventeenth century. In these experiments, Sennert was not only able to show that perfect mixtures (in this case, of gold and silver) were quite easily reduced to their original ingredients, but also that silver itself could be reduced to its atomic particles and reconstituted from them. Such reduction and reintegration demonstrated the persistence of atomic clusters through dramatic chemical transformations. Sennert's experiments, Newman argues, had a significant impact on Boyle and led him to place reduction and reintegration at "the core of his experimental activity in its interaction with theory."[75]

To associate Boyle's theory and practice so prominently with Sennertian reduction and reintegration, however, misplaces the emphasis. Boyle certainly conducted reduction and reintegration experiments. But while these experiments were crucial in proving the plausibility of his atomist philosophy, their limited agenda (which essentially evolves around the reproduction of the same) rendered them not very useful. Boyle was interested in reduction—but he was absorbed by mixture's ability to generate new qualities and bodies.[76] This ability was significant not only for Boyle's scientific theory but also for the political consequences of this theory, a subject I address in some detail at the end of the next chapter.

Boyle's interest in mixture is clearly on display in *The Sceptical Chymist*. Bathing spagyric chemistry in gently corrosive skepticism, Boyle's text takes the form of an extended conversation between friends. It is, however, not

Carneades—the character who usually speaks for Boyle—who relies on Sennert's reduction experiment in the long section this book devotes to the theory of mixture. It is the spagyrist Eleutherius, Carneades's interlocutor.[77] Their talk about mixture is prompted by Carneades's suggestion that the spagyrist's reliance on fire as the ultimate tool for the separation of bodies into simpler and purer elements is problematic. Carneades devotes over eighty pages to a careful examination of the spagyric means for achieving simplicity and purity. His discourse is varied, but he turns repeatedly to a fact that spagyrists ignore, "the Power of the Fire to produce new Concretes" (K4v). "The Fire," Carneades explains, "may sometimes as well alter Bodies as divide them, and by it we may obtain from a Mixt Body what was not Pre-existent in it" (K4r).

This argument stirs Eleutherius. It questions not only the status of fire as a privileged solvent, but, more broadly, the spagyrist principle that all bodies are made up of, and reducible to, mercury, sulphur, and salt. Getting something out of a body that was not in it, as Carneades suggests, threatens this principle. To Eleutherius, Carneades's suggestion seems at odds, in particular, with the "true Theory of Mistion," a theory that he thinks finds much support in the writings of Sennert (K4v–K5r). This theory adopts the position Aristotle criticized in *De Generatione*. If Aristotle insisted on uniformity, so that even the smallest part of a mixture is the same as the whole, the spagyrists assume "but a *Juxta*-position of separable Corpuscles, retaining each its own Nature" (K6v). Their paradigm for all mixtures is the "heap of severall sorts of Corn" that Aristotle criticized as imperfect mixture (K7r). Even Aristotle's suggestion of ontological ambiguity for the ingredients of a genuine mixture is already one step too far down the road of transformation. For the spagyrists, there is no distinction between perfect and imperfect mixture, and the ultimate ingredients that make up the mixture always retain their identity, even when the mixture acquires new qualities.

Eleutherius then turns to "Chymical Experiments" to show the truth of this theory of mixture (K8v). He alludes to Sennert's reduction experiment in the guise of an operation that refiners employ to purify gold:

> In that Operation . . . , although three parts of Silver be so exquisitely mingl'd by Fusion with a fourth Part of Gold . . . that the resulting Mass acquires severall new Qualities, by virtue of the Composition, and that there is scarce any sensible part of it that is not Compos'd of both the metals; Yet if You cast this mixture into

Aqua Fortis, the Silver will be dissolv'd in the *Menstruum*, and the Gold like a dark or black Powder will fall to the Bottom of it, and either Body may be again reduc'd into such a Metal as it was before, which shews: that it retain'd its Nature, notwithstanding its being mixt *per Minima* with the other. (K8v–L1r)

Despite the fact that the smallest parts of the silver and the gold are blended so closely that new qualities emerge, they come apart again, completely reduced to their state before mixture. Eleutherius adds a quick comparison to show us how to interpret this experiment. "We likewise see," he continues, "that though one part of pure Silver be mingled with eight or ten Parts, or more of Lead, yet the Fire will upon the Cuppel easily and perfectly separate them again" (L1r). *Aqua fortis* and fire perform the same function, revealing that mixture is always juxtaposition and therefore not genuinely transformative. Underneath qualitative change the same stuff persists.

Carneades's response is cautious. He concedes that "the Ancient Philosophers that Preceded Aristotle, and the Chymists who have since receiv'd the same Opinion" speak more sensibly about mixture than Aristotle (L2r). He submits, however, that his opinion "about the Nature of Mistion" differs "not only from the Aristotelians, but from the old Philosophers and the Chymists" (L3r). Carneades grants that "in some Mistions of certain permanent Bodies this Recovery of the same Ingredients may be made, yet I am not convinc'd that it will hold in all or even in most" (L3v). Gold and silver clearly retain their nature even under close mixture, but this case does not have paradigmatic import. Depicting mixture at the atomic level, as a meeting of clusters of corpuscles, Carneades invites us to consider other possibilities. Imagine that there are

Clusters wherein the Particles stick not so close together, but that they meet with Corpuscles of another Denomination, which are dispos'd to be more closely United with some of them, then they were among themselves. And in such case, two thus combining Corpuscles losing the Shape, or Size, or Motion, or other Accident, upon whose Account they were endow'd with such a Determinate Quality or Nature, each of them really ceases to be a Corpuscle of the same Denomination it was before; and from the Coalition of these there may emerge a new Body, as really one, as either of the Corpuscles was before they were mingl'd, or, if you please, Confounded:

Since this Concretion is really endow'd with its own Distinct qualities, and can no more by the Fire, or any other known way of *Analysis*,
be divided again into the Corpuscles that at first concurr'd to make
it. (L5r–L5v)

Carneades emphasizes the transformative ability of mixture that played
such an important role in Carpenter and Digby. Boyle's language is a little
challenging, but I think he wants to tell this story: corpuscular cluster A
meets cluster B. The relatively loose association of particles or corpuscles
that marks A attracts B. B is able to create a stronger bond with some of A's
particles than obtains among its own. This meeting does not result in a
complete union—Boyle is careful to note that only some of the corpuscles of
A create a strong bond with B—and the resulting body is therefore heterogeneous. Yet the result is fully transformative for both clusters: a new, third
kind of body is created, with new qualities and a coherence beyond the human art of separation. This mixture defies the assumptions of both Aristotelians and spagyrists because it is not uniform and yet generates a new
body that, despite its heterogeneity, resists all attempts at separation or
reduction.

Boyle supports this description of generative corpuscular tangling with
an experiment: "If you dissolve *Minium*, which is but Lead Powder'd by the
Fire, in good Spirit of Vinager, and Crystalize the Solution, you shall not only
have a Saccharine Salt exceedingly differing from both its Ingredients; but the
Union of some Parts of the *Menstruum* with some of those of the Metal is so
strict, that the Spirit of Vinager seems to be, as such, destroy'd" (L6r).[78] The
mixture of the vinegar with the lead is partial, the vinegar is unrecoverable
(Boyle's emphasis hints that the lead might not be), and the body that results
is "exceedingly" different from both ingredients, a fact Boyle dramatizes when
he notes that the sourness of the vinegar has been completely replaced by "an
admirable Sweetness" (L6r). The mixture of lead and vinegar yields a new
body with completely different qualities that cannot be reduced to its original
ingredients.

In *The Sceptical Chymist*, then, Boyle associates the reduction of bodies
with the spagyrist need to demonstrate underlying sameness despite qualitative change. While he grants that such underlying sameness may occasionally
be demonstrated, Boyle emphasizes theories and experiments that show how
mixture generates new bodies that cannot be reduced to their original ingredients. Later in the same text, Boyle's gentle skepticism regarding the spagyrist

quest for reduction hardens into the assertion that we need to move past the distinction between mixed and simple bodies. Such a distinction, Boyle now contends, ought to be replaced by the recognition that all bodies possess different densities and levels of mixture.

Boyle invites us to recognize the ubiquity in nature not only of mixed bodies, but of complexly mixed bodies. He refers to these complex bodies as "decompounds," a term that, he notes, he borrows from grammarians to designate substances made up of more than one body.[79] To illustrate this point, Boyle has Carneades draw on the figure of digestion. We should remember, he recommends, "that in the Bowells of the Earth Nature may, as we see she sometimes does, make strange Mixtures; That Animals are nourish'd with other Animals and Plants; And, that these themselves have almost all of them their Nutriment and Growth, *either* from a certain Nitrous Juice Harbour'd in the Pores of the Earth, or from the Excrements of Animalls, *or* from the putrify'd Bodies, either of living Creatures or Vegetables, *or* from other Substances of a Compounded Nature."[80] Digestion, which Boyle sees as a chemical process, illustrates how routinely nature produces decompounded bodies by the direct incorporation of bodies into one another. Nature herself is a relentless mixer. The assumption by Aristotelians and spagyrists that "all Mixtures must be of Elementary Bodies" has blinded natural philosophers to the actual complexity of bodies, and Carneades urges that there are "a greater Number of De-compound Bodies then men take Notice of."[81]

Boyle had been anticipated in his emphasis on decompounds by Thomas White, a close associate of Digby's whose work I will discuss in the next chapter. White explained Digby's ideas on generation in 1647 by describing how "many mix'd bodies are united into one *more-compounded* body," or, as he also called them, "*demix'd* bodies."[82] Characteristically, Boyle takes this point one detailed step further by emphasizing the different orders of bodies that can combine into one decompounded body. "Some Bodies," Carneades points out, "are made up of Mixt Bodies, not all of the same Order, but of several; as (for Instance) a Concrete may consist of Ingredients, whereof the one may have been a primary, the other a Secondary Mixt Body . . . or perhaps without any Ingredient of this latter sort, it may be compos'd of Mixt Bodies, some of them of the first, and some of the third Kind."[83] In Boyle's vision, first-, second-, and third-order mixed bodies can combine freely and increase the variety and complexity of decompounds to such an extent that any pursuit of simplicity and purity becomes quixotic. Heterogeneity and multiplicity are normal. Nature does not need elemental simplicity because "she may produce the Bodies accounted mixt out of one another by Variously altering and contriving their minute parts."[84] The various combinations of compounds and decompounds, Boyle suggested, "afford a way whereby Nature varies Matter, which we may call *Mixture*."[85] As a result, establishing the identity of a body hinges not on reducing it to its form or essence, but on grasping it as "one *collective Thing*."[86]

Boyle matched these theoretical considerations with a program of experimentation that privileged mixture over separation. The spagyrists, Boyle argued toward the end of *The Sceptical Chymist*, deserved to be "reprehended . . . for their over great Diligence in purifying some of the things they obtain by Fire from mixt Bodies." "Though such compleatly purifyed Ingredients of Bodies might perhaps be more satisfactory to our Understanding," he went on, "others are often more useful to our Lives, the efficacy of such Chymical Productions depending most upon what they retain of the Bodies whence they are separated, or gain by the new associations of the Dissipated among themselves."[87] Arguing against purification as an operation too heavily indebted to our desire for mental clarity, Boyle contended for the practical superiority of the mixed and the impure. The remnants that continued to cling to chemically separated substances and the new associations that sprung up among the dissipated parts of a body often offered greater benefits to our lives than its reduced and purified constituents. Because no ultimate or even approximate simplicity could be reached, Boyle advocated the direct combination of complex bodies. "This way of combining Bodies not Simple or Elementary," he argued, "will be acknowledged capable of being made much more fertil in the production of various Qualities and *Phaenomena* of Nature."[88]

Boyle demonstrated such fertility in the experiments he described in *The Origine of Forms and Qualities* (1666), a book in which he expresses some frustration with reintegration experiments, but waxes whenever he can report on the creation of new bodies through mixture. In a section devoted to experiments, Boyle hopes that he can clarify the "ill understood doctrine" of mixture.[89] Attempting to create vitriol in the laboratory, Boyle shows that merely "by the associating and juxtaposition of . . . two Ingredients" he succeeded. Once they are juxtaposed, "Metalline and Saline Corpuscles" "compose divers Corpuscles of a mix'd or compounded Nature, from the Convention of many whereof, there resulted a new Body."[90] This "factitious" vitriol possessed "the same Qualities and Properties" as natural vitriol (219). Boyle makes much of this experiment not only because bare juxtaposition and association are usually considered incapable of generating a new body, but also because this new body—nothing but an "exquisite mixture," as he points out (220)—is not distinguishable from its natural counterpart. Aristotle's strictures on mixture are thoroughly contradicted in this experiment: a new body is created with qualities that are not related to its ingredients, and yet these ingredients are only juxtaposed and recoverable from the mixture. Mixture—even loose mixture that doesn't permanently transform the mixed parts—can generate substance. This insight prompts the research agenda that comes out of this experiment, the production of "variety of Vitriols" and "Salts of new shapes" through different mixtures (240, 236).

From vitriol and salts, Boyle turns to one of his favorite examples, gunpowder. Gunpowder, he observes, features "an exceeding slight Contexture" of three ingredients, each "retaining its own Nature in the Mixture." Yet such slight mixture still produces a "new Body, whose Operations are more powerful and prodigious, then those of almost any Body of Natures own compounding" (242). Gunpowder shows that an imperfect mixture can produce a new body with unprecedented powers and qualities. While the ingredients of gunpowder are recoverable, this is not the case with Boyle's next example. Glass is a body "more lasting and more unalterable" than many produced by nature, yet it can be made "in less than an hour" by what Boyle describes as the "bare commission of the Corpuscles of Sand with . . . Saline ones" (242, 243, 183). Cohesion and long life spans may result from quick generations brought about by simple mixture.

Boyle goes out of his way at this point to argue that many of the artificial bodies chemistry is able to produce "are endow'd with more various and more noble Qualities, then many of those, that are unquestionably Natural" (243). "A slight change of Texture," he continues his theme of transmutation, "may not onely make a Specifical difference betwixt Bodies, but so vast a one, that they shall have differing Genus'es and may (as the Chymists speak) belong to differing Kingdoms" (244). To illustrate this point, Boyle turns to nature. While corals are "soft and tender" like plants when they are under water, as soon as they are exposed to air they turn into "a Concretion" (245–246). Close to Sumatra, he reports, worms have been seen to transform into trees, and the trees, when plucked up, into stone (246). In Brazil, some grasshoppers become vegetables (247). In a lake on the Chinese island of Hainan, crawfish, once they are drawn out of the water, turn into stone (248). From these natural examples, Boyle returns to glass and gunpowder and recalls a memorable experiment by van Helmont of "turning Oyl of Vitriol into Allom, by the Odour (as he calls it) of Mercury" (249).

The sequence of these experiments and the recurring emphasis on substantive transformation caused by slight change show how much Boyle was drawn by the lure of transmutation and how limited his interest in reduction and purification was.[91] Boyle believed that it was not at all absurd to assume that, "by the Intervention of some very small *Addition* or *Substraction* of Matter, (which yet in most cases will scarce be needed,) and of an orderly *Series of Alterations*, disposing by degrees the Matter to be transmuted, almost of any thing, may at length be made Any thing" (95). In the theoretical parts of *The Origine of Forms and Qualities*, Boyle spoke about the relative stability of corpuscular clusters, but his passions were ignited by the practical possibilities of metamorphosis. Considerations of structure and anatomy played an important role in his work, but they were usually overwhelmed by the powers of atomic motion and fluidity.[92] Without this acknowledgment, our understanding of Boyle remains lopsided.

It remains lopsided, too, if we do not recognize the debt Boyle owed to the Renaissance tradition of natural magic, which had given mixture a prominent role and had a marked influence on Digby.[93] Natural magic was a strain in sixteenth-century science that, in Charles Webster's words, highlighted "the transcendental potentialities of science in both its pure and applied forms" and "became the vehicle for the projection of the term magic into the normal vocabulary of the sciences."[94] This tradition gained renewed visibility in the 1650s, when many of its texts were translated into English for the first time. In *De Occulta Philosophia* (1529, translated 1650), for example, Cornelius Agrippa of Nettesheim wrote about the benefits that could be derived from "the Mixtions of naturall things."[95] While he held on to the distinction between perfect and imperfect mixture, Agrippa believed that perfect mixtures were in the purview of human art. After mentioning some examples of mixtures—two trees that become one by grafting, animals that have turned to stone, the ebony tree, which is partly wood and partly stone—Agrippa concluded that anyone who "makes a mixtion of many matters under the Celestial influencies . . . doth indeed cause wonderfull things."[96]

Joannes Jonstonus (John Johnston), whom Hakewill suspected of having plagiarized his *Apologie*, illuminated the role of the scientist in natural magic.[97] In *Thaumatographia Naturalis* (1632, translated into English in 1657), he defined the true natural philosopher as an agent of practical transformations.[98] Such a philosopher "knows how to augment, and multiply the Winds, to produce new mettals, to make mineral Waters; Artificial, of Vitriol, Brimstone, Allum, &c. and to bring forth new plants and animals . . . and can hasten the times of maturity, clarification, putrefaction, concoction, and germination."[99] Boyle, who proudly recounted his transmutation of gold into silver and was keen to produce artificial salts, did not demur.[100] "The true naturalist," he noted in *Some Considerations Touching the Usefulness of Natural Philosophy* (1663) "can Performe many things that other men cannot Doe; being enabled by his skill not barely to understand several Wonders of Nature, but also partly to imitate, and partly to multiply and improve them." "Man is but the Minister of Nature," Boyle continued, but the skilled naturalist may "do such wonders, as another man shall think he cannot sufficiently admire."[101]

One of the most famous and influential natural magicians was della Porta, who has already made an appearance in this chapter. His *Magiae Naturalis* (1550, translated 1658) was practical in outlook.[102] It included sections on how to perfume objects, how to temper steel, how to make monsters, how to preserve foods, and how to make people beautiful. It made mixture central to the improvement of the things around us. Like other exponents of natural magic, della Porta believed that mixture was transformative and that, by combining different bodies, he could create powers that did not exist in them separately.[103] He showed that mixed breeds were stronger, that mixture domesticated the wild, that it mended faults and defects, and that it made iron stronger.[104] "The commissions or copulations," he pointed out, "have divers uses in Physick, and in Domestical affairs, and in hunting: for hereby many properties are conveyed into many Creatures."[105] The natural philosopher "marries and couples together . . . inferiour things by their wonderful gifts and powers . . . and by this means he, being as it were the servant of Nature, doth bewray her hidden secrets, and bring them to light, so far as he hath found true by his own daily experience."[106] Unlike Boyle, della Porta was guided by the resemblance and correspondence between things in his quest for improving mixtures, but his debt to the occult tradition notwithstanding, his experimental program of mixture resonated with Boyle's. "To work Miracles," della Porta suggested, "is nothing else . . . but to turn one thing into another."[107] In a related vein, Boyle criticized the schools in 1661 for rejecting the "transmutation of one species into another" and pointed out that his corpuscular chemistry was highly "favourable to . . . working wonderful changes and ev'n transmutations in mixt Bodies." In fact, Boyle stressed that his chemistry was compatible with "some of the principal of the Hermetick Opinions" regarding transmutation.[108] If della Porta pursued such transmutations by exploiting the cosmic resemblances between different levels and manifestations of existence, Boyle pursued them by manipulating the atoms that created the infinite variety of the world.

Boyle was familiar with della Porta's work, but he often displayed a skeptical attitude toward the tradition of natural magic. Della Porta's comments on the generation of animals, which we heard earlier, belonged for Boyle in the realm of romance, not science, and he placed della Porta in a group of "notoriously fabulous Writers."[109] Yet the skepticism of such statements hides a more complicated attitude.[110] I think it is worth recalling, for example, that Boyle cared about romance. He wrote a romance as a young man and revised it for publication in 1687.[111] In his more theoretical writings on genre, Boyle recognized the advantages and disadvantages of romance. He compared the relationship of the experimental philosopher to nature to a reader reading romance.[112] If della Porta belonged to a group of romancers, he was also a renowned member, along with Galileo, of the Academy of Linceans (founded in 1603) whose kinship with the Royal Society was pointed out by its secretary, Henry Oldenburg, in a letter to Boyle.[113]

Boyle's relationship to natural magic seems rather like Bacon's, "who, while drawing much of the inspiration for his new method from the magical tradition, . . . managed to distance himself from magic by vilifying it as much as anyone."[114] Bacon's highly popular *Sylua Syluarum* (1626), for example, was visibly influenced by the tradition of natural magic and inspired Boyle's experimental method.[115] "This writing of our *Sylua Syluarum*," Bacon noted, "is (to speake properly) not *Naturall History*, but a high kinde of *Naturall Magicke*. For it is not a Description only of Nature, but a Breaking of Nature, into great and strange Workes."[116] Bacon linked the experimental and practical orientation of his work to the concrete manipulations of nature that populated texts like della Porta's. Intrigued by "strange Changes of Bodies, and productions," Bacon echoed della Porta's program when he offered "Helpe toward the Beauty and good Features of Persons," advice on "Producing of Birds, and Beasts of strange Colours," and making "Fruits, Flowers, and Roots larger; in more plenty; and sweeter."[117] Additional signs of della Porta's influence are Bacon's assumption that spontaneous generation holds the key to all generation, his adoption of della Porta's description of African fecundity, and his belief in species intermixture.[118] Despite attempts at creating distance, Bacon's text carried natural magic into seventeenth-century science.

While Boyle rejected the fables of animal generation in della Porta and Bacon, he transferred what these fables had to say about the species-shifting powers of mixture to his corpuscular chemistry, adopting a view of the scientist and a line of experimentation that had been anticipated in natural magic. The *camelopardus* may be a romantic creature, but Boyle's argument that slight mixtures could switch not just the species but the genus of a body claimed transmutative powers that were on a par with della Porta's argument that a body could transcend its origins by mixing with another species. Breaking down the barriers between alteration and generation, natural and artificial, perfect and imperfect, Boyle's chemistry significantly increased mixture's scientific standing. The waning of the Renaissance that William Bouwsma has described as the disciplining of its liberal tendencies—its belief in diversity and human agency, its penchant to "mix materials from different cultures and systems of thought"—contains a complicated story of survival and adaptation.[119] That story is on display in Bacon's and Boyle's appropriation of natural magic.

*   *   *

Boyle's growing fame in the 1660s and his prominent role in the newly founded Royal Society helped diffuse the idea that mixture was a fundamental natural and experimental process in a circle of influential scientists and philosophers. In the late 1660s and early 1670s, the contours of scientific mixture appeared in bolder relief. Its paradigmatic and programmatic implications were seized or denounced with a firmer sense of purpose. This is visible in work by scholars associated with the Royal Society, but also in some of the critiques that appeared during a period of intensified societal self-promotion.[120]

Boyle's friends and admirers could be sanguine about the scientific prospects of mixture. Nehemiah Grew, for example, took up Boyle's emphasis on the philosophical and experimental value of mixture in twin lectures he gave to the Royal Society in 1674 and 1676.[121] Grew was a botanist who had been mentored by Boyle, and his lectures delivered a series of broad, programmatic statements on the science of mixture.[122] "The *Formation* and *Transformation* of all Bodies," Grew declared, "can be nothing else, but the *Mixture* of Bodies." Because "*Nature* worketh every where only by *Mixture*," experimental mixture was "a *Key*, to discover the *Nature* of Bodies."[123] As scientists, Grew continued, "we have nothing to *Make*; but only to *Mix* those *Materials*, which are already *made* to our hands."[124] In a section that explained "the Power and Use of Mixture," Grew stressed mixture's egalitarian and generative potential. The goals of experimental mixture were "*First*, To Render all Bodies *Sociable*, whatsoever they be. *Secondly*, To *Make Artificial* Bodies in Imitation of those of *Natures* own production. Thirdly, To *Make* or *Imitate* the *sensible Qualities* of Bodies; as *Smells*, and *Tasts*. Fourthly, To *Make* or *Imitate* their *Faculties*."[125] Grew made clear that this was serious business when he insisted that there was no qualitative difference between natural and artificial or perfect and imperfect bodies.[126] Mixture was not divided against itself, and Grew asserted its transformative possibilities when he noted—like della Porta, Carpenter, and Boyle before him—that "Two or More Bodies of different *Natures*, [may] be so combined together, as to produce a Third *Nature*."[127]

Boyle's elevation of mixture influenced others as well. One example is Boyle's friend William Petty. In the winter of 1674, two weeks before Grew gave his lecture on mixture, Petty gave a paper to the Royal Society about duplicate proportion in which he expressed the hope that mathematics could provide an "intelligible Account of the Nexures, Mixtures, and Mobilities of all the parts of the Universe."[128] Petty had initially been exposed to atomism in the Newcastle Circle in the 1640s (which included Thomas Hobbes, William and Margaret Cavendish, and Kenelm Digby), but his paper also showed Boyle's influence when it employed the distinction between compounded and decompounded bodies.[129] In *Political Arithmetick* (written in the 1670s), Petty applied mixture to the question of national union. He recommended improving the "natural and firm Union" of the nation by increasing the "Transplantation and proportionable Mixture" of the Irish and the English. "May not the three Kingdoms be united into one," Petty dreamed about a more resilient nation, "and [be] equally represented in Parliament? might not the several Species of the Kings Subjects be equally mixt in their habitations?"[130] Petty brings us close to the 1690s and beyond, when the logic underlying arguments such as these gained additional popularity, as we have seen. Along with his society colleague Edward Chamberlayne, whose popular *Angliae Notitia: or the Present State of England* (first edition 1669) made claims about the improving effects of linguistic and racial mixture, Petty extended Carpenter's suggestion that mixture should be considered a source of national perfectibility.

Yet there was also significant dissent, even from admirers of Boyle's work. To pave our way toward the more overtly political concerns of the next chapter, I would like to discuss two examples that illustrate the political fears activated by the treatment of mixture as cause and basic reality. In the early 1670s, Henry Stubbe and Samuel Gott mounted powerful critiques of the atomist philosophy. They did so, perhaps in acknowledgment of mixture's growing explanatory power, from a position that accepted mixture as a fundamental natural process. Stubbes's critique mobilized Galen's stress on complex particularity to outflank the atomists by suggesting that mixtures were so intricate that no human could comprehend them entirely, let alone manipulate them. He shied away from "determin[ing] what *God* and *Nature* do in the *production* or *mixture* of *bodies*" and warned: "To *know bodies exquisitely mixed*, and to mix them intimately is a *divine attribute*: this last is avowed by Galen."[131] Though he admired Boyle greatly, Stubbe recommended a retreat from the close scrutiny of complex bodies and experimental mixture, suggesting that they not only violated God's order, but threatened the political order of the restored monarchy.[132] Mixture was too profound for humans to meddle with. Even so, Stubbe betrayed Boyle's influence when, in a treatise defending the practice of blood-letting, he employed phrases such as "decompounded," "heterogeneous miscele," and "miscellany of heterogeneous liquors" to characterize blood.[133]

In *The Divine History of the Genesis of the World* (1670), Gott argued that mixture was God's way of creating form from chaos. Because God, in the first three days of creating the world, "Mist [the four elements] together" they could never be "wholly Unmist and Separate, as they were in the first *Chaos*." Sounding rather Boylean in a passage that argued the irreducibility of the mixtures that make bodies, Gott claimed that it is impossible "for any Art . . . to Separate these fower Elements."[134] Still, he was concerned to counteract the tendency of atomist philosophers to exclude spiritual powers. Echoing the kind of argument John White had made in 1630 when he had justified colonization by claiming that the "mixture" of the English with the heathen would ready the latter for God's spirit, Gott presented mixture as a means of refinement that made bodies "fitt . . . for the several Superior Spirits" they had to receive.[135] Even as they guided matter, these superior spirits or forms generated themselves by "Various Mistions" that made them "more Active and Operative Substances," a phrase that recalled natural magic's rendering of mixture's effects.[136] Responsible for the generation, refinement, and increased operativeness of bodies, Gott's mixture mimicked the role it played in della Porta, Boyle, and Grew, even as it was utilized to renew distinctions between form and matter.

Gott's sophisticated attempt at reconciling elemental physics with the metaphysics of form by involving them both with mixture indicates how much he had come to admire the natural philosophy of the 1660s and how much he desired to correct its course.[137] Although he praised Bacon's *Sylua Syluarum* and Boyle's experimental practice, Gott hoped to assert the "Scale and Order of Nature" against the confusions propagated by atomist philosophers.[138] He realized that this assertion had to prove responsive to the complexities that someone like Boyle had ascribed to natural processes. This is why Gott linked mixture to formative virtue, and this is why he let nature both "coordinate" and "subordinate" its bodies.[139] To achieve the desired assertion of order, Gott combined the collaborative tendencies of coordination with the hierarchical dynamics of subordination. Coordination or mixture alone could not guarantee order, and this point seems to have come home to Gott politically as well.

Gott's sister Elizabeth had married the future regicide Edmund Harvey in 1629. In 1648, Gott made one of the more important contributions to the burgeoning genre of Puritan utopias when he published *Nova Solymae*. But in the late 1650s, Gott seemed disenchanted with utopian schemes, declaring in parliament that neither the English past nor *"Oceana's* Platonical Commonwealth" offered guidance in deciding whether parliament should recognize the Protector as chief magistrate.[140] Precedent was just as helpless as James Harrington's republicanism in resolving the impasse the commonwealth had reached. Similar to Stubbe, who was openly republican during the commonwealth, Gott had lived the hopes of the 1640s and 1650s, but their collapse made him nervous about the political implications of a philosophy that made mixture, a process with egalitarian and transformative implications, so central.

One of Gott's tools in resisting these implications was a revival of the distinction between perfect and imperfect mixture. Through that distinction, he launched a forceful diagnosis of some of atomism's most symptomatic assumptions. He clearly recognized, for example, the paradigmatic hold transgenerations had gained on atomist philosophy and firmly rejected "Transpeciation, or any Transmutation, or Conversion of one Essence into another."[141] Gott turned the phrase "equivocal generation" into a mantra that comprehended all transgenerations, including a species of reasoning he called "Equivocal Causalitys."[142]

By reviving the distinction between perfect and imperfect mixture, Gott was able to criticize as insufficiently real all generations that proceeded from mere association. His chapter on generation demonstrated this point with an example that applied equally to qualities and to bodies. Gott argued that when contemplated at a distance, a meadow of flowers "may represent one Confused Color," but no matter how much our imperfect senses suggest otherwise, in reality it "hath so many several and distinct Colors." The same can be seen in the familiar example of "dry Powders of Blew and Yellow being very finely Pulverisated and Mixt together." "By a close Aggregation," Gott pointed out, these "may appear Confusedly Greenish," but a microscope easily corrected such an impression.[143] These colors were not real qualities in exactly the same way that real bodies could not spring from the juxtaposition of a few ingredients. For Gott, the meadow and the powder represented imperfect and nongenerative mixtures. No real color and no real body were generated by confusion. To treat such generations as paradigmatic, as atomists did, was delusional: it meant taking imperfect sense impressions for solid nature. By making imperfect mixture the paradigm for all mixture, Gott charged, atomists erased the distinction between generation and association, body and heap, reality and appearance. Nature, by contrast, "is certainly . . . most Genuine and Real, in all her Operations, and not, as such Uncouth Opinions would render her, only External Violence, and Imposture."[144] The paradigmatic presumptions of imperfect mixture, he claimed, turned nature into a lie.

Gott's perceptive critique prompted little response.[145] Indeed, a year after he had taken it apart, the argument that imperfect mixtures and even confusion lay at the bottom of nature's most brilliantly homogenous bodies found sensational confirmation in Newton's theory of colors.[146] The most controversial aspect of Newton's theory—first presented to the Royal Society between 1671 and 1675—was his contention that "Light it self is a *Heterogeneous mixture of differently refrangible Rays*."[147] It was "not similar, or homogeneal," as Descartes had claimed, but simply a "confused aggregate of rays."[148] This insight was extended to whiteness. Even to Newton's own mind, "the most surprising and wonderful composition was that of *Whiteness*."[149] White was simply a "dissimilar Mixture" of all colors. In fact, "because it is the most confus'd and changed by Refractions," white proved to be the most composite of all colors.[150] To capture this degree of compositeness, Newton drew on the distinction between compounded and decompounded bodies Boyle had made popular among natural philosophers.[151]

The excitement generated by Newton's thesis was considerable, and responses ranged from agitated rejection (Robert Hooke insisted that light was a "homogeneous, uniform, and transparent medium") to predictions that Newton's thesis would "produce great changes throughout al the bodie of natural philosophie."[152] Newton eventually narrowed his argument to light, but the most difficult aspect of his theory remained the problem of mixture: how could a heterogeneous mixture seem simple, pure, transparent, and homogeneous?[153] This assertion, Newton noted, "hath seemed the most Paradoxicall of all my assertions, & met with the most universall & obstinate Prejudice."[154] The obstinacy was all the greater because Newton's experiments had asserted the corporality of light and attempted to show that the heterogeneous mixture of rays that made up light did not transform the rays, which seemed to Newton immutable.[155]

To undo the prejudice that surrounded his paradoxical assertion, Newton resorted to the example Gott had used to unveil the deceptions of imperfect mixture. The mixture of blue and yellow powder was for Newton a perfect illustration of how immutable rays could produce color without themselves mutating.[156] Of all the theories that elevated the ontological value of imperfect mixture, Newton's offered the greatest provocation by making light the result of a slight and nontransformative mixture. Even gunpowder, Boyle's favorite example for the transformative powers of slight mixture, could not touch this. Newton was able to show that a body that looked completely homogeneous, simple, and even transparent was still a loose and bafflingly complex mixture of an "indefinite variety" of colors and "rays indued with all the indefinite degrees of refrangibility."[157] The differences between body and mixture, between homogeneity and heterogeneity, were undercut in dramatic fashion. Nontransformative mixture gave birth to a translucent body. Light was an imposture of nature.

*   *   *

My sketch of the fortunes of mixture in the late 1660s and early 1670s suggests how Boyle's work and his contacts in and around the Royal Society transmitted the idea of scientific mixture. Boyle's argument for mixture as cause and basic reality gained publicity in the meetings and publications of the Royal Society and of some of its critics. The political economist Petty, the botanist Grew, and the physicist Newton decisively rejected mixture's ontological inferiority and made it a central concept in natural philosophy. Several of Boyle's mentees, friends, and admirers, even if they did not agree with atomism, recognized the primacy of mixture.

No longer suspended between elements (to which it could always be reduced) and forms (to which it could never ascend), mixture was recognized as a generative cause and, as such, acquired importance in scientific arguments about the transformation of natural and social bodies. The mixture of several bodies could produce cohesive and durable unions, superior or new qualities, and even new bodies. All of this happened without the guidance of form. As mixture ascended to the status of cause, form descended and became its effect. In Carpenter's, Digby's, and Boyle's natural philosophy, the established hierarchies of form and matter, one and many, whole and part no longer governed the generation, transformation, and identity of bodies. These were now brought about by the open-ended cooperation of multiple agents. Given the right conditions, the bodies that resulted from such mixture could escape reduction to the ingredients that composed them. They could transcend their origins, the molds of the past, the grip of resemblance, the line of descent.

While mixture thus became a transformative cause in its own right, its relevance in the scientific analysis and description of bodies grew significantly. The well-worn assumption that all bodies were made up out of a few simple elements and that the work of reduction was the indispensable first step in the scientific understanding and manipulation of bodies did not correspond to the vision of the body entertained by atomists such as Boyle or Grew. Bodies were far more decompounded and sociable than most had assumed. They were often irreducibly compounded, and their complexity did more than raise serious questions about the feasibility and usefulness of reduction: it pointed to the promise of mixture as a process and cause. Because all bodies partook of each other, an almost inexhaustible fund of potential and undiscovered interactions between different bodies had to be assumed. As Aristotle had realized early, mixture's transformative potential expands radically when we believe that all bodies are essentially decompounded. The relationship between mixture as a generative cause and mixture as a fundamental characteristic was therefore close. These two dimensions of mixture gained prominence together through a brand of scientific thinking that became increasingly influential in seventeenth-century England.

This chapter has also begun to indicate another effect of the causal ascent of mixture. When generation is explained by a mixture of parts, phenomena such as mutation, deformity, multiplicity, and heterogeneity become part of the way nature works. They cease to be threatening. For Hakewill and Digby, the revaluation of mixture broke the equation between mutation and decay. For them, as for the early eighteenth-century lexicographer Nathan Bailey, mutation became part of a process of development that had improving effects. Digby and Carpenter, meanwhile, saw the increasing heterogeneity created by a generative mixture as a marker of ontogenic and phylogenic excellence. And for Boyle, multiplicity was a constitutive feature of all bodies, whose decompounded nature made reduction less useful and transmutation more promising. As we will see in the next chapter, these revaluations of mixture's conceptual horizon had a significant impact on the imagination of political bodies in seventeenth-century culture.

CHAPTER 2

The Politics of Deformity

Renaissance ideas about natural magic, misinterpretations and critiques of Aristotle, the Calvinist taste for purity, the argument that nature was decaying, the revival of atomism—all of these factors populate the intellectual field that brought a number of seventeenth-century scientists to recognize mixture as a legitimate cause and fundamental reality. Whether that reality appeared as loose contexture, irreducible union, or heterogeneous assemblage made no ontological, theological, or moral difference. This view was radical. It threw out the idea that a proper body depended on the subordination of parts to whole, many to one, and matter to form. Atomists such as Kenelm Digby and Robert Boyle did not believe that order, union, and identity depended on subordination. They believed that the open-ended cooperation of multiple parts was not only sufficient for the production and reproduction of bodies, but vital for the improvement of nature. As we have begun to see, their arguments have a tendency to integrate multiplicity and heterogeneity, deformity and mutation into nature.

In this chapter, I try to understand the political meaning of these arguments. I will move more decisively into mixture's conceptual horizon and pursue the semantic shifts made possible by its reinterpretation. I am interested, in particular, to find out how this reinterpretation changed the way that political bodies were imagined and justified. Sixteenth- and seventeenth-century Englishmen were accustomed to thinking about political bodies in terms of natural bodies. They often compared, for example, the monarch to the soul, the heart, the head, or the stomach—single organs that ensured the body politic's function, health, and unity.[1] Yet such explanations of the body politic through the human anatomy acquired a potent competitor in the revival of atomism in the 1630s and 1640s. Those atomists who recognized mixture as cause and fundamental reality changed the rules that determined what counted as a proper body. This change helped those political writers who wished to advance arguments about the agency and cohesion of political bodies that departed from the anatomical paradigm and its tendency to figure political power through subordination and functional differentiation. As we shall see, the controversial revival of mixed government in seventeenth-century England as a weapon in the fight against unbridled royal power provides an important example of the benefits that the political imagination reaped from the scientific revaluation of mixture.

A closely related benefit moves us further into mixture's conceptual horizon and offers a first glimpse of the link between the revival of atomism and the revival of mixed government. This benefit applied to a political body that was even more controversial than the mixed body politic. Seventeenth-century Englishmen were increasingly worried about the unruly and socially diverse crowds that protested injustices and lambasted authorities in the streets of London.[2] Because they seemed to lack subordination and form, these crowds were referred to as "the multitude." They were easily associated with unshaped, chaotic matter. Christopher Hill has shown that, in the wake of the peasant unrests of the late sixteenth and early seventeenth centuries and the dawning turmoil of civil war, the anxiety about the multitude produced a seemingly endless string of derogatory adjectives, from "hydra-headed" and "many-headed" to the "senseless," "furious," "dissolute," "ignoble," "base," "mad," and "rude" multitude (the list goes on).[3] The multitude was deformed, fluid, monstrous, irrational, rebellious. Horace had dubbed it *bellua multorum capitum*, Shakespeare described it as "the blunt monster with uncounted heads, / The still-discordant, wav'ring multitude."[4] The King James Bible (1611) and its commentators suggested that the "mixt multitude" that accompanied the Jews on their way out of Egypt caused corruption and mutiny.[5] Royalists loathed the multitude, and even some republicans were taken aback.[6]

For much of the seventeenth century, the multitude presented the terrifying image of a deformed, mutable, and heterogeneous political body. Countless commentators who believed in strict unity at the top of the political hierarchy presented the multitude as the monstrous figure that lurked behind all political bodies in which sovereignty was shared between several partners. Included among such bodies was mixed government, which entailed the blending of the three kinds of government, monarchy, aristocracy, and democracy. In the English tradition of mixed government, political power, agency, and legitimacy were created by such mixture.[7] This idea went through two revivals, in the 1640s and 1680s, both times as a means to resist the absolutist aspirations of the Stuart kings. But to many royalists and absolutists, mixed government meant divided sovereignty, deformity, and dysfunction.

Thomas Hobbes's work articulates in more detail the logic that fed the critique of both mixed government and multitude. Though his political theory was sophisticated and his political reputation diverse, Hobbes was blunt in condemning mixed government. Blaming the civil war on the erroneous idea that governmental powers were "divided between the King, and the Lords, and the House of Commons," he compared mixed government to a monstrous body he had seen (most likely Lazarus Coloredo and his parasitic twin John Baptista, who were widely popular in the late 1630s and early 1640s).[8] Hobbes described the brothers as "a man that had another man growing out of his side, with an head, arms, breast, and stomach of his own." Even this, however, did not do justice to the deformity of mixed government. To achieve an accurate representation, Hobbes prodded, we have to imagine yet "another man growing out of his other side."[9] Probably aware of the common argument that monstrous births resulted from an excess of matter, Hobbes argued that no effective political agency could issue from multiplicity. Cohesion could not express itself in deformity.[10]

Hobbes is an interesting witness, not least because he was one of the first political thinkers in England to respond to the incentives atomism provided toward the reimagination of political bodies. In his early treatise *The Elements of Law Natural and Political* (first circulating in manuscript in 1640, at a time when he still aligned himself with the royalist camp), Hobbes took on the challenge to think about the generation and nature of the body politic by beginning with raw political matter, with the multitude. The radicalism of this approach is hard to overlook, especially in an environment of high anxiety about the multitude. What is less readily seen is that Hobbes denies the multitude—in this early text more deliberately than in *Leviathan* (1651)—the status of a political body. The multitude is not a body, he argues, but an "aggregate" or a "heap" of "particulars" that lacks unity, causal ability, and legal standing. "When they say ours," Hobbes explains, no doubt with an eye to contemporary unrest, "every man is understood to pretend in several, and not the multitude." The multitude is a loose collection of numerous particulars that can never incorporate as such. Even though a multitude of separate individuals stands at the beginning of the generation of a body politic, the multitude is not the cause of the body politic and cannot make legitimate claims within the body politic. Hobbes is careful to point out that, "when the multitude is united into a body" by the agreement of all the particulars, it is no longer a multitude but "a people." "The rights and demands of the particulars do cease" at this point and "he or they that have the sovereign power, doth for them all demand and vindicate . . . that which before they called in the plural, theirs." The transformation of many dispersed bodies into one body is complete once subordination and functional differentiation take hold.[11] And with that, the multitude ceases to exist.

Hobbes's argument about multitude relies on the same logic that informed his critique of mixed government. Both these political bodies violate the fundamental truth that absolutists and many royalists were making their own in the first half of the seventeenth century: the truth that sovereignty was indivisible and could not be shared among several partners.[12] Sovereignty was naturally one. Without oneness, no sovereignty—no functional, shapely, or even legitimate body politic. From royalist and absolutist perspectives, the triple-headed monster of mixed government promised almost the same disunion and dysfunction as the many-headed monster of multitude. Mixed government and multitude thus presented closely related flash points for theories of political agency and cohesion that cleaved to the superiority of whole over parts, one over many, and form over matter.

The issue for those who feared the rising tide of absolutism in seventeenth-century England was to justify, against powerfully intuitive charges of disunion and monstrosity, political entities that featured at least some of the openness, multiplicity, and unpredictability of more democratic structures. It was with regard to this justification—amounting to no less than an argument for the political virtues of deformity—that the revaluation of mixture by figures such as George Hakewill, Digby, and Boyle became politically useful. Hakewill's early intuition about the political values of a conceptual horizon on which mixture, mutation, and deformity appeared with positive meanings was firmly grasped later in the century. Beginning in the 1640s, a range of political writers recognized that such a conceptual horizon helped them to justify the divided sovereignty that marked multitude and mixed government. It even allowed them to theorize a collaborative relationship between these two deformed political bodies, thus confirming Hobbes's instinct about the kinship between mixed and multitudinous political bodies.

This chapter establishes the connections between the science and the politics of mixture by excavating the political attitudes behind the scientific emancipation of mixture and by establishing a scientific context for the defense of political deformity in the debates about mixed government in the 1640s. The argument for mixture as cause and basic reality, we shall see, authorizes multitude in science and in politics. I show that the scientific and the political advocates of mixture learned to share and rely on a religious framework that is not often associated with the battle against absolutism. Developing a motif I have already touched on, I argue that scientific and political writers realized in the first half of the seventeenth century that a Calvinist metaphysics was unhelpful in elevating mixture and extending agency to parts, matter, and many—to multitude. They found more robust support for the legitimation of self-moving and self-organizing bodies in a metaphysics with deep roots in the Catholic tradition.

One of my basic claims will be that Catholic and Arminian thinkers such as Kenelm Digby, Thomas White, Thomas Jackson, and John Bramhall made important contributions to the political emancipation of mixture in the first half of the seventeenth century (Digby has already emerged as one of the main early proponents of mixture's generative capacities). Because they relied on the Catholic idea of a mediated relationship between God and world, these thinkers were more likely than orthodox Calvinists to acknowledge that human beings were free to combine and create governments in whatever shape they wanted.[13] Drawing on counter-reformers such as Luis de Molina and Robert Bellarmine, they endorsed a metaphysics that turned out to be highly valuable to Protestant political thinkers such as Henry Parker, William Bridge, Samuel Rutherford, and Philip Hunton as they sought to promote political mixture and multitude in the 1640s. For these political thinkers, mediation—even explicitly Catholic mediation—was the key to advancing their claims for the sovereignty of the people.

In a country as rich in Catholic paranoia as England—from Gunpowder to Popish Plots, Gordon Riots, and Gothic novel—mediation is quickly associated with the oppressions of Catholic hierarchy and priest-craft. I would like to resist such instincts. Mediation is not automatically oppressive. While the Reformation stress on a more immediate relationship between world and God, individual and scripture, helped loosen the grip of worldly hierarchies, it was of limited use in formulating a right of resistance or envisioning a society in which political power was shared widely.[14] Against the continued valorization of immediacy on the left, I would like to remind us that immediacy is not always democratic. As the Catholics, Arminians, and Presbyterians who gather in this chapter testify, there are powerful democratic possibilities embedded in mediation, possibilities that, in the seventeenth century, do not place the individual, but the collective, at the center of political action. The dominant strain of atomism in seventeenth-century England, I contend, does not provide philosophical backing for the atomist individual, cut off from the larger social whole, inaccessible in his or her private shell. That old myth needs to be laid to rest.[15] The politics of atomism are not the politics of liberalism.[16] Rather, the strain of atomism that I follow here is concerned with collective ideas of agency and identity, with a concept of the body in which the many and the one could not be separated—and therein lies its political significance.

I have learned much from Antonio Negri and Michael Hardt's theorizing about multitude, but their political history is rather too critical of mediation when it identifies this concept with the counter-revolution against the "immanent, constructive, creative forces" unleashed by Renaissance humanism.[17] I show, by contrast, that in seventeenth-century Protestant England a highly mediatory metaphysics of Catholic provenance authorizes the political agency of mixture and multitude and extends the forces of Renaissance humanism—not only in science, but also in politics.

My argument involves a large cast of characters and an admittedly ambitious attempt to think simultaneously about religious, scientific, and political concerns. To ease our way into this complex picture, I propose to focus initially on the political meanings of Digby's science in its interaction with religion. We can understand these meanings more easily by placing Digby's work in conversation with Thomas Browne (an opponent) and Thomas White (an ally). Digby and White have not figured prominently in our accounts of seventeenth-century science and politics, but in the semantic history of mixture I pursue in this book their work looms large.[18] It strikingly models the tactical alliances between religious, scientific, and political truths that a revaluated mixture could sponsor. Through Digby's and White's writings of the 1640s, we can access the theoretical platform that pushed the legitimation of heterogeneous, impure, and discontinuous political bodies. This platform, I will argue at the end, also lets us see the politics of Boyle's science from a different perspective.

*   *   *

Hobbes's old friend Digby publicly invoked the political meanings of his science on January 23, 1660.[19] On that day, he gave a lecture to the Society for Promoting Philosophical Knowledge by Experiments, soon to be renamed the Royal Society. His lecture became the first publication formally authorized by the society.[20]

Digby was Catholic and had supported the crown in the 1640s. While in France in 1641, he had killed Baron Mont le Ros in a duel for calling Charles I the "arrant[est] coward in the world."[21] When he returned to England in 1642—a year of tense standoffs between king and parliament—Digby was twice arrested for his political and religious views.[22] During his second, year-long prison term, he wrote a reply to Thomas Browne's *Religio Medici* (1642) and drafted *Two Treatises* (1644), which promoted his Christian-Aristotelian atomism. The political content of both works will interest us soon.

Digby's social and political attitudes have always seemed elitist and royalist, but some aspects of his biography complicate such assumptions. Digby's father, for example, had been executed for participation in the Gunpowder Plot, the attempt to blow up parliament and reintroduce Catholicism in 1605, a fact Digby later justified by pointing to his father's "zeal for his country's ancient liberty."[23] Digby was also an admirer and devoted friend of Thomas White. White was a Catholic priest and atomist philosopher who was notorious—among other things—for a political treatise dedicated to Digby in which he argued that the multitude was free to choose whatever form of government it desired (one of Digby's descendants noted with surprise in 1896 that Digby may have agreed with White's argument).[24] Digby's advocacy of Catholic toleration, meanwhile, led him to befriend Oliver Cromwell, to whom he was close in 1654 and 1655.[25] And a few years earlier, he had offered to purchase a laboratory for the son of Samuel Hartlib, one of Boyle's friends and a key figure in a millenarian group of Puritan scientists who, as Charles Webster has shown, were hoping to revolutionize knowledge and perfect the condition of mankind.[26]

The range of these affiliations intimates that a contextualization of Digby's thought may lead us into a picture of the entanglements between science, religion, and politics in seventeenth-century England that differs from the one offered by Webster, who represents a historiographical tradition that has staked everything on the association of Puritanism with the scientific revolution and a progressive social and political agenda. By contextualizing Digby's thought, I hope to show that the scientific revaluation of mixture floated on theological and metaphysical currents that were sourced by the Catholic tradition, and that this tradition nourished social and political beliefs that became useful in the struggle against the Stuarts in the 1640s and beyond.

Digby's lecture in 1660 concerned the vegetation of plants. He began by restating his view, first articulated sixteen years earlier in a theory of generation that had made mixture a central actor, that the seed had no affinity with the plant or tree because development was a complex process in which constantly shifting circumstances produced a series of mutations, each of which had no obvious relationship to what preceded it.[27] He then revisited a scene he had already painted in *Two Treatises* when he described a bean that grew into a plant. The difference was that the 1660 version of Digby's description sprouted a political allegory that commented on the period of the commonwealth and the imminent restoration of Charles II. Once the bean was in the ground and exposed to moisture and warmth, Digby explained, its skin

> must needs crack and tear to afford way and liberty to the dilatation of the swelled body: which having thus obtained room for it self to perform such actions as in those circumstances are naturall and necessary to it (whereas, before it was shut up and fettered in a cold, dry, and hard outside) it followeth presently its own swing; and in that little naturall body, we may read the fate which hangeth over political ones, when the inferiour Members that should study nothing but obedience, have gotten the power into their hands: for then every one of them following their impetuous inclinations, the whole is brought into confusion; and that is destroyed which every one in their tumultuary way aimed to gain the Mastery of; unlesse a superiour Architect, as in the present case of our bleeding Nation, *everso missus succurere seclo*, do come to draw light and order, out of that darknesse and confusion. It will happen then to this swollen Bean, now broken prison, that the fiery parts of it will work to gain dominion of the watry ones.[28]

With a little help from Digby's royalist bias, it might be possible to argue that this description turns on a contrast between the bean and the "inferiour Members" of the commonwealth. The dutiful bean is not tumultuous; it merely responds to necessary circumstances. With a little help from Digby's earlier, not so political bean story, a more likely reading opens up. Digby's story from the early 1640s stressed, again and again, the mechanical necessity of concurrent causes to explain the bean's growth.[29] But in 1660, this stress decreases significantly. What moves to the foreground, instead, is the bean's liberation into motion. Initially fettered and shut up, the bean cracks, tears, and swells through the necessary influence of heat and moisture and gains room to perform its actions. Through circumstances acting on it, the bean acquires liberty and becomes an actor. The trigger for Digby's analogy is the moment when the bean follows "its own swing": it is at this point of realized self-motion that the natural body teaches us a lesson about political bodies. The bean's empowerment, Digby suggests, is like the empowerment of the common people during the commonwealth. The political confusion such empowerment produced requires the intervention of a higher agent, the Stuart king, to bring order back. Having made this point, Digby abruptly switches back to the bean. The liberation script resumes. The bean has broken out of its "prison," its fiery elements now attempting to dominate the watery ones. Have the inferior members returned to their tumultuous ways? How likely is it that Charles's restoration will change anything?

We can hear in Digby's lecture anger and relief: anger that the inferior bodies of the commonwealth dared to do anything than study obedience, and relief that Charles II would restore order. These are the emotionally dominant notes. But in an oblique manner, Digby also comments on the political meanings of his science. No matter how much he might resent the independent motions of the inferior members, Digby's analogy suggests that his philosophy had made room for them. Digby's explicitly political language in 1660 concedes that his laborious stress on the mechanic necessity of concurrent causes in the early 1640s could not prevent the prison break of the little bodies. It could not ban liberty from nature. In truth, Digby knew early on that the mechanic determinism he occasionally dramatized was halfhearted. It did not really suit his philosophy, which was too deeply committed to liberty and free will to hand everything over to necessity.[30]

Digby agreed with Hakewill's basic argument that God's omnipotence displayed itself in the relative freedom He extended to second causes (those forces, including human ones, that effect most of what happens in the world).[31] In *Two Treatises* he had warned: "Let us not . . . , too familiarly and irreverently ingage the Almighty Architect's immediate handy-work in every particular effect of nature."[32] God worked only mediately, through the ordinary causes He set up at the beginning of the world. He was the author of these causes, but they worked without divine intervention. For Digby, even the miraculous phenomena at the heart of Christian theology—the end of the world, the resurrection of the dead, beatitude in the next life—were explainable through the action of natural causes.[33] The most striking illustration of this highly mediatory relationship between first and second causes was the comparison between God and the clockmaker that Digby seemed to borrow from Hakewill (who had appropriated it from Godfrey Goodman).[34] Contrary to what we might expect of such a comparison, it was not intended to emphasize the control of the divine clockmaker but to show that God's abso-lute power was not operational after the assembly of the clock, after the act of creation. The clock moved by itself, following its own swing, and it were a poor clockmaker indeed who would have to intervene "at every hour, to make the Hammer strike the Bell."[35] God's first cause opened up a space for the independent action of second causes.

Digby could be slightly nervous about this. The "extasie of admiration" he displays over the "multitude and swarm of causes" that have to come together to produce a human embryo pays tribute to the wonder of God's creation, but it is equally informed by the dramatically increased potential for failure when the generation of complex living things depends on multiple cooperating causes. If only one of these causes "went never so little awry," Digby notes, "the whole fabrick would be discomposed and changed from the nature it is design'd to."[36] In a world that depends on the cooperation of numerous parts, a lot more can go wrong. Digby accepted this truth. In 1638 he explained: "Although the lawes that gouerne [materiall things] are in the generall certaine, yet in the par-ticular they are subiect to contingency and defection."[37] Hakewill had made the same point more dramatically in 1635 when he argued that there were "many more wayes . . . for the production of Monsters in what kinde soever, whither of man or beast, then to bring either of them forth perfect in their kinde, (as there are more wayes to miss the marke then to hitt it)."[38] Adopting a highly mediated relationship between first and second causes, Hakewill and Digby realized, meant normalizing mutation and deformity.

Digby was Catholic. Hakewill was a conformist Calvinist who could be virulently anti-Catholic.[39] Their agreement on a mediatory metaphysics speaks to a growing impatience in the 1620s and 1630s with the strict predestination that many leading English Calvinists had embraced in the late sixteenth and early seventeenth centuries. Understanding this impatience a little better will prove helpful. Let me begin with William Perkins, the influential "prince of Puritan theologians."[40] Perkins explained predestination by contrasting it to Stoic fatalism. While the Stoics held that God's agency was constrained by the action of second causes, Perkins pointed out, Calvinists believed "that all sec-ond causes depend vpon and are ordered by God."[41] Although he invoked free will and contingency, Perkins always returned to the idea that a preceding divine necessity enveloped liberty.[42]

His stance is articulated well in the eleventh article of the Church of Ireland (1615), which Puritans such as William Prynne and William Twisse quoted with approval. It stated that "God from all eternitie, did by his vnchangeable counsell ordaine whatsoeuer in time should come to passe" but did so "as thereby no violence is offred to the wills of the reasonable creatures, and neither the libertie nor the contingencie of second causes is taken away, but established rather."[43] The sticking point is that God ordained everything that comes to pass, even before the fall: contingency and liberty find their limit there. As Twisse put it, God did not decree contingency as a formal feature of the world, but concretely decreed "the thinges contingent."[44] The strict predestinarian strain in English Calvinism thus found it difficult to acknowledge genuine unpredictability, genuine liberty.

The impatience with this brand of predestination grew after Jacobus Arminius's 1612 challenge to Perkins gained notoriety in England.[45] In 1618, Archbishop Abbot noted that James I was "marvelously inflamed" against the "graceless positions" of the Arminians. Among these positions was the idea that Arminius placed "our perseverance not in God's hands, but our owne," a reference to one of the most controversial arguments by Arminius according to which God's grace was not irresistible. "Grace is so attempered and commingled with the nature of man," Arminius had written, "as not to destroy within him the liberty of his will."[46] Such graceless positions did not remain unanswered. In 1619, the Calvinists struck back. That was the year when the Synod of Dort, an international Calvinist conference, came out condemning the doctrines of the Arminians.[47] Yet the synod's declarations could not prevent the pamphlet war over Arminianism that broke out in England in the mid-1620s. While he had begun to promote Arminian ministers, Charles I issued a declaration in 1628 that attempted to calm, in particular, the agitated debates over predestination.[48]

This did not stop Thomas Jackson, one of the leading Arminians in England. In 1629, two years after Hakewill had published his *Apologie*, he challenged strict predestinarian views and fanned the flames of controversy (Twisse attacked the "vanitie" of Jackson's persuasions in 1631). Jackson widened the distance between first and second causes to show that necessity and contingency coexisted in the world. He relied prominently on the language of mixture to capture such coexistence. God had not ordained whatever came to pass, Jackson argued. Rather, He had ordained a genuine "mixture of contingency with necessity," or, as Jackson also phrased it, "a mixture or multiplicity of possibilities," a "mixture of contrary possibilities."[49] God's game was not "absolute necessity," but "mixt possibilitie or contingency," and His relationship with humans was cooperative, not determinative.[50] By giving agency to second causes, the Arminian God displayed greater omnipotence, Jackson thought, than the Calvinist God, who was more narrowly tied to the effects on this earth.[51] Jackson's God did not decree contingent things, but embraced "absolute contingency." God "hath printed a resemblance of his freedome," he pointed out, "in the mutabilitie of this inferiour world."[52] Jackson, too, would seem to integrate mutation and deformity into a world marked by freedom.

In slightly different but, I would argue, fundamentally related ways, Catholics like Digby, conformist Calvinists like Hakewill or Nathanael Carpenter, and Arminians like Jackson employ a mediatory metaphysics to give both liberty and necessity their due influence, to authorize mixture and multitude, and to normalize mutation and deformity.[53] To clarify the social and political content of this shared horizon, I would like to examine Digby's response to Browne's *Religio Medici*. Browne's text reflected the Calvinist rejection of a mediated relationship between first and second causes.[54] Digby's disagreements with Browne were formulated while he was imprisoned by an independently acting parliament. They reveal the extent to which the mediatory character of Digby's Catholicism promoted the legitimacy of mixture and multitude. They also show how challenging these concepts remained even for someone as flexible and syncretic as Browne, who went out of his way to emphasize the underlying unity of Catholic and Protestant beliefs.[55]

Whereas Browne privileged direct divine intervention in human cognition, Digby distrusted visionary knowledge. He took nature and reason to be better guides to truth than the "*Revelation of Spirits*."[56] "The bitter *Wood* of *Study*, painefull meditation, and orderly consideration" were far superior to the sudden flashes of illumination Browne seemed to favor. Grace, Digby argued more broadly, was not infused into the soul by God, but was simply "the whole complex of such reall motives . . . that incline a man to vertue, and piety."[57] The painful and tedious attention to natural phenomena and the gradual acquisition of knowledge were the only paths to truth and salvation.[58]

Browne was tempted to leave this path. He confessed that he often judged it "a vanity to waste our dayes in the blind pursuit of knowledge" when some day we "shal enjoy that by instinct & infusion which we endevour all here by labour and inquisition."[59] To Digby, such a position disregarded the liberty and free will God had given humans. God's infinite superiority expressed itself in self-moving agents who had to rely on toil, not divine inspiration, to achieve the knowledge that led to salvation. Fittingly, Browne's ontology permitted "no liberty for causes to operate in a loose and stragling way," be they human or natural. First and second causes were intimately related, Browne argued. "An easie Logick may conjoin heaven and earth in one argument," he claimed, and "resolve all things into God." God's "concourse" may be a general influence, but it is not passive. It "subdivide[s] it selfe into the particular actions of every thing, and is that spirit, by which each singular essence . . . performes its operation." "Bad construction and perverse comment" on the place and role of second causes, Browne added, had led too many into atheism and atomism.[60]

What irked Digby was that Browne's interventionist God encouraged not cooperation but isolation. Browne's notion that second causes can be fully understood only with the help of illumination from above struck Digby as elitist. A capacity for social condescension notwithstanding, Digby embraced an egalitarian epistemology. When he quibbled with Browne's notion of eternity, Digby argued that such notions cannot come from "Theologie" or "beatifike vision," but only from the "principles of Nature and *Reason*." This mattered because such principles were accessible to "the lowest Soule of the ignorantest wretch." The knowledge of eternity should not be confined to the learned or the saved. It is "a bold undertaking," Digby conceded, but he was confident that he could explain eternity to anyone based on natural reason alone.[61] Because we were all naturally rational, knowledge and truth were accessible to the ignorant and the sinners just as they were to the learned and the saved. Browne's tendency to link cognition to divine agency was not just misleading. It kept knowledge in the select few.

Digby's distrust of claims for exclusive knowledge played a more aggressive role in his arguments for the superiority of Catholicism. But here, too, his inclination was to think about knowledge as a communal effect. The religious knowledge of the Catholic church was infallible, Digby thought, because it did not depend on the interpretation of scripture or the authority of church fathers. It relied instead on oral tradition, transmitted by "perpetuall succession" through "such a multitude of men as contayne in them all the variety of dispositions and affections incident to the nature of man."[62] Such diversity did not undermine, but secured truth because it muted individual passion and private interest. A "tradition that is diluered by handes" in this manner ensured that the rule of faith was "within the peoples kenning."[63] The church "is composed of all sortes and of all degrees of persons," Digby noted, and the knowledge that was needed for salvation had to be accessible to everyone, the "learned" as well as the "unlearned."[64] Infallible knowledge, to his mind, meant possessing "the greatest certitude . . . that man's nature and the course of second causes can afford him." In this, religious knowledge ought to be like the knowledge of practical arts such as agriculture or navigation, and it could be so only if it relied on the multitude as a sifter of knowledge.[65]

Egalitarian strains also informed Digby's quest for scientific knowledge. Forming the right understanding of fundamental scientific concepts, Digby argued, required "examin[ing] what apprehensions all kinds of people" have of them. Comparing the empirically minded scientist to a cook who has to purchase the ingredients for even the most refined dishes on "the course Market," he argued that it is "the indisciplin'd Multitude that must furnish learned men with natural apprehensions and notions to exercise their wits about." Digby's comment simmers with condescension, but that should not make us question the seriousness of his argument. In a second stab at the relationship between multitude and scientist, Digby demands: "the first work of Scholars is, to learn of the People." This does not mean that we let "the ignorant Multitude judge" the knowledge produced by scholars. But it does mean letting the multitude judge "of the natural notion, which serves learned men for a basis and foundation to build Scientifical superstructures on."[66] Knowledge that is built up from the multitude is thus superior for two reasons: it relies on information drawn from a wide social spectrum ("all kinds of people"), and it collects the concrete insights of men devoted to a practical life: merchants, craftsmen, laborers.[67] Clear divisions of labor and rank, but equally clear dependencies, regulate the production of scientific knowledge between multitude and scholar. Knowledge is the fruit of cooperation.

Such involvement of the multitude in the search for knowledge was hard to accept for Browne (as it was for Hobbes).[68] Browne professed strong aversions against the multitude. After a beautiful passage (Digby found it "affected") that describes how his even temperament has made him the happy companion of all nationalities and the unperturbed consumer of even the most unusual ethnic foods (locusts and grasshoppers are welcome variations), Browne wonders where the limits of his social and gustatory tolerance might lie.[69] He claims that he "consorts, and sympathizes with all things" and then asks himself: "is there any thing among those common objects of hatred that I can safely [say], I doe contemne and laugh at?" He answers:

> That great inquiry of reason, vertue, and Religion, the multitude, that numerous piece of Monstruosity, which taken asunder, seemes the reasonable Creatures of God; but confused together make but one great beast, and monster, more prodigious then *Hydra*; it is no breach of Charity to call those fooles, it is the stile all holy Writers

have afforded them, set downe by *Solomon* in the holy Scripture, and a point of our faith to beleeve so. Neither in the name of multitude do I only include the base and minor sort of people; there is a rabble even amongst the Gentry, a sort of Plebeian heads, whose fancy move with the same wheele as these men, even in the same Levell with Mechanickes.[70]

Browne suggests that the multitude puzzles philosophy, morality, and religion because it transmutes reasonable individuals into an irrational, shapeless monster. Such shapelessness is a direct result of a lack of subordination, and the leveling of social differences that the multitude represents clearly worries Browne. His statement appeared in print in the early 1640s, during a particularly eventful period of mass political action in the streets of London.[71] In this context, Digby's embrace of cooperation with the multitude in the opening pages of *Two Treatises*—pages that may well have been written while he was imprisoned—gains additional resonance. Unlike Browne, we might say, Digby acknowledged that the enjoyment of superior dishes, just like the production of refined knowledge, depended on cooperating with the multitude.

Browne would have none of this. In fact, his attack on social multitude was consonant with other basic aspects of his thinking. Like the Paracelsians and Helmontians I described in Chapter 2, Browne saw the act of creation as "a separation of the confused masse into its species." Natural hierarchy was created when "the fruitfull voyce of God separated this united multitude into its severall species" (the leveling of social kinds in the multitude produces, by contrast, a monstrous body).[72] For Browne, who believed that species identity was secured by "seeds and principles in the wombe of nature," mixture was not capable of generating form, a sense he confirmed in his essay on language, in which he rejected arguments that praised the mixed nature of English.[73] "Nations that live promiscuously, under the Power and Laws of Conquest," he argued, suffer "confusion, admixtion, and corruption" in their languages. England's long exposure to the French effected the "grand mutation" of English, "yet this commixture, though sufficient to confuse, proved not of ability to abolish the Saxon words." Browne pinned his hopes for a recovery of purity on Saxon words, a trajectory he also applied to mixed bodies, which hid spiritual purity underneath drossy materiality.[74]

Digby's philosophy had a different outlook. Like Browne's, it recognized a paradigmatic link between mixture and multitude on social, epistemological, and ontological grounds. But it could reach different conclusions because

it relied on a metaphysics that posited a highly mediated relationship between first and second causes. The authorization of mixture and multitude
and the normalization of mutation and deformity in Digby's natural philosophy were made possible by this metaphysics. The ontological truths secured
in this manner were for Digby allied to an epistemological truth. In religion
and science, he argued, effective and certain knowledge depended on the
involvement of a social multitude. Digby's mediatory metaphysics thus
had equalizing and integrating consequences for the world of second causes.
For human beings, it contained an unambiguous mandate for cooperation
because cooperation was the only adequate response to the divine gift of
human liberty.

While Digby thus extended natural and social agency to the multitude,
he did not tip his hand on the political consequences of such empowerment.
Digby's discussion of the multitude's relationship to judgment shows traces
of Aristotle's remarkable comments on this topic in his *Politics*, comments
Aristotle prefaced by conceding that there were some good reasons why the
"multitude ought to be in power." Aristotle argued that the multitude's judgment was superior because it transcended individual passions and was based
on practical wisdom.[75] This view was reiterated in one of the most notorious
political tracts of the late sixteenth century, George Buchanan's *De Jure Regni*
(1579), which argued for the superior judgment and power of the multitude by
comparing it to the superior virtues of highly compounded medicines.[76] But
the traces of this argument about multitude in Digby's work do not add up to
a clear political statement. As his comments to the Royal Society in 1660 indicate, Digby had misgivings about the exercise of judgment by the "inferior
members" during the commonwealth. His friend and collaborator Thomas
White pulled him in a different direction. In two books, one scientific and one
political, White tried to show Digby what the political consequences of his
natural philosophy were. He made clear, in particular, that treating mixture
as a cause meant legitimizing the actions of the multitude.

In 1647, White published *Institutionum Peripatecarum*, which intended
to explicate Digby's *Two Treatises*. Invoking the mediated relationship between first and second causes, White argued that "the government of God is
sweet, and offers no violence to the natures of naturall causes."[77] "Neither the
Contingency of naturall causes, nor the *Liberty* of rationall Creatures," White
explained, "is infring'd by this government of God."[78] So far, White remains
close to the formulations of Calvinists such as Twisse. But he soon articulates
the differences. Similar to man, who "*determines himself* and moves himself"

and is therefore free to choose between good and ill, second causes may or may not produce proper bodies.[79] Since "the action of God is only to infuse Being," White argued, "God is not the cause of any imperfection and *not-being*, or ill." Deformities have to be resolved instead "into some defect in *being* of the Creature, and not into God, as its *cause*."[80] White thus related the freedom of human action to the freedom of natural second causes. Both illustrated the sweetness of God's government. Like Digby, he presented deformity not as God's doing, but as a symptom of nature's relative freedom. He probably would have agreed with Jackson's point that God "hath printed a resemblance of his freedome in the mutabilitie of this inferiour world."

White's book contained an appendix that discussed the creation of the world. Here, too, he showed himself a diligent student of Digby's. Nature's freedom expressed itself concretely for White in the role mixture played as a generative cause in the beginning of the world.[81] Against the likes of Browne, who emphasized that the creation of the world was mysterious and instantaneous, White insisted that it happened gradually, through the contingent agency of second causes in processes of mixture.[82] Starting with the basic element earth, White argued that "many kinds and *species* of Earths" came about by earth and water "being *unequally* mixt and remixt, with continual agitation." Joining necessity to liberty, he stated that such mixture "must, by the law of *contingency* have produc'd . . . Stones, Metalls, Mold, and concrete Iuyces." He turned next to plants and animals, whose development he attributed to spontaneous growth from "most aptly tempered and dispos'd" earth. Thus "plants proceeded from the very springing fecundity of the Earth . . . without any extraordinary and miraculous concourse of God." And because animals are "nothing but a *more-compounded Plant*," they, too, spring from a highly fertile earth. To make such equivocal generations more plausible, White noted that they no longer happen so frequently because the earth has become less fertile, but explained that even today "*Mice* and *Frogs*, and sometimes new fashion'd Animals" were produced by equivocal generation. The same point was then applied to the "very muddy" waters that existed in the early days of the world, which "must have sprung into Animals fit to inhabit them."[83]

White's explication underscores the political consequences of Digby's theory of generation. Digby's emphasis on mixture, mutation, and a multitude of causes argues that hierarchy is not natural, form not predetermined. They are not implanted by God into nature. The spontaneous leap from the mixture of parts into various living things argues instead that liberty, equality, and collaboration are inscribed into nature from the start. Species are not immediately created by God, but evolve gradually, out of the semi-independent motions of second causes.[84] The political meaning of such a stance was obvious not only to White. In a 1662 book that took on White, Hobbes, and Hugo Grotius, Roger Coke repeated charges that John Maxwell and Robert Filmer had made earlier when he observed that natural equality could make sense only to "an *Egyptian*, who held (from the example of divers Creatures generated out of the river *Nile*) Men at first were generated from equivocal generation, or that he had sprung out of the ground."[85]

Nine years after White published his explication of Digby's natural philosophy, he underscored its political truths with *The Grounds of Obedience and Government* (1655). The book was published while Digby was close to Cromwell, and it drew Charles II's ire, prompting White to flee England at the Restoration. Many saw it as a justification of Cromwell's rule, but White's aims were broader. He dedicated the book to Digby, addressing him as "my most honoured and best Friend." White explained that he wrote the book in response to "the many attempts you have this long time made upon me" to explain the "principles of Obedience and Governement."[86] At a moment when Digby's political affiliations had shifted, White wished to show his friend that the forms of government were freely made by the multitude. The multitude was politically sovereign.

White motivated this argument by drawing on a highly mediated relationship between first and second causes. When he attacked the belief that social and political hierarchies had a divine origin, for example, he argued that such belief was symptomatic of a confusion between first and second causes. What seemed like "Gods doing a thing is many times onely the course of naturall second causes," he pointed out. God gives "direction and motion" to these second causes, but that does not mean that He "doeth . . . all that is done by them."[87] To understand government, White suggested, we ought to look more to nature than to God.[88] This meant that the principle of political power derived from the first cause, but that its exercise was vested in the "rationall multitude" as a second cause by God. This "rationall multitude"—a phrase aimed at correcting the negative associations of multitude—was naturally free and equal and possessed an inalienable political power to make and remake government.[89]

White insisted on the inseparability of the political and the natural. Man was naturally a social and political animal, he argued with Aristotle and against his friend Hobbes.[90] There was no Hobbesian transcendence of nature in the establishment of civil society; the political right of the multitude persisted. As White explained it, the close relationship between the natural and the political ties the institution of government to the "improving of nature," not its transcendence. Government should be "connatural to a rationall multitude," he argued. While "the Governour is the highest and noblest part," White pointed out, he is "but a part; the People is the whole, the End, . . . the Master and Lord, for whom those who are Lords by office are to be vested and devested in Lordship, when it is necessary for the common good: who thinks other wise, deserves not the name of man."[91]

White's two books thus made a compelling case for the political meaning of Digby's science. The causal elevation of mixture, the empowerment of multitude, the normalization of mutation, and the consequent dethronement of form found for White a clear political echo in the freedom and equality of man and in the multitude's ability and right to generate whatever form of government it desired. In both nature and politics, a highly mediatory metaphysics was the enabling factor. Digby had his regrets about the political meanings that spilled out of his natural philosophy, but his remarks in 1660 also show that he recognized the spill. White made explicit what Digby kept implicit.

*   *   *

Digby's and White's appreciation of mixture and multitude is indebted to the traditional Catholic belief that man is naturally equal and human life essentially cooperative.[92] After Aristotle's *Politics* became available in Latin translation in the second half of the thirteenth century, scholastic philosophers strove to integrate its insights into their theology. Aquinas, for example, treated the multitude as the collective expression of man's natural equality and the origin of the cooperative action that was needed to maintain human life.[93] Following Aristotle, Aquinas argued that man was a political animal. There was no pre-political stage (as there was for Hobbes) and therefore no strict division between nature and society. The multitude could not be dismissed as merely natural, and its ability to establish political society was fully acknowledged. While Aquinas had also argued that the multitude lost its sovereignty in the transfer of power to a ruler and had praised monarchy as the best form of government, his integration of Aristotle's politics helped subsequent thinkers such as Marsiglio of Padua and Bartolus of Saxoferrato to produce more radical arguments for popular sovereignty.[94]

This tradition of political thought also stands behind Jesuit writers such as Luis de Molina, Francisco Suarez, Robert Bellarmine, and Robert Persons, who were notorious in early seventeenth-century England for arguing that the multitude was sovereign.[95] White had been exposed to their thought when he attended Jesuit colleges abroad.[96] As Richard Tuck has shown, Molina and Suarez disliked the idea "that the power of a sovereign over his people is a natural unitary power, transferred by them to him." For Molina, Tuck explains, "political authority was not a unified entity. It was much more complex, and could be divided in all sorts of ways between a ruler and his subjects, so that one did not have to say that it had been *either* retained *or* transferred."[97] This argument for the divisibility of sovereignty legitimized both mixed government and the continuing claims of the multitude in civil society.[98] Like Molina, Bellarmine and Persons believed in a mediated relationship between first and second causes and used this relationship to justify the original freedom of the multitude to constitute the forms of government.[99] Invoking the Bible, Persons wrote, for example: "As on the one side the Apostle doth plainely teach that the magistrates authority is from God, by his first institution, in that he sayeth, vve must be subject to them for Gods cause, so on the other side, he calleth it a *humane creature* or a thing created by man, for that by mans free choise this particuler forme of gouerment (as al other also) is appoynted in euery common wealth . . . which maketh it rightly to be called both a humane creature, and yet from God."[100] God is the first cause of political power. As second cause, man makes the forms of government freely, "through the medium of human wisdom and choice," as Bellarmine put it.[101] Or as Persons put it elsewhere: "the ordination of God by the law of nature, doth give politicall *Power* unto the multitude immediately, and by them mediately to one, or more."[102] The result of such mediation harmonizes with what Jackson called a "mixture of contingency with necessity."

Given that there was no separation between the natural and the social in the Catholic political tradition, it is not surprising that Digby and White could not write about natural bodies without also thinking about human community. If the Christian-Aristotelian atomism they both embraced empowered mixture and multitude, this had to have political consequences. Interestingly enough, the mediatory metaphysics Digby and White featured had influenced other early proponents of atomism. Lisa Sarasohn has shown, for example, that Molina had considerable influence on Pierre Gassendi, one of the most important early advocates of atomism. Gassendi saw the usefulness of Molina's mediated causality and made it central to his Christianized version of Epicureanism.[103] Either through Gassendi (who had considerable influence on English thinkers and was in contact with the Newcastle circle, to which Digby belonged) or the longer arm of the Catholic tradition, or both, Digby and White made the same connections.[104] Highlighting a mediatory metaphysics that combined liberty and necessity, they elaborated atomism as a theory of collective, semi-autonomous agency that had social, political, and epistemological consequences. The political consequences of this marriage between Catholic mediation and atomist philosophy were especially vivid in White's thought. White recognized that the ontological elevation of mixture and multitude aligned with the political arguments for popular sovereignty made by Jesuit thinkers such as Bellarmine and Persons. Sarasohn rounds out the picture here, too. She notes that the nexus of mediation, atomism, and popular sovereignty was also invoked by Gassendi. Despite considerable eclecticism in his political thought, Gassendi associated the highest power in the state not with government, but with "the multitude who make laws."[105]

As we have seen, the mediation between first and second causes also found its way into Protestant thought. Though the Church of England was theologically dominated by Calvinism into the 1620s, the doctrine of predestination came under pressure after Arminius's attack on Perkins. In England, Arminianism emerged as a public force in the 1620s and 1630s, when it found an institutional foothold through Charles I's patronage.[106] Arminian thinkers such as Jackson defended liberty and contingency against Calvinist necessity by adopting a mediatory metaphysics. The political results of their adoption were less certain, but it is clear that Jackson's *Treatise on the Divine Essence* defended the political and religious value of concepts such as equality, liberty, multiplicity, and cooperation.

Although many Catholics and Arminians sided with Charles I and criticized parliament during the crises of the 1640s, I agree with Hugh Trevor-Roper that the Arminian alliance with Charles was "not the logical consequence of [Arminian] doctrine." It resulted instead from a devil's bargain with Charles, who offered his patronage in exchange for political support.[107] That Arminian ideas had no inherent relationship to royalism is indicated by the fact that they were associated with republicanism in Holland.[108] In England, the example of John Milton shows that republican thought was more than compatible with Arminian doctrine.[109] Before I pursue the political uses of mediation into even deeper Protestant territory—into some of the central arguments of the early 1640s for the virtues of political deformity—I would briefly like to examine an example of Arminian politics that seems even more instructive than Milton's.

The political limits of a mediatory metaphysics are clarified by the royalist and Stuart supporter John Bramhall. In 1645, in a meeting at the Paris apartment of William Cavendish, Marquess of Newcastle, Bramhall debated Hobbes. He countered Hobbes's assertion that necessity determines even those actions that seem voluntary and free by arguing for a mediated relationship between God and the world. Like Jackson, Bramhall hoped to secure "the Liberty and Contingency of second causes" without diminishing the ultimate sovereignty of the first cause.[110] In his lengthy reply to Hobbes, he repeatedly identified Hobbes's position with Calvinist necessity.[111] Securing genuine liberty and contingency for second causes against such necessity, Bramhall stressed, provided clear protection against the political consequences of Hobbes's absolute necessity. Hobbes's argument for the absolute power of the "Sovereign Magistrate" in *De Cive* (1642) was unacceptable to Bramhall.[112] His own statement that kings derive their power from God notwithstanding, Bramhall argued that "the law hath a directive power over [Princes]" and that the people may resist "Tyrannical Lawes."[113] "I hate [Hobbes's] doctrine from my heart," he cried, "it destroyes liberty, and dishonours the nature of man."[114] Bramhall's Arminianism was clearly on display in the relative freedom he accorded second causes and the genuine contingency this introduced in the world. It was this belief as much as Hobbes's absolutist logic that roused the royalist Bramhall to this fervent defense of liberty.

But Bramhall did not only reject absolutism. Two years before he debated Hobbes, Bramhall had attacked the parliamentarian Henry Parker. He charged Parker with following Buchanan and Bellarmine, the guiding lights of Protestant and Catholic radicalism.[115] But despite much bluster directed at those like Parker, who wished to make the commonwealth "an *Amphisbena*, a Serpent with two heads" by promoting the sovereignty of the two houses of parliament, Bramhall's attack remained tellingly ineffective. Echoing the beliefs he would press in the exchange with Hobbes, Bramhall embraced at the outset a mediated relationship between first and second causes. Yet this embrace troubled his defense of royal sovereignty and his rejection of the rights of the multitude.[116]

On the one hand, Bramhall criticized Parker for making "strength and power the rule of what is lawfull," thereby giving "the People the last Judgement of necessity." On the other hand, he granted that in cases of national emergency "the last exercise or execution of Power . . . is in the People."[117] Regarding Parker's contention that "the People is the Fountain and efficient of Power," Bramhall faintly objected that this "is not universally true."[118] Meanwhile, he joined Parker in subscribing to Cicero's "universall and perpetuall Law of *salus Populi*" and expressed agreement with several others of Parker's arguments.[119] Whenever Bramhall accepted the terms of natural law, he found himself close to Parker.[120]

In defending royal privilege, Bramhall sought refuge in common law, custom, and prescription—even as he conceded that such national law was ultimately inferior to natural law.[121] On the grounds of national law, Bramhall contended that parliament is neither superior nor equal but "subordinate" to the king.[122] And yet he also suggested that legislative power is shared between king and parliament and advocated the "mixture of Government" as a protection against tyranny (if that did not help, tyrannicide was permissible).[123] These uncertain crossings between royal and popular right, natural and national law, monarchy and mixed government indicate that Bramhall's political ontology could not offer firm support for the subordination of parliament and people under one king. They illustrate the political tendencies of Armininan metaphysics. Bramhall could not sever second causes from political agency. His mediatory metaphysics made it impossible to strike decisively at popular power. It is now time to connect such a metaphysics to a group of Protestant writers who made a powerful contribution to promoting the virtues of political deformity.

Around the time that Bramhall offered his unwilling acknowledgment of the political tendencies of mediation, several opposition writers realized that mediation did, indeed, provide sturdy support for mixed government and popular sovereignty. A group of political authors that were neither Catholic nor Arminian—Henry Parker, William Bridge, Charles Herle, Samuel Rutherford, and Philip Hunton—pushed mediation into Protestant politics, despite the fact that some of them were suspicious of Catholics and publicly attacked Arminianism.[124] These authors understood that the mediated relationship between first and second causes supported an agenda that legitimized political bodies in which mixture, multitude, and mutation were vital forces.[125] They realized that the atomist redefinition of the body had momentous implications for their attempt to imagine and justify a body politic that did not depend on the primacy of form, whole, and one.

One of the prominent critics of those who argued for mixed government and popular sovereignty was John Maxwell. He charged that these arguments came directly from Jesuit writers such as Bellarmine and Suarez. From them, Parker and his ilk had imbibed the belief that political power did not originate in hierarchies but derived "immediately" from the multitude and "mediately from God."[126] Parker, Rutherford, and Bridge were not intimidated by this association with Jesuits. Though the Pope was for him the anti-Christ, Rutherford freely owned his agreement with Molina, Suarez, and Bellarmine on the mediation of political power through human agents.[127] Bridge followed suit. In the space of fifteen pages, he declared that he was eager to "destroy those nests of Jesuits and Jesuited persons," quoted Rutherford to support his contention that "the first seat and receptacle of ruling power under [God], is the whole people or body politicke," and approvingly cited Molina on the difference between paternal and civil power.[128] Like Rutherford, he drew support from William Durandus of Pourcain, who wrote in the thirteenth and fourteenth centuries and had been a polemical reference point for anti-Catholic agitators in the first half of the seventeenth century. Durandus had argued for a mediated relationship between first and second causes and had embraced, as Rutherford pointed out, the political consequences: political power was instituted by God, but its uses and forms were determined by man.[129]

Adding to these debts to the Catholic tradition, Michael Mendle has suggested that Parker may have derived one of the more important slogans he used to argue for popular sovereignty—"*quicquid efficit tale, est magis tale* [the cause of something is the greater thing]"—from Suarez.[130] Parker was also influenced by Richard Hooker's *Of the Laws of Ecclesiastical Politie* (1593), whose famous and initially unpublished book eight he consulted in manuscript.[131] Hooker's book was intended to temper what he saw as the extreme tendencies of a still rising Puritanism. Suspected of crypto-popish ideas and popular with Arminians, Hooker gave Parker a second notorious slogan: "the King is Major *singulis, universis minor*."[132] The king is superior to each single part of the body politic, but inferior to all the parts together (a truism Hobbes would reject in *Leviathan*).[133] Hooker supported such primacy of the collective body by adopting a mediatory metaphysics. Mediation allowed Hooker to argue that, at the beginning of political society, the "multitude . . . hath under God Supream Authority" to set up freely what kind of society it desires to live in.[134]

*   *   *

Partially in response to critics such as Bramhall and Maxwell, Parker wrote his philosophically most ambitious treatise in 1644. *Jus Populi* is remarkable for several reasons. It is the first of Parker's political pamphlets that showcases a mediatory metaphysics. This allows Parker to move beyond the Puritan narrative about mixture as a symptom of the fall. It frees him to deploy mixture not only as an effective antidote to arguments for pure, clear, and absolute political forms, but as a means of improvement. Inspired by atomism—something Maxwell had recognized—Parker constructs analogies between natural and political bodies and launches a sophisticated radicalization of the idea of mixed government.[135] This radicalization turns political deformity and mutation into virtues. All of this makes it imperative to spend some time with Parker, but the following discussion will also cast new light on some of the more moderate advocates of mixed government in the 1640s.

Parker frankly acknowledges that mixture enters the world only after Adam and Eve's expulsion from paradise. It is only at this point, after humankind was forced to leave "nature in its greatest purity" that "subjection" entered human life. Government was the result of sin, and the best it could achieve was "a mixture of good and evil."[136] After the fall, Parker explained in *Of a Free Trade* (1648), "restraint, and liberty, are relative things, and not to be accounted simply good, or simply bad in themselves." He considered those wise who knew how "to distinguish betwixt that sheere, unmixt freedom, which uses to intoxicate us, and to bring detriment, and danger with it; and that allayed, or mixt freedom, which God, and Nature have made so sweet to all Generous mindes."[137] The metaphysical foundation of this mixed freedom was mediation.

Parker asserted in the opening pages of *Jus Populi* that God was not "the immediate Authour of our Constitutions." He did not so "extraordinarily intervene in the erecting of Governors, or limiting of governments, as to strangle second causes, and invalidate human acts."[138] God had too much respect for "rationall and free causes" to regulate or prescribe political or social forms.[139] "The founding or new erecting of authorities at first, and the circumscribing the same after by consent," Parker underscored, "is so farre from being Gods sole immediate act, that it is, as far as any act can be mans proper and intire act."[140] Hierarchies and subjection might be necessary, but they were neither divine nor natural. They were man-made and expressed the liberty guaranteed by the mediated relationship between first and second causes.

Critics like Maxwell made considerable political hay out of the hierarchies that seemed to structure sexual, social, physical, and political relationships, from Adam and Eve to husband and wife, from master and servant to form and matter to king and people.[141] But while Maxwell stressed that these hierarchies were obvious, clear, and proper, Parker urged the complexities of mixture. Regarding the relationship between husband and wife, for example, he mused whether there is not in "conjugall Jurisdiction . . . a strange kind of mixture, and coordination, and may not the Spouse plead that divine right as much for a sweet equality, as the husband does for a rigorous inequalitie?"[142] Just like the husband had to respect his wife's claims, he went on, "Princes who were created for the people's sake, [may not] chalenge any thing from the sanctity of their offices, that may derogate from the people."[143] A mixture of equality and inequality made good government. This was also true of the relationship between master and servant. Parker addressed the master in these terms: "If thou may'st tyrannize over him as he is thy servant, yet thou may'st not as he is man: If the misery of one capacity have exposed him to thy cruelty, the priviledge of the other capacity ought to recommend him to thy favour: If the more base relation of servant entitle thee to domineer, yet the more noble relation of man checks the insolence of that title."[144] Equality and inequality, natural and social laws were operative at the same time, Parker argued, and such mixtures had nothing obscure, ambiguous, or improper about them. They were, quite simply, the expression of our inescapably mixed condition after the fall. We lost unmixed liberty and equality through the fall, but God's institution of political power left us free, as semi-independent second causes, to cultivate mixed social and political relations. By contrast, anyone pursuing simple solutions that hinged on absolute liberty or absolute subjection strove for a distorting purity.

Parker's argument for mixture as the proper medium of human agency and liberty allowed him to present the rise of mixed governments as an achievement worth celebrating. Today, Parker noted, "there are more mixt and limited states then absolute, and those which are mixt and limited, are more civill, more religious, and more happy than those which are not."[145] Echoing a point Persons had made when he argued that mixed government was the structured reassertion of the original rights of the multitude, Parker suggested that mixed states are commendable solutions for the political problem of how to channel the natural self-motion of "the peoples moliminous body." (Rutherford agreed, and so did Bramhall.)[146] Parker understood that mixture was not something that we had to endure passively, a fixed limit imposed by unshakable law. The historical movement from absolute to more mixed forms of government was a story of progress. Our mixed condition was not tied to inevitable decay. It was dynamic, a source of improvement.

Parker was acutely aware of the consequences such acceptance of mixture had for the question of political form. The fact that "Gods hand . . .

stands with the freedome of naturall causes" led him to dismiss the superiority of form Maxwell had sought to assert for both natural and political bodies.[147] "That great Dispute . . . amongst Polititians, about the comparison of this and that Form of Government" was pointless. "The difference," Parker pointed out, "is not so much to be seen in the Forms themselves, as in the States, which make choice of those Forms."[148] Invoking one of the fundamental claims of atomist philosophy, Parker offered that "the difference of formes" was not a difference in kind, but "only in degree." In fact, "the degrees are almost as various as the severall states of the world are, nay the same states admits of often changes many times, sometimes the people gaines, and sometimes looses, sometimes to its prejudice, sometimes not; and sometimes injuriously, sometimes not."[149] If form is a matter of degree, all nations have different political shapes. Forms of government should not be classified and studied as distinct kinds. Even within a single nation, governmental forms are variable and unstable. The same state "often changes many times," and the people sometimes lose, sometimes gain in the struggle for political power. Parker proposes here that the postlapsarian dependence of form on mixture is politically liberating: it can render the body politic so fluid that its shape is determined from one moment to the next, depending on the political motions that prevail—a proposal that horrified Filmer, who had turned in disgust from such radical changeability of form.[150] The idea of mixed government, Parker intimates, might be radicalized in such a way that political power is everywhere in the body politic and subject to constant, complex, interdependent struggles.

Parker confirms this radicalization of mixed government in the discussion of political trust that follows these comments about the changeability of the state. One of Parker's opponents tried to bolster royal prerogative by arguing that "under a Monarchy much must be trusted to the King, or else it will be debased into Democracie." Parker responds: "Tis confessed much must, but all must not be trusted: the question then is, how farre this *much* extends in a Monarchy of such a mixt nature as ours is, in such times as ours now are."[151] "In such times as ours now are": with this qualification, Parker shifts the ground of the debate. The relationship expressed by the trust, he argues, cannot be addressed formally, with a disquisition on "the Lawes and Customes of the Land." Rather, the question of trust has to be answered by tending to current circumstances. "Infirme credulous, and easie Princes," Parker points out, cannot "pretend always to the same degree of power as their Ancestors have held, unless they can prescribe to their vertues also. Queene *Elizabeth* might with safety and expedience be trusted further then the King *Iames*."[152] Parker conflates the legal instrument of the trust with the literal trust a people have in their rulers and thus undermines the idea of the trust as a formalized moment of investiture with clear limits. He begins to construe trust instead as a continuous, unlimited process that depends on shifting circumstances: "such times as ours are." These comments radicalize the participatory aspects of mixed government. They interpret the "mixt nature" of England's monarchy as the description of a fluid and constantly evolving body politic. For Parker, the mixed nature of English monarchy signifies a developmental plasticity that is caused by the continuously evolving exercise of trust by the people and the different degrees of power that rulers enjoy as a result.

Although Parker occasionally invoked the Galenic vocabulary of temperance and balance to describe the body politic, his idea of political mixture clearly moved beyond the humoral paradigm that often served more conservative commentators.[153] At the same time that atomists such as Digby or White were authorizing mixture to demote form and render mutation routine, Parker leaned on mixture for closely related political effects. He belongs to those theorists of political mixture who fully grasp its utopian potential for a totalizing union that does not rest on subordination and homogeneity, but on coordination and heterogeneity. It makes sense, therefore, that Parker defines political power physically and locates it in the constant and complex interactions between multiple political bodies. Parker defined this concept of political power when he described the origins of civil society. He notes that "Power is originally inherent in the people, and it is nothing else but that might and vigour which such or such a societie of men containes in it selfe."[154] Such a physical definition of political power may not be so surprising in a discussion of the origins of government, but even when Parker talks about established civil society, he expresses his belief that political power consists in the combined physical force of all. "Power doe[s] flow from a humane naturall principle," he reminds us, and "supreme signiory" has a physical source in the people:

> The honour and splendor of Monarchs . . . are after a physicall manner derived; the more glorious and noble the people is, the more glorious and noble the chief of the people is; and this honour and glory [that] flows from the people is such as flows from the people without wasting it self, in the act of flowing. In the like manner, puissance, and force, it has a naturall production from the people . . . the more

strength there is in such a Nation, the more strong is he who com-
mands that Nation: and yet that puissance which by perpetuall consent passes into the supreme commander, does not so passe from the
people, but that it retains its ancient fire, and subject of inherence.[155]

Parker's insistence on the physicality and perpetuity of flow constructs political power in sharp opposition to those who see it as alienable by transfer or
contract. Political power is a continuous, variable, and inexhaustible current
passing from people to king and back. Just as he does with the term *trust,*
Parker transfigures the meaning of *consent:* it is not a moment of tacit or explicit authorization, but the conduit that channels a constant flow of honor
and power from people to ruler. Such an emphasis on the fluid naturalism of
political power can also be found in Herle and Bridge. Bridge notes, for instance, that "the power of ruling and governing is naturall" and depends on
"the Fluxus and Refluxus of civill authoritie . . . from and to the people."[156]
Appropriately, Parker goes on to explain that political agency is never simple.
As in nature, it always involves the action of "joynt causes" and "concauses."
The transfer from the people to the ruler does not end; political forms do not
congeal. The cause of popular sovereignty cannot exhaust itself because it is
"multiplied and gathers new strength from other concauses."[157] In nature and
in politics, Parker argues, a complex and interactive network of causes—set
free by mediation—constitutes bodies and power.[158]

Such an interactive construction of the body politic explains why Parker,
who is usually seen as an advocate of parliamentary sovereignty, so frequently
emphasizes "the totall body and collection," "this collective universality," or
"the whole community in its underived Majesty."[159] While such statements
occasionally serve to justify parliamentary right, they appeal more often to
the total force field of the political community—what Rutherford called "the
Kingdome collective"—as the ultimate reference point for the measure of sovereignty.[160] The "consideration of the whole body" is crucial because "the whole
body politicke is the general subject of authority, though it be more intimately
contracted sometimes into such a Chaire, such a Bench, such an Assembly."[161]
Power cannot be taken away or concentrated in one part of the body politic, be
it head, heart, or soul. The anatomical paradigm is too rigid. While the inevitable mixture of necessity and liberty, inequality and equality, makes a total
dispersion of power impossible, the best body politic only compresses power
at different points and to different degrees, all the while maintaining porous
borders between the points.

That Parker was serious about the porosity of borders in the body politic becomes clear when he treats the multitude as a legitimate political agent. He does so despite the "termes of derision" that "our adversaries" apply to the multitude.[162] Parker acknowledges the claims of multitude not only at the moment of the founding of civil society, but also after. He defends, for example, the need to satisfy the demands of the multitude, and he assigns the multitude a constitutional role that limits parliament's sovereignty.[163] In a passage that praises the ability of parliaments to reconcile the diverging interests of multitude, gentry, and aristocracy, Parker notes that, although "the multitude hath only a representative influence, so that they are not likely to sway, and yet some influence they have, and that enough to preserve themselves from being overswayed."[164] The multitude cannot be overruled by parliament because parliament is supposed to represent the interests of the multitude. In addition, Parker suggests that the violation of parliamentary privilege by the king could be legitimate grounds for the multitude to exercise its inalienable political power.[165]

Parker's recognition of the political rights and powers of the multitude explicitly applies to the unruly and extra-parliamentary forces that so many Englishmen, from royalists to aristocratic republicans, denounced as monstrous.[166] For Parker, the mixed nature of the body politic makes it impossible to exclude anyone from power, and he accused the royalists of pursuing such ends by dividing the body politic.[167] Parker's comments on the multitude reflect his understanding of political power as a compressible, but indivisible physical force that belongs to everyone and can mutate into various forms, forms that are not necessarily well proportioned or symmetrical, and that can contract or dilate, bulge or flatten in different places according to shifting circumstances.[168]

The view that Parker is an advocate for parliamentary sovereignty or even, as Mendle has suggested, of parliamentary absolutism, provides only a partial perspective on his thought.[169] Although Parker pressed for parliamentary rights, he retained a lively sense of the horrors of absolutisms of any kind. He was too convinced of the mixed nature of political power, of the complex entanglement of necessity and liberty that characterized human life, to advocate political solutions à la Hobbes that relied on sharp contrasts between body and heap, one and many, society and nature. His body politic was made up of various smaller bodies—groups and individuals, institutionalized and not—whose interactions determined its shifting shapes. Parker believed in independent political motions, in the freedom of second causes, and in form as an effect. While there were some advantages to be gained by structuring the body politic, these structures could never remove themselves from the origins of political power in the people's free and underived motion. To be just, these structures had to remain responsive to the mixed nature of political power and collect merely into closer circles the authority that was needed to realize the common good. Liberty and subjection had to coexist, but Parker hoped to give liberty as much space as mixture could produce. For this reason, deformity becomes the expression of a just body politic.

Because Parker connects the independence of second causes to the shifting physics of power in even a single commonwealth, he rejects a balance of forces as the guarantee of durability, an idea that was sometimes expressed by more conservative theoreticians of mixed government. There is no ultimate durability, no escape from the forces of history. Rather, like Rutherford and Bridge, Parker believes that "men have an active power of government by nature" and that this power makes up the life of the commonwealth.[170] While that life has to find forms to function (parliament, for example), these forms are never independent and always subject to mutation. In the end, the changing forms of government are simply the effects of the people's motions. Parker's radicalization of mixed government thus releases the body politic into the fullness of historical circumstance and human participation.[171]

As Mendle's formulation of parliamentary absolutism indicates, Parker is not typically seen as someone who is closely engaged with ideas of political mixture. In fact, one of the most influential theoreticians of mixed government in seventeenth-century England, Phillip Hunton, advocated moderation against what he saw as Parker's extreme arguments for parliamentary sovereignty.[172] Still, Hunton's vision of the mixed body politic exhibits important similarities to Parker's. Like Parker, Bridge, Herle, and Rutherford, Hunton endorsed a mediatory metaphysics that stressed the collaborative agency of "con-causes" and "joint causes" in political and natural bodies.[173] Though less decisively than Parker, Hunton also employed the language of political mixture with a sense of its physical and transformative character. When he writes that the "Authority of this Land is of a compounde and mixed nature in the very root and constitution thereof," he asserts the concreteness and irreducibility of England's mixed power. The mixed nature of English government needs to be distinguished, he elaborates, from the idea of limited monarchy, which relies on the imposition of legal restraints on the king.[174] An exclusive reliance on legal devices strikes Hunton as dangerous. "Limitation without mixture of another constituted power" makes "no provision for the indemnity of the people."[175] The concrete union of King, Lords, and Commons in what

Hunton calls "*radicall mixture*," on the other hand, provides such indemnity because it relies on a more physical sense of connection.[176]

That it provided such indemnity showed in situations of national crisis. In case of a conflict in which the three estates cannot resolve their "crossing and jarring," Hunton argues that no governmental authority can be appealed to. "No Constituted, Legall, Authoritative Judge of the fundamentall Controversies arising betwixt the three Estates" may exist, for that would turn mixed into absolute government. Hunton concedes that this is an inconvenience of a radically mixed state, but it is not a wholly unwelcome inconvenience. An irreducible mixture between King, Lords, and Commons keeps sovereignty in the people. In case of an unresolvable conflict, Hunton argues, "the Appeale must be to the Community, as if there were no Government."[177] Hunton leaves the strictly mixed state open to the total body of the community. If the triple-headed body politic fails, the many-headed multitude takes over. Hunton's emphasis on the radical mixture of powers between King, Lords, and Commons reflects and protects the ultimate irreducibility of political power, which always rests in the many. By projecting itself into the future time of constitutional crisis, Hunton's theory confirms the kinship between multitude and mixed government that thinkers like Persons or Parker had traced in the past.

Though Hunton possessed a more formal sense of mixed government, he deployed the vocabulary of mixture in a manner that resembled Rutherford's or Parker's. Mixture's ability to cross the absolutist fence that kept many and one, parts and whole, matter and form, heap and body apart gave it a central role in the writings of these thinkers. Though they occupied different positions on the spectrum of political opposition, Parker, Herle, Bridge, Rutherford, and Hunton made crucial contributions to the fight against absolutism by adopting a Catholic scheme of mediation that let them legitimize political bodies that were not defined by subordination ("*subordinates* make no *mixture*," Hunton wrote) and possessed more than one head.[178] They understood that they had to deploy such a scheme to authorize mixture and multitude and normalize mutation and deformity. For Parker, Rutherford, and Hunton, as for White (and, reluctantly, Digby), mutation and deformity were political virtues. This political vision owed a significant debt to the redefinition of the natural body by an atomism that was newly ascendant because of its reliance on a mediatory metaphysics. The debt was especially clear to White, Digby, and Parker. Mediation allowed mixture to become a transformative cause that sponsored cooperative and mutable unions by letting the multitude go to work.[179]

*   *   *

How does Robert Boyle, the most influential promoter of scientific mixture in the second half of the seventeenth century, engage the relationship between science, religion, and politics I have been tracing in this chapter? This question is inescapable at this point of my argument. Boyle wrote very little about political issues and could seem actively dismissive of political concerns (he once quipped that the government of kingdoms was a "solemn trifle" compared with the spiritual mysteries God gave us to contemplate).[180] Considering the overlaps between scientific, theological, and political knowledge in seventeenth-century culture, however, it is unlikely that Boyle was not aware of the political meanings of his science. As Richard Kroll has emphasized, the revival of atomism in seventeenth-century England was animated, to a significant degree, by the systematic aspirations of Epicurus's and Gassendi's works, which hoped to integrate religious, moral, physical, and epistemological considerations.[181] Boyle, too, believed in the ultimate unity of knowledge. In *Occasional Reflections upon Several Subiects* (1665), for example, he argued that theological, moral, political, economic, and physical truths were related and capable of illuminating each other.[182] Analogies produced knowledge. That Boyle wrote comparatively little on political issues should therefore not prevent us from understanding his politics.

Historians have recognized that Boyle's science had political meanings, but some of the most influential arguments—by Carolyn Merchant, Margaret Jacob, James Jacob, Steven Shapin, Simon Schaffer, and John Rogers—have presented Boyle as a conservative thinker whose political instincts moved him away from the politics of a White or a Parker.[183] Margaret and James Jacob, whose focus on political ontology is closest to my concerns, have prominently argued that Boyle's corpuscular philosophy grows out of a politically conservative desire for stability and harmony that excludes democratic possibilities. This desire expressed itself, they contend, in a metaphysics that emphasized God's power over nature. Boyle made "a providential God . . . responsible for all motion in the universe" and effectively banned the self-motion of atoms and therefore the political agency of the multitude.[184]

This interpretation of seventeenth-century atomism, however, no longer seems credible. Twenty-five years ago, John Henry showed that a broad swath of scientists, including Boyle, Walter Charleton, Henry Power, Thomas Willis, John Mayow, Robert Hooke, and William Petty, argued for self-moving atoms (I would like to add Samuel Gott, John Wallis, Robert Midgley, Kenelm Digby, and Thomas White).[185] Confining self-motion to the radical fringe, as the Jacobs and more recently Rogers have done, is no longer feasible.[186] By situating mediation in the historical context in which it gained prominence, I have been able to show that a mediated relationship between first and second causes did not put God in charge. Rather, mediation freed up the self-motion of natural and political bodies in a Christian culture that had been shaped by the Calvinist and Lutheran tendency to tie second causes to the first cause. It is this context that also helps us understand Boyle's politics. Boyle rejected Calvinist predestination, embraced free will, and endorsed a mediatory metaphysics.[187] This basic orientation stands behind Boyle's ability—examined in the previous chapter—to make mixture a legitimate cause, dethrone form, and normalize mutation.

Boyle's thinking aligns in other ways with a conceptual horizon on which mixture, multitude, mutation, and deformity shed their threatening aspects. He argued, for example, that the generation of monsters was a perfectly natural occurrence. "When a Woman is with Child," he observed in a passage that seems to recall Hakewill, "the Aim of *Nature* is, to produce a Perfect or Genuine human Foetus; and yet we often see, that Nature widely missing Her Mark, instead of That, produces a Monster. And of This we have such frequent Instances, that whole Volumes have been publish'd, to recount and describe these gross and deform'd Aberrations of Nature."[188] Yet to Boyle, such monsters were not deviations, but "the Genuine consequences of the Order, [God] was pleas'd to settle in the World."[189] Monsters, earthquakes, pestilences, and famines were neither "*Praeternatural* Things" nor nature malfunctioning.[190] Nature was not an agent for Boyle. It was nothing but a "Compounded Accident" whose effects did not spring from specific intentions or aims, from some intelligent principle residing in or above nature, but from numerous, interactive, semi-independent atoms who had no idea what they were about.[191] For Boyle, the universe was not filled with intentions, and the boundary between form and deformity did not mark essential differences.

Boyle also advocated scientific cooperation with the social multitude, whose knowledge he considered indispensable to scientific progress.[192] Boyle was not immune to what Richard Ashcraft has called the "prudential fear of the giddy multitude," but like Digby's, Boyle's aristocratic status did not bar egalitarian beliefs nor did it impair his ability to recognize the moral advantages of republican forms of government.[193] And like Digby, Boyle imported the concept of multitude into different fields. He used multitude, for example, to tell a creation story in which God divides matter "into an innumerable multitude of very variously figur'd Corpuscles." Once endowed with motion, this multitude arranged itself into the phenomena of this world.[194] Perhaps more tellingly, Boyle frequently used multitude to evoke the sublime variety of identities and interactions in an atomist universe. Boyle was awed by the spectacle of multitude. "An innumerable multitude of singly insensible Corpuscles"; "the most familiar Bodies may have Multitudes of Qualities"; "there [are] actually in the Universe great Multitudes and Corpuscles mingled among themselves"; "a Multitude of Associations"; "so great a multitude of differences": phrases like these can be found everywhere in Boyle's work.[195]

Boyle even used multitude to describe his writing style. In his introduction to *Certain Physiological Essays* (1661), he argued that he has "oftentimes, contrary to my Reason and Genius, deliver'd things, to make them more clear, in such a Multitude of words, that I now seem even to my self to have in divers places been guilty of Verbosity." Whatever its demerits, however, such a multitude of words responded to the challenge of clearly capturing the complexity of atomic realities in language. Boyle's verbose sentences "comprise," as he put it, "what I thought requisite to be delivered at once."[196] Freed from the guiding hand of form, the agency of the many created a cooperative intricacy that found expression in sentences that strove to represent such complexity faithfully, through a similarly unformalized stream of words. Verbal multitude reflected natural multitude. The plain style recommended by some Puritan writers was unsuitable to Boyle's ontology, even as anti-formalism was a value central to both.[197]

In these and other ways, Boyle participated in the revaluation of mixture's conceptual horizon through a mediatory metaphysics. Boyle was no politician, but he was reminded of the political content of such a metaphysics in 1677, when he asked Presbyterian and eventual nonconformist leader John Howe to write a treatise on God's foreknowledge that repudiated its determinative hold on human action.[198] Howe conceded that God possessed "Almighty Power" that could "immediately work, without the subordinate concurrence of any second cause," but such immediacy was the exception rather than the rule.[199] In nature, politics, and religion, Howe claimed, the self-motion of second causes was the norm.[200] Howe did not draw any radical political

conclusions from this position, but he was quickly identified with such conclusions by the Calvinist Thomas Danson, who traced his theological roots
back to Twisse.[201]

In an excited exercise of Calvinist scholasticism, Danson accused Howe of
relying on "Durandus his Opinion, which was, That God concurs remotely
and mediately with second Causes, (*viz.*) no otherwise than as he confers and
conserves their Essence and Power of action, by which they themselves act
nextly and immediately."[202] This was a politically resonant charge. As we have
seen, Rutherford and Bridge had mobilized Durandus's support in their arguments for the rights of the people to choose their government. Not surprisingly,
Danson also charged Howe with Arminianism and atomism and concluded
that he "justled [God] out of his proper place; I mean, of being the first cause
of all the Creatures actions." "The Creature [is] put in his stead," he continued, and is "able to use its power, as it pleases."[203] Andrew Marvell rushed to
Howe's defense, condemning Danson's discourse for displaying the "humor
of Tyrants."[204] Even in Boyle's immediate surroundings, the political meanings of a philosophy raised on the semi-independence of second causes were
plain.

This does not mean that Boyle was unworried about these meanings. He
was worried. But we would be mistaken to place these worries at the center of
Boyle's thought. This is the troubling implication of William Newman's insistence that Boyle's scientific program revolved around the repeated demonstration that all bodies could be reduced to their atomic constituents, and it
is the Jacobs' when they contend that Boyle's desire for stability banned the
transformative possibilities of self-motion. Boyle was interested in the persistence of atomic clusters through profound chemical transformation, and he
was anxious, as were most Englishmen in the seventeenth century, about political stability. Ontological and political stability were important, linked issues.
But any interpretation that makes stability a motivating concern of Boyle's
philosophy is misguided. The phenomena that most actively engaged Boyle's
curiosity were not structure and stability, but motion, cooperation, and mutation. In the final analysis, these phenomena dominate Boyle's atomist world
picture. Let me drive this point home by looking closely at one of Boyle's ren-
ditions of this picture.

In *The Origine of Formes and Qualities* (1666), Boyle prepares us for this
picture by stressing that the "Fruitfulnesse and Extent of our Mechanical
Hypothesis" can be grasped only when we understand that "the World we

live in is not a Movelesse or Indigested Mass of Matter, but a . . . Self moving
Engine, wherein the greatest part of the common Matter of all Bodies is al-
waies . . . in Motion."[205] "Local Motion seems to be indeed," Boyle explains,
"the Principal amongst Second causes, and the Grand Agent of all that happens in Nature."[206] Here is how Boyle depicts his self-moving engine:

> From the various Occursions of those innumerable swarms of little
> Bodies, that are mov'd to and fro in the world, there will be many
> fitted to stick to one another, and so compose Concretions; and
> many . . . disjoyn'd from one another, and agitated apart; and multi-
> tudes also that will be driven to associate themselves, now with one
> Body, and presently with another. . . . If a parcel of Matter do but
> happen to stick to one Body, it may chance to give it a new Quality,
> and if it adhere to another, or hit against some of its Parts, it may
> constitute a Body of another Kind; or if a parcel of Matter be knockt
> off from another, it may barely by That, leave It, and become it self of
> another Nature then before. If, I say, we consider these things on the
> one side; and on the other side, that (to use *Lucretius* his Compari-
> son) all that innumerable multitude of Words, that are contain'd in
> all the Languages of the World, are made of the various Combina-
> tions of some of the 24 Letters of the Alphabet; 'twill not be hard to
> conceive, that there may be an incomprehensible variety of Associa-
> tions and Texture of the Minute parts of Bodies, and consequently a
> vast Multitude of Portions of Matter endow'd with store enough of
> differing Qualities, to deserve distinct Appellations.[207]

The clustered atoms that swirl around in this crowded field transform or become bodies with each little collision, each shifting coalition, however temporary it may be. They perform a productive, chancy dance, open to contingency.
While the ultimate building blocks of Boyle's world—the smallest particles of
matter—are invisible, indivisible, and uniform, the atomic clusters they compose create "an incomprehensible variety of Associations and Textures," and
with that, qualities and bodies. The "Seeds or immediate Principles" Boyle invokes to emphasize the stability of his atomic clusters earlier in this text are
now displaced by ceaseless motion.[208] They dissolve into the stirring spectacle
of casually infinite metamorphoses.[209] It is not just new qualities that emerge
from this swarming dance, but new kinds. By "sticking" to one body, a parcel

of matter may give that body a new quality, and by "adhering" to another, it
may set off a transformation in kind—or it may not. The possibilities and
variations are infinite in this vast self-moving engine.

Stability is not a dominant concern in this picture. It authorizes instead
the local motions of the multitude to make, unmake, and remake bodies on
a routine basis, with even the smallest of movements or shifts. The gentle
enthusiasm that radiates from Boyle's depiction of small, invisible bodies, his
attention to their travels, adventures, and transformations, undo the passivity
of matter Boyle tries to foreground initially. As he gets into his description,
Boyle lets stability be the worry of another day and celebrates the transformative dance of matter in motion. He may assert on other occasions that "matter, how vastly extended, and how variously shap'd soever, is but a brute
thing," but his description shows that such assertions were easily overcome by
a profound sense of wonder over the contingent productivity of moving and
mixing atoms.[210] Boyle explains such wondrous generative variety by referring to Lucretius, who had compared it to the multitude of words that can be
created out of twenty-four letters. But his description is indebted to Lucretius's
De Rerum Natura in another sense as well. Like Lucretius's poem, Boyle's
description aspires to make visible the invisible.[211]

Boyle's world picture should help us view his concern about political
stability with different eyes. I turn to one of the few sustained and rarely analyzed political meditations in Boyle's oeuvre, an episode in *Occasional Reflections*. Boyle's occasion for this meditation is the adventure of a boat ride. He
tells the story of a few friends who go on a ramble in the countryside. At one
point, they decide to hire a sailboat to reach promising fishing grounds. The
boat runs into trouble. A sudden storm, the drunkenness of the captain, and
the incompetence of his assistant create an increasingly unstable situation.
When it becomes clear that the two steersmen (one of whom is drunk) have
little control over the ship and that even their communication with each
other is breaking down, some of the passengers begin to expostulate with
them. Confusion rises, and the situation gets even more precarious when
these passengers stand up and threaten to destabilize the boat. At this point,
a passenger named Lindamore intervenes, instructing the others to sit still
and let the two boatmen do their work. He has seen enough cases, Lindamore urges, in which such disagreements between passengers and steersmen
have overset the boat. "This counsel was thought very reasonable," Boyle
ends the story, "since the greater the Wind was, and the less the Steerman's
dexterity, the more necessary it appear'd, that we should be orderly and quiet,

and by leaning our Bodies sometimes one way, and sometimes another, as occasion requir'd, do what in us lay to keep the Vessel upright." The journey ends safely.[212]

The story's political lessons are literally conservative. If the people in charge of government are incompetent and reckless, it is best to remain quiet. Active resistance (standing up) is especially dangerous. The preservation of the body politic has to be the primary goal of every subject. These lessons are clear. They are qualified by the subsequent discussion between the friends who were in the boat. Lindamore is the first to comment on the political truths contained in the adventure. Government, he argues, is charged with managing "free Agents." Because such agents often pursue "interests or designs of their own, distinct from those of the Prince, and many times repugnant to them," government is an inherently difficult art. So difficult, Lindamore adds, that misgovernment is more likely than not. Still, the "publick Infelicities of declining States, are not always wholly due to the Imprudence of the Ruler." "Oftentimes," he goes on, "those that most resent such Imprudency . . . encrease the publick Disorders." It is unclear, Lindamore concludes, which causes more damage: imprudent "States-men" or an impatient "Multitude."[213]

Boyle believes that these reflections are appropriate to the adventure of the boat ride. It seems to me that they revise what initially seemed like a flat rejection of popular resistance. The starting point for Lindamore's interpretation is the fundamental fact of human freedom. Sounding a skeptical Tacitean note, Lindamore argues that the multiplicity of interests and designs pursued by individuals makes government an inherently difficult art that might well be impossible to master.[214] The confusion in the boat is thus regrettable, but it is also an expression of human freedom. The trouble the boat runs into is a natural consequence of the inherently difficult business of sailing. When Lindamore urges that the multitude behave quietly or, later on, that the "vulgar" are incapable of understanding the complex circumstances that inform the actions of government, he invokes reason of state and the superior cognition of an educated aristocracy, but he does not question that the multitude is exercising a basic right.[215] Even if they destabilize the boat, the multitude's actions are the legitimate expression of free agents.

These views are reflected on by the two other participants in the conversation. Eugenius confirms that we owe "Reverence and Submission . . . to Senates, or Princes." But such reverence, he notes, does not apply to reason, which he views as essentially free to judge whatever matters present themselves. "The Tribunal of reason," he argues, "has a Jurisdiction that reaches to

Thrones themselves."[216] The most conservative contributor to the conversation, the divine Eusebius, bemoans the "disturbing Vicissitudes of Government" one finds in countries whose fates are determined by "whoever could get Interest enough in the Souldiery, or the Multitude." Yet he acknowledges that governments can be changed by the people. His evaluation of different forms of government uses the criterion of relative stability to recommend a heritable crown.[217]

It is not easy to parse which of these speakers Boyle feels closest to. It is clear, however, that all three accept some fundamental truths. Human beings are free agents. They may pursue their interests and designs, even if this creates conflicts in the state. Conflicts and power struggles, indeed, are inevitable, and forms of government are changeable and equally legitimate (senates and princes both deserve submission). It is useful to evaluate these forms by the degree of stability they offer, but neither the wish for stability nor the condemnation of ill-informed actions changes the freedom of human beings to resist or change government.[218]

Boyle's concern with stability is often seen as a response to the turmoil of the commonwealth period. I think this is only partially true. Boyle's concern has deeper roots in his belief in human freedom. His recognition of the inevitable challenges that such freedom poses to the art of government makes him prize stability. He fully realizes, in other words, that instability is the inevitable condition of a civil society made up of free agents. Societies may be able to limit instability by adopting devices such as a heritable crown, but no sanctity attaches to such forms. They are only means to an end. If different forms promise better, there is no reason why societies should not adopt them. The ultimate source of political power lies in the free individuals that gather in societies.

This last point is underscored by the most interesting moment in Boyle's simile of the boat ride, the ending. The weather is dire, the captain is drunk, and the ship of state is out of control. One might expect that Boyle's apparent familiarity with the Tacitean tradition would prompt him to seek a solution in which necessity and emergency justify a radical suspension of the existing order. But the solution Boyle advocates is to utilize all the forces at hand. The multitude may be uninformed and giddy, but the cooperation of all is needed to reach safe shores. "By leaning our Bodies sometimes one way, and sometimes another," the passengers trim the boat. Civil society may require the adoption of legal structures or an active recognition of the duty to obey, but moments of crisis reveal that such requirements do not change the natural political power every individual possesses. Such moments dramatize the collective nature of the body politic. They show that the health of the commonwealth depends on all. Strict subordination does not suit free agents. Active cooperation does.

Boyle's meditation on the cooperative nature of the body politic illuminates the politics of a passage in which Boyle contemplates the problem of stability in natural bodies. To illustrate what he calls "the coherency of the heap"—the stability of bodies whose cohesion results from constant particulate motion—Boyle turns to a simile.[219] Consider a swarm of bees, he invites us: viewed from a distance, it "seems to be one entire masse or body," but a closer view reveals "that the particular Bees that swarm have most of them their distinct and peculiar motions . . . when one of the more innermost Bees removes, as she lets go her hold from those that she rested on before, and goes away from those that rested on her, so she meets with others on which she may set her feet, and comes under others that in like manner set their feet on her, and so by this vicissitude of mutual supports their coherence and their removes are made compatible."[220] This simile of body-like cohesion through individual, particulate motion and shifting mutual supports matches the political logic of Boyle's boat ride as much as the "innumerable swarms of little Bodies" that populate his world picture. Instability is a feature of the world. It cannot be fixed—not by forms, not by chains of antecedent causes. But that doesn't mean that the world is chaotic. Undoing the difference between heap and body does not mean the destruction of cohesion and order. Instead, it means the elevation of a cooperative order that achieves a degree of stability by trusting the only thing that can be trusted: the constantly shifting "vicissitudes of mutual supports."

Boyle's description of the swarming of bees rewrites the political lessons Samuel Purchas had drawn from the bee swarm. In Purchas's *A Theatre of Politicall Flying-Insects* (1657), the order and functionality of the swarm depended on a leader, not the cooperation of equals.[221] In this, Purchas aligned himself with a well-established tradition that associated bees with monarchy.[222] Two years before Purchas's book appeared, Boyle's friend Hartlib had tried to draw different political lessons from bees. In a chapter on swarming, Hartlib's *The Reformed Common-wealth of Bees* (1655) argued that a functional and industrious commonwealth resulted from an "unarmed" king who was "shut into a little den" and, under such restraints, unleashed "wonderful diligence in the Bees." Boyle was familiar with Hartlib's book, but even if that were not the case, Boyle's belief in the divinely guaranteed unity of all truths makes it highly likely that the cooperative self-motion of a swarm of bees contained a political lesson for him.[223] Unlike Hobbes, Boyle sees coherence in the heap and accepts the bee as a political animal.[224]

By treating multitude, monster, heap, and swarm as the natural expressions of a divinely ordered universe marked by liberty and cooperation, Boyle articulated a political ontology that rendered deformity legitimate and functional. He joins thinkers such as Hakewill, Digby, White, and Parker, for whom the rejection of the difference between form and deformity—and thus of the moral, theological, political, and ontological difference between form and matter, one and many, whole and parts—was central. This rejection contradicted those theorists who denied political agency and right to the multitude and insisted on the singular, homogeneous, clearly subordinated body as the naturally superior foundation of good government. Fanned by the fame it achieved in the 1660s and 1670s, Boyle's philosophy thus contributed to the growing acceptance of a mixed body politic that, to those who insisted on an indivisible sovereignty, could only seem monstrous.

CHAPTER 3

Locke's Mixed Liberty

My argument has shown that the attempt in seventeenth-century England to imagine and justify political bodies that share sovereignty between multiple parts was assisted by changing scientific definitions of natural bodies. Adopting a mediated relationship between first and second causes, a diverse group of natural and political philosophers in the first half of the century sought to legitimize mixture and multitude and normalize heterogeneity, deformity, and mutation. Their vision of natural and political bodies offered a fundamental challenge to the norms of political order promoted by royalists and absolutists. To be unified, powerful, and civil, the anti-absolutists argued, political bodies did not have to subordinate the many to one, parts to whole, matter to form. Nature indicated that bodies could establish, maintain, and transform themselves through the cooperation of parts instead. To describe such cooperation, natural and political philosophers resorted to the new language of mixture, which sustained a clear and broadly applicable counter-program to the idea that order depended on strong boundaries, clear forms, and sovereign essences. The programmatic possibilities of a redefined mixture helped to align religious, scientific, and political truths in support of an idea of order that included permeable borders, deformity, and mutable essences. These possibilities also opened up, under the pressure of acute political crisis, acknowledged and unacknowledged areas of agreement between royalists and parliamentarians, Catholics and Protestants.

In this chapter, I would like to examine how these shifting definitions of natural and political bodies affected the politics of mixture in the second half of the seventeenth century. One way to approach such a task would be to focus on the second revival of mixed government between 1678 and 1685, which occurred in the context of a renewed absolutist threat raised by the possible succession of James, Duke of York. But while this second revival is an important event in the history of mixture in seventeenth-century England, it is not going to be my main focus. Apart from the fact that this revival has already received considerable attention from political historians, I would like to continue to pursue a semantic history of mixture that follows the migrations of this concept across different areas of inquiry, into the various intellectual contexts in which it unfolded its new meanings.[1]

To this end, I propose to examine the works of John Locke, one of the best-known proponents of mixed government. Locke is important to my story because he reaped extensive and varied benefits from the widening recognition of mixture's scientific and political value. The writings Locke produced during the political crisis of the early 1680s present the most original contribution to the revaluation of mixture in seventeenth-century culture. With greater clarity and ingenuity than any of the figures I have discussed so far, Locke realized that accepting mixture as cause and basic reality has far-reaching consequences. Largely unrecognized in Locke scholarship, this realization permeated core areas of Locke's ontology, epistemology, and politics. As extensive and varied as the benefits were that Locke reaped from the explanatory value mixture had gained, however, these benefits still confirm what I have argued throughout: the scientific authorization of mixture is intertwined with the political history of seventeenth-century England. Locke's friendship with Boyle, his membership in the Royal Society, and his eventual embrace of atomism certainly contributed to his appreciation of mixture's value.[2] But it was Locke's involvement in the political battle against the absolutist threat contained in James's succession that made the most decisive contribution to this appreciation.

While Charles II's restoration in 1660 had returned the nation to a sense that a strong monarchy was its destiny, it did not take too long before the old conflicts resurfaced. James had declared his Catholic faith in the 1670s and was secretly promoting, in concert with his royal brother, England's return to Catholicism. Catholicism had shed many of its radical associations and was now firmly expected to lead to absolute government. When evidence of a Catholic plot to kill the king and to establish the Catholic faith emerged in 1678, mass hysteria ensued. Under the leadership of Anthony Ashley Cooper, First Earl of Shaftesbury, the Stuart opposition introduced a bill in 1679 to exclude James from the succession. It triggered a serious political crisis. The multitude reared its many heads, and mixed government rose with it. After an early attempt by the restored Stuart court to expunge the idea of shared sovereignty from the political conversation, political mixture became once again a rallying cry for the Stuart opposition.[3] Many of the political pamphlets that circulated in the 1640s were republished, including Phillip Hunton's *A Treatise on Monarchy* (1680), Robert Persons's *A Conference About the Next Succession* (1681), and several of Robert Filmer's treatises. Many new ones were added, and Locke's *Two Treatises of Government* (1689) was initially designed to join the fray.

In the course of this crisis, Charles's illegitimate son, the Protestant Duke of Monmouth, came to embody the best hope for an escape from the twinned threats of popery and unbridled royal power. I have elsewhere shown in detail that between 1678 and 1685, the bastard prince became a powerful symbol of the mixed sovereignty that opposition writers held up against the looming threat of absolute government.[4] Monmouth's illegitimate body was used by Whig and Tory writers to represent a body politic in which no clear distinctions between many and one, form and matter, parts and whole existed. Such use was possible because, despite the arguments by Kenelm Digby and William Harvey earlier in the century, Aristotelian assumptions about sexual generation continued to dominate popular culture. In this context, the illegitimate child (also known as the "love child") was viewed as issuing from an illicit sexual contact whose highly passionate nature prevented the male from asserting his formal agency. The bastard prince had issued instead, it was widely asserted, from an equalizing mixture of male and female parts. He was frequently depicted as an irreducibly mixed creature, half man, half woman, half noble, half base, and quickly compared to animals or substances that resulted from mixture. Monmouth's illegitimacy and the ambiguities produced by it became serious political capital. It fostered Monmouth's remarkable popularity with the multitude, which seemed to throng around him wherever he went in London or in the countryside, and it allowed Tories and Whigs to appropriate Monmouth as a representation of social, sexual, and political mixtures that made tangible the prospect of a more egalitarian society. The Tories reactivated the full catalogue of negative associations mixture possessed; the Whigs tried to make mixture virtuous.

As a trusted aid and friend of Shaftesbury, Locke was closely involved in the political drama around Monmouth and the exclusion of James. Locke helped plan Monmouth's progress in the west in July 1680, drafted instructions for the final exclusion parliament in Oxford, and—after slipping into Holland under threat of political persecution—materially assisted Monmouth's rebellion.[5] One of Locke's pupils at Christ Church, James Vernon, was Monmouth's secretary, and Locke and Monmouth conducted their financial business in Holland through the same banker, Thomas Dare. Dare was one of the leading English radicals in Amsterdam, and Locke trusted him not only with his money, but also with a draft of his *An Essay Concerning Human Understanding* (1690).[6] Court spies reported regularly on Locke's contacts with various radicals while he was in Holland. Though Locke may not have had "high thoughts" of Monmouth, as his friend Jean Le Clerk reported, he supported Monmouth's cause.[7] Charles II, meanwhile, believed that Locke had a bad influence on Monmouth. Monmouth's diary records a conversation with his father that took place after the plan to assassinate the king and his brother had been discovered in 1683. Monmouth confessed his knowledge of the plot to his father Charles. He wrote in his diary that Charles "received me pretty well; and said Locke and [Robert] Ferguson were the causes of my misfortune, and would ruin me. After some hot words against them," the conversation ended.[8]

Locke's proximity to the political struggle to remove James from the succession gave him many opportunities to observe firsthand the politics of mixture unfolding around and beyond Monmouth. It may not have taken too much, in fact, to convince Locke of mixture's political value. In one of the earliest drafts of the *Essay* dating from 1671, Locke had already given mixture a central place in his philosophy.[9] Comparing man's mental and physical powers, he wrote: "The Dominion of Man, in this little World of his own Understanding, being muchwhat the same, as it is in the great World of visible things; wherein his Power, however managed by Art and Skill, reaches no farther, than to compound and divide the Materials, that are made to his Hands; but can do nothing towards the making the least Particle of new Matter, or destroying one Atome of what is already in Being."[10] I will argue in more detail in the following that Locke's use of the word *compounding* in this comparison of the little and great world of human doing is already informed by the revaluation of mixture in seventeenth-century culture. If Locke believed in the expansive and transformative possibilities of mixture—and we will know soon whether he did—this seemingly modest statement on human agency would contain more daring possibilities. In 1671, however, Locke had not fully grasped these possibilities and their implications. That would change during the political struggle he joined in the late 1670s. Faced with the prospect of absolutism and, soon enough, of political persecution, Locke began to develop a connected argument in *Two Treatises* and the *Essay* in which the possibilities of human liberty are defined in terms of our ability to generate ideas, things, and political relations through mixture. In so linking Locke's major political and philosophical statements to the revaluation of mixture and the exclusion crisis, I hope to develop a fresh perspective on the unity of Locke's thought.

Such unity has been as often proposed as it has been denied. Peter Laslett has been prominent among the deniers. In Laslett's view, Locke was simply not a systematic thinker who aspired to the kind of coherence Hobbes strove for when he identified natural matter with political multitude. In his groundbreaking edition of Locke's *Two Treatises*, Laslett noted that Locke worked simultaneously on his political and philosophical projects, but he diagnosed a basic incompatibility between Locke's embrace of natural law in *Two Treatises* and his polemic against innate ideas in the *Essay*.[11]

Those who have argued for a meaningful relationship between the philosophical and the political Locke include Ruth Grant, Richard Ashcraft, and Robert Albritton.[12] These scholars argue that the *Essay* lays the epistemological and moral foundations for the formulation of political truths. Like so many pursuing a more unified Locke, they prioritize the political work.[13] The *Essay* plays a subservient role: it is the basement of the political house that Locke built. There is a clear division of labor. While the *Essay* deals in epistemology and morals, *Two Treatises* deals in politics. These arguments are not unpersuasive, but the division of labor they propose stands in the way of a more cross-disciplinary integration of the political and the philosophical Locke. Such integration offers a greater chance of capturing characteristic ways of thinking about the world. I pursue it in the following by approaching Locke without privileging one half of his thinking over the other and without assuming that political issues play no major role in the *Essay*. Following the trail of mixture, I carry out a strategic de-differentiation that connects levels and aspects of Locke's thought that are not usually considered to be in conversation. Thus, I recover the political meaning of Locke's discussion of mixed species and mixed modes in book three of the *Essay* and apply this meaning to his frequently criticized use of labor as an agent of mixture in *Two Treatises*. I will initially focus on texts that were written in the context of the political struggle over James's exclusion. This context has always been central to understanding *Two Treatises*, but I will argue that it also helps us understand significant portions of the *Essay*, and in particular book three.

This approach distinguishes my work from the most powerful argument for the unity of Locke's thought, James Tully's *A Discourse on Property: John Locke and His Adversaries* (1980). Though Tully also privileges *Two Treatises*, he offers a compelling synthesis when he argues that Locke's thinking about the little world of understanding and the great world of doing employs a workmanship model. Locke has a "maker's theory" of human agency that applies to the way we make ideas and to the way we make things. On both levels, Tully argues, Locke asserts that we are exercising our God-given dominion over the world by combining its ingredients and making (but not creating) something new.[14] Much of my thinking about Locke is influenced by Tully's deeply learned book. Unlike Tully, however, I argue for the paradigmatic significance of the relationship Locke posits between making and mixing. Tully does not comment on this relationship, not even when he discusses Locke's comparison of the little and the great world.[15] In focusing on Locke's realization of the philosophical and political values of mixture, I do not propose to improve on the synthesis Tully achieves. Following the links between natural and human agency and between ontology, epistemology, and politics, I aim instead to reveal a wider and more varied landscape of relatedness within Locke's thought. I will begin this task by descending into Locke's highly topical polemic against a dead author.

*   *   *

Locke's *Two Treatises* was written in response to a remarkable royalist propaganda hit: the publication of Robert Filmer's *Patriarcha* in 1680, some forty years after it had been composed. Questions of kinship and sexual generation had become intensely political around the campaign for and against Monmouth. The differences between legitimate and illegitimate, between close kin and distant kin, were vigorously asserted by James's supporters. Kingship was heritable, and James was next in line. As a bastard without a formal relationship to the Stuart family, Monmouth was out of line. Filmer's insistence on the patriarchal, univocal, and heritable nature of political power strengthened these assertions. Locke's treatise pushed against them.

In the first part of *Two Treatises*, Locke attacked Filmer's argument that inheritance and succession are natural forces that exist independently of human construction. In a passage that echoed the rhetoric of contemporary opposition pamphlets against hereditary succession, Locke exposed as vague and uncertain the kinship values that were supposed to order inheritance and succession. I would like to join Locke as he poses a series of probing questions about the relative rights of older and younger brothers, male and female lines:

I go on to ask whether in the inheriting of this *Paternal Power*, the *Supreme Fatherhood*, the Grand-Son by a Daughter, hath a Right before a Nephew by a Brother? Whether the Grand-Son by the Eldest Son, being an Infant, before the Younger Son a Man and able? Whether the Daughter before the Uncle? or any other Man, descended by a Male Line? Whether a Grand-Son by a Younger Daughter, before a Grand-Daughter by an Elder Daughter? Whether the Elder Son by a Concubine, before a Younger Son by a Wife? From whence also will arise many Questions of Legitimation, and what in Nature is the difference betwixt a Wife and Concubine? For as to the Municipal or Positive Laws of Men, they can signifie nothing here. It may farther be asked, Whether the Eldest Son being a Fool, shall inherit this *Paternal Power*, before the Younger a wise Man? And what Degree of Folly it must be, that shall exclude him? And who shall be judge of it?[16]

Locke presents a crushing list of cases that would seem to escape, contradict, and destabilize what Filmer claims to be the self-evident standards of succession.[17] He rejects the idea that the bloodline can speak for itself and establish rank and privilege independent of human intervention. Since Monmouth is the oldest son of Charles by one of his "concubines," Locke's questioning of the distinction between mistress and wife, illegitimate and legitimate, is highly topical and politically inflammatory. Under natural law—for Locke the most authoritative law—no one can withhold title from the illegitimate whoreson. Locke makes a related point elsewhere in his treatise when he mentions the biblical story of the "Bastard" Jephta as an example that contradicts the divine right of kings and highlights the elective and conditional nature of kingship.[18] Locke's questioning of the values we attach to kin and the rules of descent they organize amounts to the assertion that they are not natural. The differences we make between grandson and nephew, true-born and bastard, are conventional and cannot naturalize inheritance, whose patterns vary from one society to the next and even within a single society.[19] They cannot provide what Filmer claims they do: a natural source of legitimacy, social hierarchy, and political power.

Locke underscored his argument about the social construction of kinship values in a journal entry of 1681, the year in which he likely concluded composition of the first treatise of government.[20] Polygamy, Locke argued, was no sin in the state of nature. It only became a vice "in a societie wherein modestie the great Vertue of the weaker sex has . . . other rules and bounds set by custom and reputation than what it has by direct instances of the law of nature in a solitude or an estate separate from the opinion of this or that societie." John Marshall has suggested that these reflections may have been prompted by Locke's perusal of John Dryden's *Absalom and Achitophel*, which intervened in the exclusion crisis late in 1681.[21] Dryden had opened his poem with a mock defense of the polygamy by which King David (Charles II) propagated his image throughout the land. The most famous result of such polygamy was of course Absalom, for Dryden and many others the biblical type of Monmouth. Locke did not condone Charles's philandering, but he insisted that illegitimacy was not a fact of nature. It was a social fact. Monmouth's birth could seem problematic only because English society had developed conventions that discriminated against polygamy. These conventions, meanwhile, were not unchangeable.

The demonstration that kinship structures were imposed on nature, however, did not reach the heart of Filmer's assertions. Locke believed that Filmer's attempt to naturalize hierarchy was most powerfully supported by the fact of sexual difference. The ultimate source of Filmer's claim that we are born into hierarchies and are therefore "not naturally free" is the act of begetting, Locke argued. Filmer's patriarchal right originates in the male because, in Filmer's own words (here quoted by Locke), he "is the Nobler and Principal Agent in Generation" (180). Essentially Aristotelian ideas about the agency of the male in generation constitute, Locke claimed, "the main Basis of all [of Filmer's] Frame" (176). Filmer's reliance on these ideas kept succession clear and sovereignty singular. If the male act of generation creates patriarchal power and if that power is political, the one always trumps the many, in families and in kingdoms. "There is, and always shall be continued to the end of the world," as Filmer put it, "a natural right of a supreme father over every multitude."[22] That the multitude possessed political rights was for Filmer the preposterous assertion of Jesuits like Robert Bellarmine (Bellarmine's argument that humankind had imposed inequality on natural equality was attacked early and prominently in *Patriarcha*).[23]

Given the continued pull of Aristotelian ideas of generation and the highly visible political stage they entered in the drama of a bastard prince who challenged the true line of succession, it is not surprising that Locke felt the need to suggest an alternative model of generation. Echoing arguments that had surfaced forty years earlier, *Two Treatises* contended that the woman has an equal if not "greater" share in the process of generation. It is in "her own body, out of her own Substance" that the mother provides the "Materials and Principles" of the child—an important point since the mother provides not only matter, but also something more spiritual (180). That made her equal to the male. "The Mother," Locke argued, "cannot be denied an equal share in begetting of the Child, and so the Absolute Authority of the Father will not arise from hence" (180). As we shall see in more detail soon, Locke would come to favor a model of generation in which the "mixture of Male and Female" was procreative.[24] In the context of royalist attacks on Monmouth that denigrated his origins by associating them with an equalizing sexual mixture, such a model did more than contradict Filmer.[25] It undermined further the alleged boundaries between illegitimate and legitimate by contending that cooperative sexual mixture was not a deviation from the norm, but the norm itself. From this perspective, Monmouth's mixed origins were no flaw. His "mounting spirits bold," as Dryden's poem had suggested, were not locked in agonizing battle with his "Mothers Mold."[26]

Locke recognized that this biological argument strengthened the claim that Adam and Eve were equals. Against Filmer (and with Filmer's contemporary Henry Parker), Locke argued that Adam and Eve were equal recipients of God's grant of dominion. God's command to take possession of the goods of this world did not go just to Adam, but to "them." Eve was "Lady, as well as he Lord of the World" (161). Biological and political cooperation mirrored each other. Nature and theology agreed that sovereignty was always shared.

*   *   *

Locke's argument that biology and theology suggested an equal and cooperative universe can easily look like an expedient and perhaps uncharacteristic counter-claim to Filmer's argument. Feminist critics have argued that Locke was by no means a convincing advocate of sexual equality, and political philosophers have claimed that Locke was not lured by the "naturalistic fallacy," the belief that political lessons could be drawn from natural processes.[27] Before we go further in our reconstruction of Locke's evolving attitude to mixture, we have thus occasion to ask whether Locke's biological argument was less indebted to deep convictions than to a highly localized set of circumstances that included the exclusion crisis, the publication of the forty-year-old *Patriarcha*, Shaftesbury's patronage, and Locke's acquaintance with

Monmouth. Do genuinely held beliefs underwrite Locke's polemic against Filmer's old-fashioned ideas?

I am inclined to say yes. The political circumstances in which Locke sat down to write *Two Treatises* influenced what he wound up saying, but they alone cannot explain Locke's claim for an equalizing mixture of female and male parts in generation. That claim had started to develop in Locke's thinking before 1678. While it was precipitated, along with a heightened awareness that natural philosophy was political, by the volatile events of the exclusion crisis, the claim for generative mixture did not owe its existence to Lockean temporizing. Indeed, the argument for a generative, equalizing mixture soon became an integral part of Locke's passionate and principled critique of species distinctions in book three of the *Essay*. This critique, in turn, resonated with the representation of Monmouth as a mixed species and what it symbolized about the egalitarian promises of mixed government. Grasping and sorting these connections between the passionate, the occasional, and the principled—between the political street fighter and the aloof philosopher—is critical to understanding the political content of Locke's *Essay* and the philosophical bent of *Two Treatises*. Before returning to *Two Treatises*, I would like to use this section and the next to address the political content of the *Essay* in more detail. I begin by explaining what an argument for sexual mixture has to do with a critique of species distinctions and how Locke came to see both as simultaneously political and philosophical problems. At stake, ultimately, is Locke's idea of liberty.

In the late 1670s and early 1680s, the royalist press had a good time sliding from the product of sexual mixture, Monmouth, to the claim that he was a mixed species. The anonymous *Grimalkin, or, the Rebel-Cat* (1681) returns us to Giambattista della Porta's world, though it firmly rejects the positive effects that the magical tradition associated with mixture. It represents Monmouth as a leopard, in della Porta's phrase a "bastard brood" that springs from the union of panther and lion.[28] As the "Bastard Leopard," this pamphlet explains, Monmouth was the "natural son" of the "true-born Lyon" and the base panther.[29] For *Grimalkin* and many other texts, such species mixture signified a violation of natural hierarchies, which in turn signified the leveling of social and political hierarchies. The conclusion was that Monmouth's mixed species stood for a radical and degenerative equality.[30]

This was imaginative political satire, but in extrapolating from sexual mixture to mixed species *Grimalkin* also made sense. In the Aristotelian model of generation, after all, the male is the source of form. He specifies female matter. In an age yet unfamiliar with the idea that species are preserved by genetic differences, arguing against the male's or the seed's primacy opened the gates to species mixture. Locke came to acknowledge this consequence gradually. He asserted it more aggressively only after he had become involved in the political fight against the Stuarts in 1679, in his intense polemic against species in book three of the *Essay*. Let me sketch, as far as I can, the development of Locke's thinking about mixture and species up to that point.[31]

Locke's initial drafts of the *Essay* date to 1671. They already delineate some of the basic parameters of Locke's thinking about species distinctions. Although nature, he points out, may "make many particular things which do agree one with another in many qualitys or simple Ideas, yet it is men who takeing occasion from those qualitys wherein they finde them to agree that distinguish them into species." The crucial point is that nature does not make the species we recognize as such: we do. Nature produces particular things that share qualities; man observes a certain number of shared qualities between different particulars and collects these particulars into a species. Although we may persuade ourselves otherwise, our species names do not designate anything existing objectively out there. Locke underscores this later in the same paragraph. "But notwithstanding we sort [these particulars] thus according to our collections of simple Ideas into kindes or species, it is yet certain that many of those Individuals which are . . . received as being one species have yet qualitys as far differing from others of that species & name, as they have from other things from which they are accounted to differ specifically."[32] Our collection of the qualities by which we determine species, Locke argues, is limited. An incomplete set of observed resemblances is all we have. This explains why two particulars that we class in the same species on the basis of such a set may at the same time possess diverging qualities that could differentiate these particulars as clearly from each other as two different species. For this reason, different cultures may well divide the natural world into classes of particulars that we would find utterly strange.[33]

All of this, of course, concerns only processes of human understanding and does not directly address the question of what nature, in fact, makes. Five years before Locke formulated his critique of species names, he seems to have believed that nature does generate species through seminal principles, which he considered the actors behind complex natural processes. But he also acknowledged at this time the generative capacity of the "bare mistion of ye parts." This happened shortly after he read Boyle's *Origine of Formes and Qualities* (1666), a book that was fascinated, as we have seen, by the transformative powers of simple mixture.[34] Yet it seems that, subsequently, Locke's belief in the ability of seminal principles to preserve the order of species declined. Mixture rose. Some of the journal entries made during his travels in France between 1675 and 1679 indicate as much.

Locke's journal entry of September 19, 1676, reiterates his belief that our names for species have little to do with the actual constitution of natural things and far more with our ideas about these things. Turning from human knowledge to natural processes, he argues that animate things are kept by nature "in the distinct classes by the order of generation." Animals and plants are made by "that internall principle that organizes the parts . . . and is the principall cause of generating the like." This is different, however, for inanimate things. Because such things consist merely of "several collections of matter without any organicall constitutions [they] may be capeable of infinite variety within the same species, there being a latitude for a great variety of mixtures."[35] The collections of matter that make up minerals lack the principle that would perpetuate clear species boundaries. Mixture is here generative. Still, in 1676 Locke is obviously attached to the notion of a superior formal agent that ensures the reproduction of like animate things.

A year later, on November 19, 1677, Locke renews his meditations on species. The distinction he made between animate and inanimate things seems to be weakening. He suggests that "the Idea of nature by which she forms and distinguishes" things is realized in animals "with more constancy and exactnesse than in other bodys and species of things." In vegetables, he now observes, such constancy and exactness is absent, for "we finde that severall sorts come from the seeds of one and the same individuall [producing] as much different species as those that are allowed to be soe by philosophers."[36] The idea of nature—the seed or the form—does not control the generation of plants. Different kinds, fully satisfying the philosophic definition of species, may come out of the same seed. This statement qualifies Locke's belief in "that internall principle that organizes the parts" of animate things. Whatever determines the species of a vegetable, such determination, Locke argues now, does not happen through a univocal agent. Vegetables are capable of the same infinite variety as minerals. The clear line Locke drew a year earlier between inanimate and animate things has been crossed, and the epistemological critique of species names is joined by a broadening doubt about the ontological stability of species boundaries.

In 1678—about a year before he returned to England and immersed himself in the opposition struggle against the Stuarts—Locke described an actual instance of species mixture in animals. He noted in his diary that he saw "a beast got between a bull and mair" that sported, among other things, "a taile [that] had a mixture of both species."[37] Is it possible that Locke asked himself in 1678 whether even in complex living things the "idea of nature" was less exact and constant than he had assumed? His position on species in book three of the *Essay* makes this likely.

Composed in the mid-1680s, book three shows that Locke was willing to abandon his earlier belief in a single, superior formal agent, even in the making of complex living things.[38] In a polemically charged passage, he argues that sexual generation is not governed by the transmission of an idea, form, or essence. *Grimalkin* might dwell with horror on the "unevenness and incongruity" that results from "Nature's mis-matching of Creatures," but for Locke such combinations are no longer scary.[39] They are simply part of the way nature works:

> Nor let any one say that the power of propagation in animals by the mixture of Male and Female, and in Plants by Seeds, keeps the supposed real *Species* distinct and entire. . . . If History lies not, Women have conceived by Drills; and what real *Species*, by that measure, such a Production will be in Nature, will be a new Question; and we have Reason to think this not impossible, since Mules and Gimars, the one from the mixture of an Ass and a Mare, the other from the mixture of a Bull and a Mare, are so frequent in the World. I once saw a Creature, that was the Issue of a Cat and a Rat, and had the plain Marks of both about it; wherein Nature appear'd to have followed the Pattern of neither sort alone, but to have jumbled them both together. To which, he that shall add the monstrous Productions, that are so frequently to be met with in Nature, will find it hard, even in the race of Animals to determine by the Pedigree of what *Species* every Animal's Issue is; and be at a loss about the real Essence, which he thinks certainly conveyed by Generation, and has alone a right to the specifick name.[40]

The ontological instability of species is greater than ever before. It matches here Locke's epistemological critique of species. Our mistaken ideas about species, Locke argues, derive from false assumptions about sexual generation.[41] Generation is not the exact or constant reproduction of essences that descend from the male into a passive womb that merely provides the raw materials of life. There are no natural hierarchies that control the jumbling of diverse elements and the crossing of divisions. Form does not preexist generation, and this is why the mixture of male and female parts from different species can produce new species. Without the guiding hand of form, there is not only no firm barrier that keeps mandrill and woman, cat and rat from having offspring, there is also nothing that should prevent such offspring from assuming the dignity of a new species. After all, we already recognize mules and gimars as distinct species without worrying about their origins in species mixture. Locke's observation in France of "a beast got between a bull and mair" supports a clear recognition of the ontological instability of species.

Locke draws a radical (and by now familiar) conclusion from such observations. Sexual generation, he argues, can be so transformative that "some of these monstrous Productions, have few or none of the Qualities, which are supposed to result from, and accompany the *Essence* of that *Species*, from whence they derive their Originals, and to which, by their descent, they seem to belong" (448–449). The union of a cat and a rat doesn't always result in a rat-cat with the "plain Marks of both about it." Other results are possible once generation is aligned with the transformative potency of mixture. These results may well defy our ability to reconstruct pedigree or descent by a close examination of the offspring, be it human, nonhuman, or a mixture of both. "Since there has been Humane *Foetus*'s produced," Locke reminds us in book four of the *Essay*, "half Beast, and half Man; and others three parts one, and one part t'other; and so it is possible they may be in all the variety of approaches to the one or the other Shape, and may have several degrees of mixture of the likeness of a Man, or a Brute" (572–573). Mixture challenges the order of resemblance, the reproduction of the same. It undoes the superiority of form, essence, species, and descent, terms whose kinship Locke recognizes.[42] Like Digby before him, Locke uses the evidence of transgeneration to make his case for mixture as a generative cause.

Locke's eyewitness accounts of the mare-bull, the rat-cat, or his mention of a hog with a human head (454–455) have left some philosophers puzzled and incredulous. They cannot explain what Locke intended with these "improbable stories," often ignore them altogether, or contend that Locke did not really mean what he said about species mixture.[43] I have argued, by contrast, that Locke's epistemological doubt about species names is joined by a growing ontological doubt about the stability of species boundaries. However inconvenient Locke's improbable stories may be for our view of Locke as one of the beacons of enlightenment, they should not be sidelined. They make philosophical sense. For Locke, they provide striking physical proof that Aristotelian concepts of form, essence, or species cannot explain the natural world. They illustrate Locke's belief—expanding since the mid-1670s—that mixture can be generative even in the reproduction of complex natural things. And they strengthen Locke's critique of species names.

And yet, all of this is not quite enough to explain Locke's endorsement of species mixture in book three, not enough to resolve the philosophers' puzzlement, and not enough to explain the intensity of Locke's attack on species. To do that, we have to consider that Locke wrote book three shortly after he had come to realize how central Aristotelian ideas of generation were to Filmer's claims about absolute power. Filmer's success prompted Locke to look for a model of generation that suited both his broad philosophical outlook and his political stance in the battle against the Stuarts. The idea of an equalizing mixture did the job: it aligned with Locke's argument for a world in which dividing and compounding were the only expressions of human and natural agency; it assisted the Whig attempt to contest the royalist rhetoric of legitimate descent, pedigree, and natural hierarchy; and it even supported arguments for a mixed body politic whose superior virtue, in the phrasing of Algernon Sidney (one of Monmouth's co-conspirators), sprang from the mixture of the different "species" of government.[44]

If any of Locke's Whig friends read chapter three of the *Essay* in 1686, when it existed as a draft, they would have understood the political meaning of Locke's biology. Because a tremendous amount of political leverage was available to Tories and Whigs through Charles's bastard son, the biological analogy of political mixture became highly visible in the 1680s. Such visibility was only increased by the publication of Filmer's *Patriarcha*, which integrated biological and political arguments with such public success. Locke responded by embracing a biological argument that suited the political need to justify the illegitimate prince and a mixed body politic as much as it fit his anti-Aristotelian philosophy. The stridency of Locke's polemic against the illegitimacy of mixed species in book three of the *Essay*, I submit, grows out of the political context in which Locke acted.[45] It was built on Locke's realization that natural philosophy had become openly political during the exclusion crisis and that his long-standing anti-Aristotelianism harmonized with his evolving political beliefs (I shall say more about this harmony soon).

Isaac Kramnick noted a while ago the marked attachment, among cultural and political critics in early eighteenth-century Britain, to the idea of the chain of being. Henry St. John, Viscount Bolingbroke, for example, stressed the chain of being as a normative expression not only of natural, but also of social and political hierarchy. He did so, Kramnick notes, in response to Locke's insistence on natural equality. Bolingbroke considered the argument for political equality unnatural. He associated it with a confusion of species distinctions that violated the chain of being and produced monstrous social and political consequences. Referring to Jonathan Swift's *Gulliver's Travels* (1726), he made his point that a "belief in natural freedom and equality would destroy . . . fixed social and political distinctions" by noting that "Gulliver's horses made a very absurd figure in the place of men, and men would make one as absurd in the place of horses."[46]

When Locke turned to the chain of being in book three, he placed the emphasis elsewhere. He foregrounded those creatures on the chain that crossed hierarchies and distinctions, including "Fishes that have Wings, and are not Strangers to the airy Region," "Birds that are Inhabitants of the Water" whose meat tastes so much like fish that "the scrupulous are allow'd them on Fish-days," "Porpoises [that] have the warm Blood and Entrails of a Hog," and "Brutes, that seem to have as much Knowledge and Reason, as some that are called Men" (447). Locke used the traditional image of the chain of being to make a metaphysical point about the "magnificent Harmony of the Universe," but he did so in a fashion that would have troubled Bolingbroke, who tried to limit mixture's connection with liberty.[47] Locke's description, by contrast, points to a social and political world in which the combination of differences and the crossing of boundaries is evidence of order and liberty.

It is true, of course, that Locke at least twice assures readers of book three that he does not deny that "Nature, in the constant production of particular Beings, makes them not always new and various, but very much alike and of kin one to another" (462).[48] And it is also true that he invokes the idea of a "real essence" and the notion of a "particular Constitution, which every Thing has within it self, without any relation to any thing without it" (442). Yet such assurances that Locke believes in a real constitution that may define a stable and reproducible identity remain not only occasional, but heavily qualified. For one thing, Locke makes clear that knowledge of real constitutions will never be reached by human actors, whose senses do not extend to the atomic level. For another, his argument about the relationship between things and their environment in book four emphasizes interdependence to such an extent that any real constitution would seem to lose much of its determinative power. Starting at the bottom of the chain of being, Locke argues that the ability of a real constitution to secure identity is weak, and that it gets weaker as you move up the chain:

> If inanimate Bodies owe so much of their present state to other Bod-
> ies without them, that they would not be what they appear to us,
> were those bodies that environ them removed, it is yet more so in
> *Vegetables*. . . . And if we look a little nearer into the state of *Ani-
> mals*, we shall find, that their Dependence, as to Life, Motion, and
> the most considerable Qualities to be observed in them, is so wholly
> on extrinsecal Causes and Qualities of other Bodies, that make no
> part of them, that they cannot subsist a moment without them. . . .
> The ravage made often on several sorts of Animals, by invisible
> Causes, the certain death (as we are told) of some of them, by barely
> passing the Line, or, as 'tis certain of others, by being removed into
> a Neighbouring Country, evidently shew, that the Concurrence and
> Operation of several Bodies, with which, they are seldom thought,
> to have any thing to do, is absolutely necessary to make them be,
> what they appear to us, and to preserve those Qualities, by which we
> know, and distinguish them. . . . This is certain, Things, however
> absolute and entire they seem in themselves, are but Retainers to
> other parts of Nature, for that which they are most taken notice of
> by us. Their observable Qualities, Actions, and Powers, are owing to
> something without them; and there is not so complete and perfect a
> part, that we know, of Nature, which does not owe the Being it has,
> and the Excellencies of it, to its Neighbours. (586–587)

Concentrating on the "Confines of the Body" and thus on the particular constitution that every thing has within itself does not tell us anything about the most important qualities we can observe in a body. The identity of inanimate and of animate things cannot be found on the inside, but in the relationships between inside and outside. So close and so vital is the union between these things and their surroundings, that they are not "entire" by themselves. Every thing in nature owes its being and its qualities to its neighbors. What is extrinsic to a body, Locke argues, is the most important source of knowledge about it. The distinction between inside and outside all but evaporates in such radical interdependence.

Locke's belief in interdependence rests on what I have described, with regard to Boyle's philosophy, as the swarming of atoms. Boyle's influence is noticeable in Locke's discussion, which explains interdependence by referring to "those invisible Fluids" that constantly move through bodies (585) (a subject Boyle was deeply interested in), by alluding to Boyle's vacuum experiments, and by noting that our lives depend on "the duly tempered motion of Particles" streaming toward us from the sun at a certain distance and angle (586). When Boyle argues that "an individual Body . . . needs the assistance, or Concourse, of other Bodies . . . to perform divers of its Operations, and exhibit several Phaenomena's that belong to it," he makes Locke's point, albeit with more restraint.[49] Locke is more radical. For him, real constitutions do not control identity. The qualities, actions, and powers of a thing depend on its neighbors, and this would also seem to be the basis for Locke's belief that the same seed can produce different species. If there is some constancy in nature's reproduction of similar things, it is not guaranteed by any single agent, essence, or preexisting form. What is true of generation is thus also true of life. The shapes, qualities, and powers of things are not preformed and do not inhere in things. They result instead from complex and often unpredictable interactive processes. In this way, Locke emphasizes what we might call "developmental plasticity."[50]

I have argued that Locke's belief in the generative capacities of mixture is logically connected to his critique of species boundaries, and that the belief and the critique received a crucial impetus from the political events of the exclusion crisis. The threat of absolutism prompted Locke to highlight arguments for sexual equality in generation, and the resurgence of political mixture—so dramatically embodied by the bastard prince—made him realize the political content of his philosophizing about species.[51] This realization motivates, I believe, his heated critique of species distinctions in book three of the *Essay*. This critique counters the Tory assertion of natural hierarchy by arguing that there is no such thing. Like kinship and sexual hierarchy, species are human impositions on a world that is far more fluid and free to combine its various ingredients. Placed in the context of royalist attacks on mixed species between 1678 and 1685, Locke's argument for species mixture reveals itself as a plea for political liberty.

I have focused so far on the political ontology of book three of the *Essay*. I would now like to turn to some of the epistemological concerns that preoccupy this book. These concerns also respond to the political situation Locke found himself in after his return from France and during his exile in Holland. In his discussion of the words by which we represent our ideas, Locke contrasts the deceptions of substance names (including species names) to the potential for human liberty in what he calls "mixed modes." In the following section, I will argue that Locke models liberty in human understanding on nature's ability to shape things through mixture. If nature is producing new things by mixing given materials (including the production of new species), the same is true for the smaller world of human understanding. Although Locke argued that humans, unlike animals, have the capacity for abstraction and can distance themselves from the concrete and the natural, his belief that humans occupied a mediocre position in the universe, far removed from the superior rationality of angels, made mixture the proper means of mental elevation.

*   *   *

For many years, Locke used the term *complex ideas* to refer to what he eventually called *mixed modes*. In the two earliest drafts of the *Essay*, "complex ideas" is the phrase of choice.[52] In a diary entry from 1678 (seven years later) Locke uses "complex modes."[53] The exact year when he decided to switch to "mixed modes" is not known. According to Richard Aaron, Locke struggled with the distinction between simple and complex ideas in the early 1680s, and that struggle seems to have yielded the distinction between simple and mixed modes. The distinction debuts as such in draft C of the *Essay*, which was written in the winter of 1684, during Locke's political exile in Holland.[54] We may never have direct evidence of why Locke switched to mixed modes when he wished to describe liberty in human understanding, but it is likely that politics had something to do with it—and I do not mean only the events Locke witnessed during the exclusion crisis. By the time Locke sat down to draft book three, which he finished in 1686, he had already given mixture a central role in the definition of human liberty in *Two Treatises*, as we shall soon see.[55]

It is a little unusual to view book three as expressing a politics of liberty that is related to *Two Treatises*. A more intuitive interpretation might see book three as a cry for reform that hopes to return to order a state of linguistic confusion by reducing complex to simple ideas. Locke spends a whole chapter, after all, on the abuse of words and another on how to remedy these abuses. But while book three is clearly animated by anger over the "*learned Gibberish*" (495) that still dominates learning in seventeenth-century England, I would like to show that Locke's theory of language ultimately recognizes such gibberish as a symptom of human liberty, albeit of an abused liberty that imposed "Mists" on our understanding (497).

Locke's articulation of liberty in human understanding mimics the dialectic unity of reduction and expansion I sketched for Boyle's atomism. On the one hand, Locke's argument on human understanding involves a sweeping act of reduction: all human ideas, no matter how complex, can ultimately be reduced to simple ideas and the sensible qualities they represent. These simple ideas are the ultimate building blocks—the atoms, as it were—of human understanding.[56] To secure this ultimately binding foundation of all knowledge, Locke presents sensible qualities as animated entities that solicit our senses and enter our minds independent of our will. Light and colors, for example, are literally "busie at hand every where . . . to solicite their proper Senses, and force an entrance to the Mind" (106–107). Thus, in this aspect of its operations "the Understanding is merely passive; and whether or no, it will have these . . . materials of Knowledge, is not in its own Power" (118). "Unmixed" (119) ideas thus leave the individual no choice. If knowledge is to possess an objective ground, Locke implies, its origin has to be the involuntary or even forceful penetration of the individual.

Liberty in understanding, on the other hand, involves an act of expansion from the limits imposed by external forces. We begin to experience mental liberty during the later stages of our development by "repeating and joining together" (164) the simple ideas we receive from sensation and reflection. The formation of mixed modes is the highest form of such liberty. Mixed modes, Locke explains, are those terms that signify ideas of "Humane Actions, . . . with their various Ends, Objects, Manners, and Circumstances" (351). Hence gratitude is a mixed mode, and so is polygamy. Whenever man tries to capture the complexity of human actions and relations, mixed modes result. They comprise such a vast number of terms that a complete list would constitute "a Dictionary of the greatest part of the Words made use of in Divinity, Ethicks, Law, and Politicks, and several other Sciences" (294). Unlike substance names, mixed modes have no preexisting natural referent and therefore register cultural differences especially forcefully (nature does not recognize the difference between wife and concubine, as Locke pointed out in *Two Treatises*—some societies do, others might not).

For Locke, the human liberty to form mixed modes is fundamental. The same "liberty *Adam* had at first to make any complex *Ideas* of mixed Modes, by no other pattern, but by his own Thoughts," Locke argues, all men still have (470). In making mixed modes, human beings exercise their God-given mental liberty to its highest extent, without the constraint or the perplexity that confronts them in the contemplation of natural phenomena. Locke explains that the "Workmanship of the Understanding" can model freely in mixed modes and "with great liberty unite often into one abstract Idea Things that in their Nature have no coherence; and so under one Term, bundle together a great variety of compounded, and decompounded *Ideas*. Thus the Name of Procession, what a great mixture of independent *Ideas* of Persons, Habits, Tapers, Orders, Motions, Sounds, does it contain in that complex one, which the Mind of Man has arbitrarily put together, to express by that one Name?" (436). Locke celebrates the human liberty to mix ideas arbitrarily and to bundle numerous complex ideas under a single name. His language is infused with a sense of wonder over the heights that the human mind can climb when it combines a great variety of compounded and decompounded ideas in a single mixed mode. Using a different example two pages earlier, Locke is similarly enthusiastic about the name we have given to the procession of victorious generals returning from battle: "What a vast variety of different Ideas," Locke exclaims, "does the word *Triumphus* hold together, and deliver to us as one species!" (434). Such celebrations of "the free choice of the mind, pursuing its own ends" (431) show how strongly Locke associated mental liberty with acts of mixture that are capable of producing new species.

There is, then, a dramatic difference between the compulsion by which we receive simple ideas and the liberty we realize when we mix them. The depth of this difference raises a question. How do we reconcile the sober notion of "repeating and joining together" simple ideas with the triumphant liberty of mixed modes? Locke is aware of this difficulty. He self-consciously insists in the early stages of the *Essay* that "all those sublime thoughts, which tower above the Clouds, and reach as high as Heaven it self" (118) can indeed be produced by the combinatory activity of the mind. "In this faculty of repeating and joining together its *Ideas*," he stresses, "the Mind has great power in varying and multiplying the Objects of its Thoughts, infinitely beyond what *Sensation* or *Reflection* furnished it with: But all this still confined to those simple *Ideas*, . . . which are the ultimate Materials of all its Compositions" (164). The tension between externally imposed simple ideas and the sublime beyond issuing from them is palpable.

Locke eases this tension between the simple and the sublime, between involuntary imposition and liberty by turning to an illustration that atomists frequently used to explain the dialectic unity of reduction and expansion. Early in the *Essay*, Locke resorts to an analogy that had served Boyle to combat the charge of an improbable reduction of the glorious variety of God's creation to quality-deprived, gray atoms. Invoking Lucretius, Locke argues that the "various composition of 24 Letters" shows that a "few simple ideas [are] sufficient to employ the quickest Thought, or largest Capacity; and to furnish the materials of all that various Knowledge, and more various Fancies and Opinions of all Mankind" (132). There is no necessary tension between a few simple ideas and the infinite variety of human thought they generate.

To strengthen this assertion, Locke draws on the transformative potential mixture had acquired in atomism. This is evident, for example, in the language Locke uses when he celebrates the mixed mode "procession." Locke describes the mental work of mixing in language that applies equally to the physical realm and thus keeps alive the parallel between the little and great worlds of human agency. By using the terms *compounded* and *decompounded* to characterize ideas, Locke leans on Boyle, who had appropriated them from linguists to describe physical phenomena.[57] Like Boyle (as well as Digby and White), Locke sees the combination of simple, compounded, and decompounded materials as an activity that can produce new species. In book three, he celebrates our liberty to make mixed modes of "Things that in their Nature have no coherence" (436) by saying that such mixtures allow us to "[constitute] a Species . . . before any one individual of that Species ever existed" (430). This is the same generative potential that Locke ascribes to the mixture of animal species. For Boyle, the diagnosis that natural things were intricately compounded and decompounded was an important precondition for his experimental program of improving nature by various mixtures. Reduction and purification had their analytical uses, but they could not lead the way toward improvement. For Boyle and for Locke, the greatest promise for the improvement of the human lot lay in acts of mixture. Such acts helped realize human liberty. In strengthening the dialectic of reduction and expansion through the generative potential of mixture, Locke mobilizes the conceptual resources of atomism to explain the liberty and productivity of the mixed mode while holding on to the idea that all mixed modes are ultimately made up of simple ideas. Liberty and necessity coexist.

This solution, however, did not take care of the pragmatic problems that could plague any highly compounded entity intended for communication between human beings. The mixed mode, Locke had to concede, fared worse than substance names and certainly worse than simple ideas when we assess their potential for successful communication. Of all the ideas and names that humankind possessed, mixed modes were "most liable to doubtfulness and imperfection" because they so frequently consisted of highly "compounded and decompounded" ideas (477–478). If mixed modes could be produced by the human mind without any restrictions on the degrees and kinds of mixture, communication was easily threatened. The flipside of liberty was confusion. Having no limits on new species, in nature as in language, could be worrying.

This is clearly a powerful concern. Yet in the end Locke decides to shelve his worries about complex ideational generations, just like he had ultimately shelved his concerns about species mixture. Following his concession about the dangers of mixed modes, Locke considers the imperfections of substance names at some length (481–488). He concludes that, ultimately, mixed modes are capable of more accurate signification because they refer only to what we can know: human actions and human relations. With mixed modes, he explains, human beings "need but know the combination of *Ideas*, that are put together within their own Minds" (517). Substance names, meanwhile, impose on the speaker the impossible task of "enquir[ing] into the whole Nature, and abstruse hidden Constitution, and various Qualities of a Thing without them" (517). In substance names, the potential for irremediable mistake and confusion is higher than in mixed modes.

Even the fact that mixed modes are only "fleeting and transient combinations" of ideas turns out to be a good thing in the comparison with substance names. The fact that mixed modes "have but a short existence any where, but in the Minds of Men, and there too have no longer any existence, than whilst they are thought on" is a plus for Locke (291). It means that, unlike substance names, mixed modes are less likely to promote the false appearance of independent existence and unity. There certainly is a rich fund of examples that indicates the degradation of mixed modes into a kind of second nature, but the reasons for such degradation do not inhere in mixed modes. The potential of mixed modes to promote human liberty is not changed by the fact that human practice has allowed some mixed modes to congeal into dogma or fizzle into confusion.

Locke explains such potential in politically telling language. The names of mixed modes, he notes, make a "precise multitude" (289).[58] We can understand this statement better if we extend Locke's habit of connecting physical and mental workmanship. The virtues of mixed modes, we might say then, derive from the fact that they do not invoke distinctions between matter and form, many and one, parts and whole (unlike substance or species names). That is what a *precise* multitude achieves. For Locke, this means that the identity of mixed modes switches with the addition or subtraction of a single element: "any of the Ideas that make the Composition of the complex [idea], being left out, or changed, it is allowed to be another thing, i.e., to be of another species"

(501). Mutability joins hands with precision. The species of a mixed mode represents a one-ness and whole-ness that does not reduce or subordinate the many. Rather, the many define the one; they are the whole. The utopian potential of mixed modes has to do with their ability to produce form, essence, species, identity (or whatever else you want to call it) as the shifting effects of mixed parts.[59] Using mixture and multitude to describe the most noble products of the human mind aligned Locke with the revaluation of these terms in seventeenth-century science and politics. It allowed him to achieve for ideas what these areas of inquiry had achieved for natural and political bodies: the liberation of matter from the dominance of form. In Locke's philosophy, abstraction realizes human liberty when the many make one, when the parts define the whole.

Locke believed, then, that mixed modes operated in a manner that came closest to the way the world was constituted and to the way man's liberty fit the world. They could live up to the possibilities of human liberty in a world that tied agency to mixture. The deceptions imposed by substance names, meanwhile, ran so much deeper because they suggested a world in which things had inherent unities. Veiling the world that God made, they had helped to persuade us that essences, species, forms, and identities were sovereign and governed the world. Locke's distinction between substances and mixed modes follows the logic that informs his distinction between the old-fashioned belief in species as an unchanging, male order of resemblance and the belief in species mixture as an opening for the new and the superior. In Locke's epistemology and ontology, mixture demonstrates the truth of multitude and combination against the deceptions of the Aristotelian tradition, deceptions that, Locke knew, were deployed to produce political support for the absolutist aspirations of the Stuarts.[60]

I return to the question I posed at the beginning of this section. Locke's decision to replace "complex ideas" with "mixed modes" was indebted to the realization—prompted by the Whig resistance to the absolutist threat—that mixture was the language of liberty. Locke's arguments in book three of the *Essay* for species mixture and mixed modes are related responses to philosophical and political problems Locke wrestled with in the early 1680s. The explicitly political value of mixed modes and the degree to which Locke created overlaps between his discussion of physical and mental species cast a bright light on the political meanings of book three. These meanings are illuminated further when we consider that, by the time Locke sat down to write book three, he had already established the tie between mixture and liberty in *Two Treatises*, to which I now return.

*   *   *

Not content with countering Filmer's biological and theological argument for the indivisible sovereignty of one, Locke sets out in the second treatise of government to search for "another rise of Government, another Original of Political Power."[61] He finds it in the state of nature, in an act of mixture. Every individual, he argues, naturally possesses his or her person. When this possessive self mixes with its environment, a fundamental political relation is created. Locke describes this founding moment of political right as follows: an individual has "mixed his *Labour* with [an object], and joined to it something that is his own, and thereby makes it his *Property*" (288). Despite the fact that everything in the state of nature is common property, more defined powers and rights emerge once the individual moves beyond simple self-possession. In Locke's foundational political myth, creating property in things hinges on the extension of the possessive self into its environment. Locke's description, indeed, seems to suggest an actual transfer of something human to a nonhuman object—mixture as a concrete joining of different substances.

This suggestion has always seemed highly problematic. David Hume noted in 1739 that "we cannot be said to join our labour to any thing but in a figurative sense." Laurence Sterne poked fun in *Tristram Shandy* (1761), suggesting that it was the sweat of the finder that "mix'd" with the apple and created the property.[62] Twentieth-century political philosophers have had similar problems with Locke's description. They have been arguing about Locke's theory of property for a long time. While the stakes of these arguments are high—from the fate of distributive justice to the ethical development of individuals—very few philosophers have been willing to accept the basic terms of Locke's claim about the origins of the right of ownership.[63] Even committed defenders of Locke's theory of property concede that all this talk about labor as an agent of mixture is a little awkward and shouldn't be taken literally.[64] Widely scrutinized and debated, Locke's mixture is at worst a philosophical error and at best a misleading use of figurative language.

Such assessments do more than fault Locke's word choice. They ignore Locke's meaning. Throughout the section on property, Locke's formulations indicate that he sees mixture as a literal, not a figurative term. How else would

we explain his constant habit of presenting the process of appropriation as a
"joining" and "annexing" of the self-possessed human to objects in the state of
nature? In mixing labor with an object, man has "joyned to it something that
is his own" and the object "hath by this *labour* something annexed to it that
excludes the common right of other Men" (288). When a man has practiced
agriculture in the state of nature, he has "annexed to [the land] something
that was his Property, which another had no Title to, nor could without Injury take from him" (291). Because labor is "the unquestionable Property of
the Labourer, no man but he can have a right to what that is once joyned to"
(288). Locke's natural self-possession thus presents an individual who, by mixing with an object, can materially extend him- or herself.

Still, Locke's material sense of mixture as the origin of rights and powers
may seem a little odd. Does he really mean to say that there are possessive
atoms passing from the laboring human figure to the object he or she is working on? Perhaps not. But I do not see what good it does to treat literal and
figurative meanings as mutually exclusive options when Locke seems to work
deliberately with both dimensions, not only here, but elsewhere in his work.
We have seen how Locke relies on mixture in his theory of natural (more
literal) and ideational (more figurative) making, and that such reliance has to
be understood in the broader context of the joint material and symbolic elevation of mixture in seventeenth-century science and politics. That such reliance should also inform Locke's story about the origins of political powers
and rights illustrates how much Locke was drawn to the equation between
making and mixing as a way to undo the superiority of one over many, whole
over parts, form over matter. Locke's consistent gravitation toward a sometimes more literal, sometimes more figurative mixture, I believe, is at least in
part indebted to what Michael Ayers has called Locke's "systematic opposition" to Aristotelianism.[65] A quick glance at Aristotle, in fact, provides some
additional reasons why we should respect Locke's suggestion that labor is an
agent of mixture. Aristotle had not only excluded mixture from the generative actions Locke ascribed to it, but had directly compared sexual generation
to physical labor, arguing that both have nothing to do with mixture. Aristotle
explains his assertion that the "semen is not situated inside the egg and mixed
up with it" by comparing sexual generation to house-building:

> The carpenter is close by his timber, and the potter close by his clay;
> and to put it in general terms, the working or treatment of any mate-
> rial, and the ultimate movement which acts upon it, is in all cases

close by the material, e.g., the location of the activity of house-building is in the houses which are being built. These instances may help us to understand how the male makes its contribution to generation; for not every male emits semen, and in the case of those which do, this semen is not part of the fetation as it develops. In the same way, nothing passes from the carpenter into the pieces of timber, which are *his* material, and there is no part of the art of carpentry present in the object which is being fashioned: it is the shape and the form which pass from the carpenter, and they come into being by means of the movement in the material. It is his soul, wherein is the "form," and his knowledge, which cause his hands (or some other part of his body) to move in a particular way. . . . In a similar way to this, Nature acting in the male of semen-emitting animals uses the semen as a tool.[66]

Aristotle's emphasis on house building as an activity that takes place inside the house serves to defend his claim that, despite their proximity, there is no material mixture between female and male parts in generation. Even though the carpenter works inside the house, Aristotle argues, nothing material passes from him into the structure he is creating. No part of the carpenter physically enters the structure he is building. What he contributes instead is the motion and form that make the house. Like the semen, the carpenter shapes undifferentiated matter, and he does so without communicating anything of his own substance to the object he is creating. His motions, his labor impart the form that is located in his soul to matter. In the same way, though the semen is physically close to the "building materials" provided by the female, it "is not part of the fetation as it develops." Like the carpenter and his labor, the semen is not actually mixed up with the female parts, and male form acts without interference by the female.

Even if Locke was not familiar with this passage, he would have found Aristotle's comparison in a text he closely studied, William Harvey's *Anatomical Exercitations Concerning the Generation of Living Creatures* (1653).[67] Though Harvey rejected the Aristotelian notion of the male as the principal generative agent and elevated the female role, he explicitly embraced the idea that an immaterial principle or form is the primary cause of generation.[68] In support of this argument, Harvey drew on the same analogy Aristotle had invoked. "The Species, or Forme of the Chicken is in the *Uterus*, or *Egge*," he wrote, "without any matter at all: as the reason of the Work is in the Artificer, and the Reason of the House, in the Brain of the Builder."[69] The immaterial form of the chicken—the principal cause of its generation—is insulated from any concrete entanglement with matter and work.

Interestingly enough, Harvey expands Aristotle's comparison beyond biological and physical to ideational making. He urges us to view the immaterial conception of the womb in analogy to the conceptions of the brain. The womb, Harvey nudges, "is a no lesse admirable Organ than the Braine," and nature "hath framed it of a like constitution to execute the office of conception." "Both their functions are equally called *conceptions*, and both are *Immaterial*," he points out.[70] Harvey will subsequently shrink from the implications of this comparison, but the material point for my discussion is that Harvey's book exposed Locke to a theory that mobilized the superiority of immaterial form to think in a unifying manner about biological, physical, and ideational kinds of making. Indeed, Harvey prominently used the term *workmanship* to articulate this theory, though he defined it in a way that replicated Aristotle's hylomorphism.[71] The immaterial forces at work in Harvey's generations exclude material mixture from assuming generative functions.

Locke's decision to make mixture generative in biological, ideational, and physical settings thus counters, on the one hand, the systematic aspirations of maker's theories in the Aristotelian mold and promotes, on the other, the political value Locke began to see in mixture during the exclusion crisis.[72] The closeness with which political questions bore on biological ones in the period leading up to Locke's composition of *Two Treatises* pressed mixture on Locke, but it must have been a clarifying pressure. It helped Locke to see that his opposition to Aristotelianism harmonized with his developing political beliefs and his eventual embrace of atomism. Because it dispensed with a superior formal agent, a maker's theory that authorized mixture painted a fundamentally different picture of the world, a picture in which not the drawing or preservation, but the crossing of boundaries becomes productive. It is this picture that political philosophers miss when they ignore Locke's equation of labor with mixture.

But let me return to my starting point and take a closer look at how the human mixes with the environment in Locke's state of nature. Locke opens his case for the natural foundations of property by highlighting the limits of use right. He appeals to God's gift of the world in common and for man's use, but contends that the use right that man received from God has to entail a right before use: "Though all the Fruits [the earth] naturally produces . . . belong to Mankind in common . . . and no body has originally a private

Dominion, exclusive of the rest of Mankind, in any of them, as they are thus in their natural state: yet being given for the use of Men, there must of necessity be a means *to appropriate* them some way or other before they can be of any use, or at all beneficial to any particular Man" (286–287). The necessity remains elusive. It is not clear why God's gift of the world for man's use has to entail a right beyond simple use right, as Locke claims it does. Locke proceeds to argue for this necessity with an example: "The Fruit, or Venison, which nourishes the wild *Indian*, who knows no Inclosure, and is still a Tenant in common, must be his, and so his, *i.e.* a part of him, that another can no longer have any right to it, before it can do him any good for the support of his Life" (287).[73] The necessity is still a little hard to see. Why do exclusive rights to the fruits of the earth have to be established before these fruits have actually supported life? Why is simple use right insufficient? Locke doesn't explain. The need to stretch possessive right beyond the context of actual use is created by Locke's desire to establish property before the arrangements of civil society take hold and thus to naturalize political rights (against Hobbes, who had offered the opposite case). This desire forces him to contend that the rights to the fruits of the earth cannot be restricted to the point and place of actual consumption. In order to strengthen political right in the state of nature, Locke needs to carve out a more extensive sphere of rights that stretches beyond this point and place.[74]

Locke's argument for the state of nature as the enduring source of inalienable political right can't be supported by an isolated individual whose rights are confined to such elemental acts of self-preservation as eating. Locke wants to get beyond ingestion as the natural point of inalienable right, but he is also attracted to ingestion because it literalizes inalienability: to take away something that has already given another person nourishment and thus has incorporated with that person's body is virtually impossible. Locke's insistence that, even before consumption, the Indian's fruit "must be his, and so his, *i.e.* a part of him, that another can no longer have any right to it" indicates a desire to model appropriation on incorporation—to expand property in the state of nature beyond the immediate context of actual use without losing the physicality of ingestion and the dramatic sense of injury that it enables. The fruit has to be "part of him" before actual consumption, but to be part of the Indian in a decisive sense, Locke has to try to present the act of appropriation as natural and physical as ingestion. In this way, property before actual use could become as compelling and natural as property established by actual use.

Locke's solution to this problem is to extend the rights of nourishment (and thus of self-preservation) beyond the here and now of actual ingestion. In the state of nature, Locke points out, individuals can "consume [no] more than a small part" of the overall resources available in common (292). Even when they go beyond the immediate limits of use, they are unlikely to disadvantage anyone. Therefore, claims to property may extend to goods that are not immediately useful if these goods eventually turn out to be useful. On the other hand, whenever man's exertions overreach so that "the Grass of his Inclosure rotted on the Ground, or the Fruit of his planting perished without gathering" (295) he has infringed on the right of others. In Locke's extension of right beyond use, "nourishment" is still the limit of appropriation, though now we are permitted to reckon with future empty bellies. The effect these provisions have is that outside and inside, present and future, individual and community become part of an extended sphere of rights. Locke's natural right of property is modeled on the security as well as the limits of the belly's possessions and manages to push both beyond immediate nourishment into a more expansive temporal and spatial frame without abandoning a sense either of security or of limits. The literal blending that takes place inside the belly, we might say, is exteriorized, into an extended sphere of appropriation by mixture, a sphere that keeps the exigencies of nature and the here and now of use at bay.

Stephen Buckle has emphasized such extension. He argues persuasively that Locke's definition of property, which joins together "Life, Liberty, and Estate," has to be associated with the natural law concept of the *suum*, an extendable sphere of one's own.[75] Yet Buckle fails to see the importance of mixture, which prevents him from realizing that Locke's *suum* is not only a moral, but a physico-moral sphere.[76] Even if it appears by way of figure or metaphor, such physicality is important to Locke's overall goal of raising a natural and highly sensitive fence that can be preserved (or so Locke's myth assumes) in the transition from nature to society and thus offer fundamental protections against the encroachments of arbitrary government. The extendability of the *suum* into a physical sphere beyond the body is critical in this undertaking because it endows the inviolable core of right with a naturally concrete integrity that makes any encroachment, even where the human body isn't directly violated, appear as an attack on vital aspects of the individual. Locke's partially literal, partially figurative act of mixture endows this extended sphere of rights with a sense of reality and rhetorical force.

Thus, when Locke defines personhood as possessive, he doesn't close it off from environment or community. He opens it up to these things. Self-possession alone does not found the rights that civil society will protect. The relationship between self and thing does, and the crossing from self into thing establishes a bond that tolerates no injury. By mixing beyond the limits of the body, the self realizes its membership in a community with rights and obligations. Liberty, right, and obligation do not come out of some human essence or an enclosed self, but out of our God-given ability to mix and compound with the materials around us. Locke's idea that the self is possessive isn't meant to create a private citizen or bounded self that can withdraw into its shell whenever needed. It is there, instead, to activate the self's powers and rights through the establishment of political relations via an expansive and integrative mixture. The state of nature is thus already political.[77]

Given that such mixture is expansive, it should not be surprising that the greater sphere of rights and liberties Locke's political theory secures for the individual simultaneously serves the goal of colonial expansion. Locke's naturalization of property makes land in the state of nature appropriable. It makes possible, as I have argued elsewhere, the story of Robinson Crusoe, who, in complete isolation from the world, creates a title to a seemingly vacant Caribbean island simply by mixing his labor with it.[78] The expansiveness that secures the self's inalienable political rights of life, liberty, and estate is thus a good match for the expansionist ambitions of British empire, which, unusual among European colonial powers, justified themselves as a program of "plantation."[79]

But if Locke politicizes the natural in this manner, he also naturalizes the political, bringing his complexly combinatory vision of life also to bear on civil society. The law of nature, Locke argues in *Two Treatises*, does not cease in civil society. Despite the mutual agreements that constitute civil society and despite the transfer of certain individual rights to institutions of communal justice, the state of nature and the laws of nature are not left behind. Parts of one's "natural liberty" are to be given up upon entering society (352, 353), yet "the Obligations of the Law of Nature, cease not in Society, but only in many Cases are drawn closer" (357–358). Civil society is charged with providing more effective guarantees for the protection of property, but it does not generate any new fundamental rights nor extinguish any basic natural rights. It merely "limit[s] the Power, and moderate[s] the Dominion of every Part and Member of the Society" (412). Locke's argument recognizes the civil in the natural and the natural in the civil. Each is curled up in the other.[80]

That natural powers and rights remain functional in society even though they predate its institution is crucial to Locke's discussion of sovereignty. Hobbes, Filmer, and others argued insistently that sovereignty was indivisible, but while Locke concedes that "there can be but one Supream Power, which is the Legislative, to which all the rest are and must be subordinate," he asserts that "there remains still in the People a Supream Power to remove or alter the Legislative, when they find the Legislative act contrary to the trust reposed in them" (366–367). If liberty and subjection coexist in the relationship children have to their parents, as Locke argues elsewhere in *Two Treatises*, a closely related coexistence of liberty and subjection describes the people's relationship to government.[81]

Political power is not a unified, homogenous entity, and Locke ultimately doesn't shy away from the consequences. While Filmer contends that "there cannot be any Multitude of Men whatsoever, but that in it, consider'd by it self, there is one man amongst them, that in Nature hath a Right to be the King of all the rest," Locke argues for the rights of the multitude.[82] Turning Filmer's own words against him, he contends that the dispersed people of Babel were indeed a "confused Multitude without Heads and Governors" and that they were indeed "at liberty to choose what Governors or Governments they pleased" (247). If the government dissolves, Locke suggests, the "confused Multitude" is "at liberty to provide for themselves, by erecting a new Legislative" (411).[83] In this way, liberty and subjection coexist in society *and* in nature, in the relationship of parent to child as much as in the relationships of individuals in the state of nature or in that of subject to king.

As these observations begin to suggest, Locke's interest in political impurity, in the coexistence of contrary states, plays an important role in how he imagines the dissolution of government.[84] Political impurity allows Locke to argue for political plasticity, and that includes the possibility that the government can dissolve from within, without the application of external force or the horrors of civil war. When Locke discusses the nature of the body politic, he turns initially to Aristotelian imagery. Legislative power, he claims, is the "Soul that gives Form, Life, and Unity to the Commonwealth: From hence the several Members have their mutual Influence, Sympathy, and Connexion" (407). Such unusual and perhaps strategically conservative terms, however, quickly give way to the language of mixture. Locke realizes that the Aristotelian terms he has invoked will not help him explain the dissolution of commonwealths as an internal and nonviolent process. "It is hard to consider [such dissolution] aright," he notes, "without knowing the form of Government in which it happens" (408). For illumination, he turns to England's mixed government. In the English system, "the Legislative [is] placed in the Concurrence of three distinct Persons," "a single hereditary Person," "an Assembly of Hereditary Nobility," and "an Assembly of Representatives chosen *pro tempore*, by the People" (408). The Aristotelian overtones disappear as Locke begins to describe the coordinating relationship between English Lords, Commons, and King. They constitute a combination of oligarchy, democracy, and monarchy that originated in the people's right to "make compounded and mixed Forms of Government, as they think good" (354). In this compounded form—which Locke clearly favors—liberty and justice are insured by the interaction of parts. If such interaction produces a superior body politic, it also improves that body's chances for death and dissolution. This is important. For as soon as one of the three bodies assumes legislative agency independently of the other two, Locke claims, the legislative is in fact changed and government dissolved from the inside, without conquest or rebellion (408–410). Locke was familiar with Hunton's *Treatise of Monarchy*, and its influence can be felt in Locke's statements about dissolution.

Locke's thinking about the qualities of the mixed English body politic draws, I believe, on the ability of mixture to guarantee superior qualities that here include enhanced justice, union, and dissolvability. Mixtures can easily make and sustain bodies with superior qualities, as Boyle had taken pains to show, but their unity and identity rests on a complicated set of relationships, not on a form or an essence. That is why dissolution can occur from within the mixed body politic and doesn't require ostentatious force. Locke is concerned to address the objection that a mixed government defined in this way creates a rather too changeable commonwealth, but in a response that should no longer surprise us, he holds fast to mutability as a condition of political liberty (414). In this regard, his thinking about the mixed body politic and the promise of liberty it carries is related to his vision of mixed modes as the most sublime manifestation of liberty in human understanding. Although mutability, along with the power of the many, reaches an extreme and, as it were, utopian high in Locke's mixed mode, a more restrained version of such mutability and multitude is also a condition of liberty in the great world of political doing.

In *Two Treatises*, political mutability makes its most dramatic entrance when Locke discusses the right of resistance and the conditions under which regicide is justifiable, the most radical aspects of his political thinking. Resistance and regicide were actively discussed in opposition circles, which were plotting to assassinate Charles and James in the early 1680s (the discovery of this plot prompted Locke to flee to Holland). In a frequently repeated formulation that Ashcraft has linked more generally to radical thinking during the exclusion crisis, Locke presents the possibility of the king "revolting from his own kind to that of Beasts" (383) by entering a state of war with his own people.[85] In the case of such a mutation, the tyrant may be "destroyed as a Lyon or a Tyger, one of those wild Savage Beasts, with whom Men can have no Society nor Security" (274). Ashcraft rightly calls such language "colorful," but the political value of unstable species boundaries in the *Essay* ought to make us pause before we treat Locke's language as only rhetorical. There are a variety of reasons why Locke was drawn to such language. His anger over the abuse of power by the Stuarts played a role, as did his hope to assuage those who feared a return to the sovereign parliament that executed Charles I, and his desire to mobilize natural law's right of self-preservation. But there was also the fact, I would submit, that such imagery harmonized with book three of the *Essay*, which had theorized the instability of species boundaries as both the threat of confusion and the promise of liberty.

Once a body politic is established, Locke's idea of liberty critically depends on the possibility of "degeneration" (273) in several senses: of the human into the beastly, ruler into tyrant, people into animals, civilized into savage, state of society into state of nature or war.[86] Locke's thinking about the body politic isn't guided by a desire to insulate the states of nature, war, and civility from each other. He depends on their interrelation. They can rule each other and regress into one another, recede into the background, coexist or collapse into each other. The sovereignty of the people, long dormant under a peaceful and prosperous reign, can suddenly be activated by a single royal transgression. A thief breaking into your house can suddenly reactivate the state of nature in which the immediate needs of self-preservation legitimate taking justice into your own hands. In this way, Locke's commonwealth is defined not by what is immediately or obviously present, not by the visible limits of the body or a clear internal hierarchy. Locke distrusted the anatomical logic that underwrote the undivided sovereignty of Bodin's, Filmer's, and Hobbes's political theory. His body politic stretches in different directions, combining nature and society, democracy, aristocracy, and monarchy, past and present, and liberty and subjection.[87]

Like Hunton or Henry Parker before him, Locke wishes to reorient the search for a proper body politic. He rejects the tie between clear form, durability, and superior functionality that one can find in Bodin or Hobbes and promotes a body politic whose "*radicall Mixture*," to recall Hunton's phrase, ensures liberty as it reconciles a superior union, justice, and equality with considerable degenerative potential.[88] The impurity of political forms is the cause of their virtues, and their evaluation no longer rests on the difference between form and deformity that served so many royalists and absolutists as the scarecrow by which they frightened an anxious public.

In this way, Locke's attraction to the idea of a mixed government in which several political bodies share and coordinate power is also motivated by his philosophical stance. That stance prompted Locke to see mixture as more than the primary solvent of all essentialisms, real constitutions, and resemblances. Mixture has a positive role. It is the enabling principle of ontological, epistemological, and political compounds in which every state, body, identity, or species partakes of some other state, body, identity, or species. Nothing is complete or sufficient in itself, nothing is homogeneous, bounded, pure, or straightforwardly continuous, and the various compositions and coalitions that endow the world with a high degree of natural plasticity recommend a similar plasticity for the political world. The mutations and species switches that are programmed into Locke's strictly interactive political unity guarantee liberty.

*   *   *

I have argued that Locke wants to authorize species, ideas, and bodies that lack a sovereign essence. Because he sees mixture as the fundamental form of worldly action, Locke recognizes impurity, heterogeneity, and discontinuity as basic forces of life. Accepting these forces renders mute the dream to master the many by the one, the parts by the whole, matter by form. If, under Aristotelian premises, it was possible to define things by distinguishing between their essential and accidental characteristics, such distinction was not available in Locke's philosophy. The reduction of things to an underlying essence, substance, or form could no longer explain their identity. What could?

Locke directly addressed this question in a chapter on identity he added to the second edition of the *Essay* in 1694. To many philosophers, this chapter put the problem of identity on the philosophical map. It is still a force to be reckoned with, not just among historians of philosophy, but also among analytical philosophers. More important for my argument is the fact that Locke's chapter offered the most systematic and provocative rebuttal of the idea that identity could be tied to some essence, substance, or form. This idea underwrote, of course, what many writers had to say about the Saxon roots of English identity and English institutions. In characterizing identity as irreducible to anything simple, stable, or native, Locke also argued against the essentializing tendencies of the Anglo-Saxon argument. Indeed, Locke had criticized the application of such arguments to English identity. In the year before he added the chapter on identity, he had written an essay that advocated a general naturalization. Locke argued that the English ought to look to Holland to see what an active immigration policy could do for prosperity and reminded his audience that England was already a highly composite nation: after all, "most of . . . our Ancestors were Foreigners."[89]

I propose, then, that Locke's chapter on identity does more than argue about personhood. It provides the most detailed picture yet of the logic that underlay the provocative arguments about English identity made by such writers as Matthew Hale, Daniel Defoe, or Thomas Salmon. Samuel Clarke, an early commentator on Locke's chapter, seemed to point in this direction when he described Lockean identity by invoking the figure Hale had used to think about the composite structure of the English nation and of English law: the ship of the Argonauts that returned the same but did not contain a shred of the substance it was originally made of.[90] Locke's vision of personal identity is not insulated from larger national or political considerations, and this will also become clear by what I will argue is its basic congruence with Locke's notion of a political self that acquires rights, powers, and obligations by mixing with the environment. In this case and in others, Locke's thinking about identity aligns with his recognition of mixture as a fundamental form of human agency.

Locke begins his task by defining physical identity. He argues that a plant—an oak, for example—cannot be defined by the "Mass of Matter" that makes it up. As a "living Body," the oak's identity rests instead on "such an Organization of . . . parts as is fit to receive, and distribute nourishment, so as to continue, and frame the Wood, Bark, and Leaves, etc. of an Oak, in which consists the vegetable Life."[91] The same paradigm applies to animals, whom Locke compares, somewhat incongruously, to a watch consisting of "one continued Body, all whose organized Parts were repair'd, increas'd or diminsh'd, by a constant Addition or Separation of insensible Parts, with one Common Life" (331). Identity is supported by constant exchange, not a persistent substance or real essence. Man, too, bears this out. "The Identity of the same Man," Locke argues, "consists . . . in nothing but a participation of the same continued Life, by constantly fleeting Particles of Matter, in succession vitally united to the same organized Body" (331). Continued life, enabled by the constant addition and separation of parts, makes up identity. "Constant change" (339) is not different from identity and sameness. It makes them possible. Locke's vision of the profound interdependence of all things shapes his initial definition of identity and sameness.

It may seem that what Locke calls the "organization of parts" that supports life suggests a persistent core on which identity can rest (something like "that particular Constitution, which every Thing has within it self, without any relation to any thing without it" [442]). But as his language for describing the animal-watch makes especially clear, Locke includes this organization in the transformative traffic of parts. The animal-watch's "organized Parts [are] repair'd, increas'd or diminsh'd, by a constant Addition or Separation of insensible Parts." The range of transformations Locke permits under the umbrella of identity and sameness is considerable. Locke emphasizes the transformation of the oak from "a plant to a great tree" which is eventually "lopp'd" and yet is all this time "the same Oak" (330). If we extend this example slightly, we can glimpse the outer limits of Locke's definition of identity. Let us imagine what is not impossible: the stump left by the oak's felling, after two years of dormancy, suddenly sprouts fresh leaves. An organization of parts has emerged that, once again, can support life. By Locke's definition, we would have to call this the same tree, even if the dead trunk that once organized its life was rotting next to the new shoots, and even if these shoots grew into something resembling a bush more than a tree.

Of course, all of this applies only to physical identity, or so Locke suggests. Locke's big prize in the chapter is a workable definition of personal, not physical, identity. It is the person, not the man, who has self-possession and may communicate such self-possession to the environment. But even as he distinguishes between these two kinds of identity in the chapter, Locke's definition of physical identity keeps insinuating itself into his definition of personal identity. By a barely acknowledged movement issuing from several directions, physical identity moves in on personal identity through analogy and concrete relation until, finally, the two identities share the same definition. As in Locke's account of the mixture that gives rise to rights, powers, and obligations in the state of nature or in his argument about mixed modes, materialist models exert an irresistible draw. They are tools for thinking that lead somewhere. Let me follow this draw in more detail.

When he first defines personal identity, Locke argues that the "sameness of a rational Being" (335) consists in consciousness, which he describes as the ability to perceive that we are perceiving. This is the fundamental difference between man and person: the former is defined by constant exchanges with the environment, the latter goes beyond such physical realities. Consciousness has no substance and no location, and it might seem that such disembodiment, as Charles Taylor has argued, is the source of the personal self's power and independence.[92] But for Locke, this is not quite how the story works. He points out that, even though consciousness itself is not substantial, it still depends on what he calls "substances": the thoughts and actions that we are conscious of. Consciousness is active only insofar we are conscious of something. "It is by the consciousness it has of its . . . Thoughts and Actions," Locke points out, that the self is self to itself (336). Defined this way, consciousness is not quite that powerful and independent. And Locke soon explains that our consciousness of substances is unsteady. It is "interrupted always by forgetfulness," and we never have "the whole train of our past Actions before our Eyes in one view" (335–336). As we are contemplating one memory of a past action, we are losing sight of others. "Being intent on our present thoughts," we don't mind past actions (336). And while we sleep we have "no Thoughts at all, or at least none with that consciousness, which remarks our waking Thoughts" (336). Consciousness is a spotty, discontinuous affair: we are only conscious of some things, sometimes of none, and never of many at the same time. The substances we are conscious of shift constantly.

But even if these interruptions and shifts qualify the sovereignty of the self, our personal identity is still preserved. To explain how this is possible, Locke is compelled to compare personal to physical identity. That "different substances" are "united" by consciousness into one person works just "as well as different Bodies, by the same Life are united into one Animal, whose *Identity* is preserved, in that change of Substances, by the unity of one continued Life" (336). No matter how weak our memory is, no matter how few things we remember about our past actions, no matter how different the substances are that we are conscious of, we are still the same person, held together by what Locke will later call, in a significant verbal echo, "continued consciousness" (346).

Locke's comparison suggests that consciousness is a stomach that digests all kinds of stuff, invariably supporting continuity, sameness, identity. But his argument, pulled as it seems toward the neutralization of substantial differences in an ever-victorious sameness of consciousness, ultimately recognizes that personal identity is affected by the substances consciousness digests. Locke writes, for example: "as far as this consciousness can be extended backwards to any past Action or Thought, so far reaches the Identity of that *Person*" (335). And later on: "it is impossible to make personal Identity to consist in any thing but consciousness; or reach any farther than that does" (343). These statements acknowledge that the substances we become conscious of shape our identity. Similar to self-possession, consciousness alone cannot constitute a fully formed self: the substances it reaches are crucial. If we wanted to stay with gustatory metaphors, we might say: Locke realizes that you are what you eat. If pressed, he would have to acknowledge that the stomach, as an organization of parts, is not immune from transformation by other parts.

Locke defines the range of substances consciousness can reach generously, fully acknowledging his belief in the interdependence of all things. This range includes "our very Bodies, all whose Particles, whilst vitally united to this same thinking conscious self, so that we feel when they are touch'd, and are affected by, and conscious of good or harm that happens to them, are a part of our selves: i.e. of our thinking conscious self" (336–337). Though he distinguishes physical and personal identity, Locke does not deny that our consciousness extends to various body parts and makes them part of our sense of self. In fact, when he includes all the body's particles as potential candidates for conscious connection, he opens the gate for vital ties between body and mind rather wide. At this stage of Locke's argument, however, opening such connections between body and mind supports the main argument: it happens in service of his almost obsessive quest for demonstrating that identity is not rooted in any substance. So Locke concludes his meditation on body particles and the degree to which we can become conscious of them by arguing that the loss of any part of our physical body, even though it is part of our personal consciousness, cannot alter the fact that we are still the same person.

A little later in the chapter, however, Locke acknowledges that the loss of mental substances may have transformative effects on the self. This acknowledgment grows out of another forceful attempt to dispel the notion that personal identity is substantive. Locke anticipates an objection to his argument that personal identity is not tied to sameness of substance in the following way: "But yet possibly it will be objected, suppose I wholly lose the memory of some parts of my Life, beyond a possibility of retrieving them, so that perhaps I shall never be conscious of them again; yet am I not the same Person, that did those Actions, had those Thoughts, that I was once conscious of, though I have now forgot them?" (342). Locke answers that what the objector calls the "same Person" is really only the same man. He contends that a complete loss of the memory of certain actions makes it impossible to deploy the category "same person." Locke is cautious when he approaches the positive version of this argument—that the person after the memory loss is a different person than before it. He begins with a subjunctive clause: "If it be possible for the same Man to have distinct incommunicable consciousness at different times, it is past doubt the same Man would at different times make different Persons; which, we see, is the Sense of Mankind in the solemnest Declaration of their Opinions, Humane Laws not punishing the *Mad Man* for the *Sober Man*'s Actions, nor the *Sober Man* for what the *Mad Man* did, thereby making them two Persons" (342). The subjunctive opening is swiftly actualized by the evidence of common human practice. In law, the belief that the same man can be different persons is vital to the exercise of justice. Locke's endorsement of this belief is a necessary consequence of his argument that identity does not consist in the sameness and continuity of a substance. Identity instead consists in the occasional, partial, and discontinuous connections that consciousness entertains with different substances. That is why the complete loss of memories, beyond possibility of retrieval, can occur in the first place. When the substances consciousness connects with vary widely, we may be one person today and another tomorrow. And even when I merely lose "the memory of some parts of my life," I am, strictly speaking, no longer the same person.

Locke's decision to cut identity off from substantive continuity and sameness not only allows consciousness to lose substances, it also lets it add some, and these substances may not be gained only from the fund of our own personal experience. Consciousness, Locke contends, is capable of erasing the self's sense of the difference between an action that it did commit and an action that it did not commit. "As to this point of being the same *self*," Locke explains, "it matters not whether this present *self* be made up of the same or other Substances, I being as much concern'd, and as justly accountable for any Action was done a thousand Years since, appropriated to me now by this self-consciousness, as I am, for what I did the last moment" (341). This statement is both controversial and uncontroversial. Locke argues that, as soon as I am conscious of having committed an action that I did not commit, I am accountable for that action. Such accountability strikes me as controversial. Yet the attendant claim that our self is defined by whatever our consciousness presents as our actions (even if they are not ours) seems uncontroversial. "That with which the consciousness of this present thinking thing can join it self," Locke puts it simply, "makes the same Person" (341). On this definition, personal identity and sameness are capacious conditions, constantly evolving, and ultimately not confined to personal experience.[93]

Locke sums up his views on personal identity in a passage that recalls, in telling ways, his opening meditation on physical identity:

> In all which account of *self*, the same numerical Substance is not considered, as making the same *self*: But the same continued consciousness, in which several Substances may have been united, and again separated from it, which, whilst they continued in a vital union with that, wherein this consciousness then resided, made a part of that same *self*. Thus any part of our Bodies vitally united to that, which is conscious in us, makes a part of our *selves*: But upon separation from the vital union, by which that consciousness is communicated, that, which a moment since was part of our *selves*, is now no more so, than a part of another Man's *self* is a part of me; and 'tis not impossible, but in a little time may become a real part of another Person. (346)

Locke acknowledges that he has wound up constructing personal identity on the model of physical identity. The constant addition and separation of parts he had invoked to explain physical identity now explains personal identity. The phrase "vital Union" initially entered Locke's chapter in the description of physical identity (331), but it is here used to describe the relationship between substances and consciousness. And Locke's phrase "continued consciousness" echoes the "continued life" that defined physical identity early on.

An equally significant sign that Locke acknowledges his adoption of a unified theory of identity is his reference to the relationship between body and mind, which he uses to construct an amusing (and easily missed) parallel between physical and mental substances. Locke claims that it is "not impossible, but in a little time" a part of our bodies that we had been conscious of but are no more so because we have lost that part, "may become a real part of another Person" (the loss of a finger Locke had discussed earlier in the chapter comes to mind: 341). Locke extends his reference to the relationship between body part and consciousness into a story about the relationship between people. We have already heard, of course, that one person can become conscious of and own the actions of another person. But because the thing that is appropriated here is not an action but a body part, Locke's story smuggles in a physical version of his argument about consciousness's ability to extend itself to substances beyond our personal experience. We may not want to, in other words, but we certainly can ingest another person's body parts—a finger, say.

The confounding of personal and physical substances goes further. Locke ends his suggestion of cannibalism by noting that the lost body part may become "a real part of another Person" when, by his own strict standards, it would have to be the real part of another *man*. Locke's disregard for the difference between physical and personal substances indicates that his initial distinction between man and person has collapsed. The physical paradigm has taken over the definition of personal identity. I agree with Ayers that Locke holds back on reducing mental activity to atomic swarming, but it is indisputable that the "constantly fleeting Particles of Matter . . . vitally united to the same organized Body" (332) Locke mentions early in the chapter become a model for the way various substances connect to consciousness. The analogy between physical and personal identity cannot be dismissed as "a decorative conceit," as Ayers urges.[94] It is instead one stage in Locke's journey from distancing to approximating physical and personal identity. Both of these identities are insubstantial; they are made by the loss and gain of various substances. If there is a real constitution, it does not bear on the identity of the self. Locke's identity does not rest anywhere: it is open to mutability.

In the final paragraphs of his chapter Locke underscores and develops this position. He notes that it is only at the time of God's final reckoning with humankind that our failure to own our actions will be unveiled and "*the secrets of all Hearts shall be laid open.*" The divine sentence passed at this time "shall be justified by the consciousness all Persons shall have, that they *themselves* in what Bodies soever they appear, or what Substances soever that consciousness adheres to, are the *same*, that committed those actions, and deserve that Punishment for them" (347). Full justice, along with complete knowledge of our selves, has to wait for this moment because our earthly consciousness is fallible: it may have been connected to substances that had nothing to do with our actions or failed to connect to substances that represented our actions. Thus, final justice may include the realization that we are not guilty of something that we had always owned as our action and perhaps had even been punished for. Only divine justice will give us undeniable knowledge about who we are, about our guilt, our goodness, and our accountability.

Locke's reflections on final justice are motivated by a passage in which he throws some nervous, bold glances at the relationship between personal identity and liberty. "A concern for Happiness," Locke argues, is "the unavoidable concomitant of consciousness" (346). We are conscious of pleasure and pain and "desir[e] that that *self*, that is conscious, should be happy" (346). This desire for happiness, Locke goes on, explains why "personality extends it *self* beyond present Existence to what is past" (346). It also explains that "whatever past Actions [the self] cannot reconcile or appropriate to that present *self* by consciousness, it can be no more concerned in, than if they had never been done" (346). These statements cast consciousness in a new light. While it may still be the unreliable and haphazard operator Locke made it out to be early in his chapter, consciousness here acquires a motivation: the concern for happiness. The extension of the self beyond the present moment happens as the result of a desire, and this desire stands behind our failure or success in appropriating certain actions to our selves. It is profound misery, Locke points out, to be punished on this earth for actions that we have no consciousness of having committed (whether we have committed them or not). It is absolute justice, on the other hand, to realize at the day of final reckoning that we deserved such punishment. Similarly, it may make us happy to appropriate actions that did not belong to us, but we will ultimately have to face up to our self-deception. The relationship this argument has to the question of human liberty is not explored in an explicit manner. But the implications point clearly to Locke's workmanship model: the idea that human agency and human liberty realize themselves by appropriating and compounding the ingredients of the world, be they things, ideas, or the substances that make up our personal identity. Mixture—literal and figurative—is the way to get beyond the exigencies of the here and now.

The result of dissociating identity from sameness of substance, then, is not the construction of a sovereign, but an open and changeable self, the kind of self that also sustains Locke's argument about powers and rights in *Two Treatises*. Locke pulls identity away from what the philosopher Derek Parfit has criticized as a "one-one relation," an "all-or-nothing" criterion: you are the same or you are not. This is that.[95] For Locke, life and consciousness lack substantial definitions and are therefore highly dependent on their surroundings, through which they establish identity as a one-many relation. The one and the many are joined. Continued life and continued consciousness alone cannot constitute identity. Locke's insistence on interdependence teaches us that life and consciousness exist through discontinuities and mutations. Planted in one neighborhood rather than another, the seed of one species may produce another species. Animals that flourish in one environment may get sick in another. The same man can be different persons. By making consciousness a flawed medium with long reach, limited grasp, and equalizing effects, Locke renders the self flexible. There is no essence or substance that secures who we are. We are composite beings whose personal and physical identity is tied to the constant addition and separation of parts.[96]

*   *   *

In concluding, I would like to go back for a moment to Locke's discussion of mixed modes. The closeness Locke ascribes to the relationship between one and many in his discussion of identity recalls what he says about this relationship in his discussion of mixed modes. Mixed modes, he notes, are made up of the "fleeting and transient combinations of simple ideas" (291). The appearance of "a constant and lasting existence" in mixed modes, Locke explains, derives exclusively from their "Names." Underneath the thin cover of the name, a sublime variety of compounded and decompounded ideas can gather, but such gatherings are instable, subject to continuous losses and gains. It seems to me that the chapter on identity adapts the intimacy of one and many Locke found in the mixed mode. Locke's language regarding the "constantly fleeting Particles of Matter . . . vitally united to the same organized Body" echoes the "fleeting and transient combinations of simple ideas" collected under the name of the mixed mode. While the intimacy of many and one is extreme in mixed modes and produces species mutations with every addition or separation of a part, Locke's definition of identity—just like his portrait of the mutable body politic—is still patterned on such intimacy. In this sense, Clarke's reference to the ship of the Argonauts is apt. The oneness or sameness of this ship—its identity, essence, form, or substance—cannot be established by analytic reduction. There is nothing that such reduction could reach. The only thing we have is an organization produced by interacting, constantly changing parts. For Locke, this is both sobering and promising.

My discussion has shown the importance of mixture in Locke's vision of natural and human making, from the physical interdependence of all things and the reproduction of species, to mixed modes, mixed labor, mixed government, and personal identity. By rendering mixture productive, Locke undid the hierarchies that regulated the relationship between many and one, parts and whole, matter and form and thus created room for human liberty. We have seen Locke's commitment to mixture as cause and basic reality across different levels and aspects of his thought. This commitment was not tethered to a systematizing impulse, but Locke recognized mixture as a key concept in overcoming Aristotelian and absolutist ideas of order. If, by following the trail of mixture across aspects of Locke's thought that are not often considered together, I have suggested a unity, it is not a grand synthesis of epistemology, ontology, and politics. It is, rather, the unity of a way of thinking about the world that crystallized during a moment of intense political conflict and became portable, finding work in different places, large and small, visible and obscure. In this way, Locke capitalized on a conceptual revaluation that this study has traced back to George Hakewill and Nathanael Carpenter, who began to reverse the impotency and impurity mixture represented in the religious and philosophical traditions that dominated the early seventeenth century. Locke's philosophy extended this reversal into the eighteenth century. If the recognition that England reproduced itself through mixture was unprecedentedly broad in the early eighteenth century, Locke endowed this theme with philosophical depth.

Undividing Modernity

I set out to understand the intellectual resources that allowed early eighteenth-century Englishmen to become assertive about mixture as the source of English perfections. I have written a semantic history that has tracked the revaluation of mixture and its conceptual horizon in seventeenth-century culture. The pursuit of this horizon has taken us through a diverse terrain. We have crossed several fields of inquiry, from geography, embryology, and chemistry to political science and philosophy. We have climbed some metaphysical heights and were rewarded with the sight of unexpected political bridges between Calvinists, Arminians, and Catholics. We saw that the paths of older knowledges (mixed government, natural magic, atomism, Aristotelianism) can cross, twine, and make new knowledge. We have acquired a sense of how some of the transformative impulses of Renaissance humanism were extended into the late seventeenth century and beyond. And we have realized that not only the boundaries of religious but also those of political difference can be porous. A Catholic royalist such as Kenelm Digby, for instance, could ultimately agree with a Protestant parliamentarian such as Henry Parker that the power of the multitude has to be respected.

The point of view from which the footprints that mark this terrain became visible was raised on the merger of dusty bibliographies and gleaming electronic databases and the new perspectives that such databases are opening up for intellectual history. This combination of the old and the new has made it possible to trace the joint expansion of the material and symbolic usefulness of mixture in seventeenth-century England. Mixture's release from many of the ontological, moral, theological, and political strictures that confined it in the early seventeenth century helped legitimize natural and political bodies that were generated and ordered not hierarchically—through the primacy of one over many, whole over parts, or form over matter—but cooperatively, through the equalizing coordination among multiple actors.

This release of mixture undermined essentializing distinctions that were common among the learned, including distinctions between form and deformity, perfection and imperfection, natural and artificial. It promoted the contemplation of deformed bodies outside of the moral and theological frameworks in which they were made to signify. This normalization of deformity, I have argued, had politically liberating effects. It assisted the legitimation of political bodies such as multitude and mixed government that were viewed as monstrous and mutable by absolutists and royalists. Only a handful of seventeenth-century political thinkers dared to present the multitude in a positive light. Yet the stigma of deformity waned, and in the second half of the century mixture was increasingly claimed as the generative force and ultimate ground that stood behind superior breeds, languages, and polities. Multitude, mutation, and heterogeneity ceased to be the telltale signs of inferiority or imperfection.

This revaluation of mixture's conceptual horizon in seventeenth-century science and politics helps explain how so many early eighteenth-century Englishmen could be excited, alarmed, or blasé about the idea that theirs was a culture that reproduced itself through mixture. The notion of England's mixed genius could enter the national conversation so nimbly and widely—in its linguistic, racial, social, religious, and political aspects—because of a change in the value and uses of mixture itself. More local historical forces such as the debates about toleration and naturalization in the early eighteenth century were surely crucial in focusing many educated minds on the problem of mixture, but the assertion that mixture perfected English culture drew on wider-ranging semantic shifts. My hope is that my history of these shifts has made Pliny's remark about the debt that excellence and identity owe to difference less paradoxical.

In this chapter, I would like to reflect on two questions that address some of the historiographical implications of the early modern appreciation of impurity. What lessons can be drawn from the revaluation of mixture for our thinking about modernization and enlightenment, concepts that have framed so many of our inquiries into the seventeenth and eighteenth centuries? And what do these lessons tell us about our current fascination with concepts such as mixture and hybridity, our belief that these concepts help us understand and shape modes of identity and agency in a globalizing world?

*   *   *

Exquisite Mixture has told a positive story. It has described a significant sharpening of the intellectual tools that could authorize liberty, diversity, equality, and cooperation in early enlightenment England. Though it concentrates on a slightly earlier historical period, this book is related to a number of studies that have, over the past ten years or so, begun to redeem the enlightenment from the withering critiques it suffered in the second half of the twentieth century, especially in the wake of Max Horkheimer and Theodor Adorno's absorbingly bleak *Dialectic of Enlightenment* (1947). Studies such as Sankar Muthu's *Enlightenment Against Empire* (2003), Stephen Eric Bronner's *Reclaiming the Enlightenment* (2004), Jennifer Pitts's *A Turn to Empire* (2005), or, even more recently, Daniel Carey and Lynn Festa's *The Postcolonial Enlightenment* (2009) have tried to paint a more nuanced picture of an enlightenment that had become a punching ball for critics from the political left and right.[1] I find it remarkable that, as little as twenty-five years ago, it would have been difficult to imagine a broad following for such a redemptive effort.

Back then, we had stopped believing in the grand liberal narratives about enlightenment as the unshackling of the individual from ignorance and inequality. Our disbelief, in fact, had become so fervent that we delighted in nothing so much as in unmasking enlightenment as secretly unenlightening. Whatever looked to previous generations of scholars like a triumphant march toward greater freedom and knowledge looked to us like a funeral procession in disguise. We had sharper, warier eyes that looked beyond the pretty flags, the confetti, and the rousing speeches, down to where the real operations of "enlightenment" took place. The seeming increase of individual freedom in the seventeenth and eighteenth centuries, we argued, was the result of transplanting power and oppression from external institutions such as church or monarchy into newly individualized hearts and minds. Modern individuals were both freer and infinitely more oppressed. And whatever had looked to previous generations of scholars like the dark, premodern days of institutionalized deception, violent oppression, and social injustice acquired for some— most famously and influentially, Michel Foucault—the nostalgic patina of the good old days when modernization had not yet unleashed its perfidious police operation on the admirable heterogeneity of traditional society.[2] From this perspective, the normalization of the deformed and the monstrous I have presented as politically liberating could only appear as a loss, a loss that we had to mourn because it robbed the world of wonder.[3]

I once shared the fascination with enlightenment's subtle perfidy, but I have lost my faith in a relentlessly cunning modernity. I find myself relieved that the glory days of the hermeneutics of suspicion are ending and that there is room for a more genuinely dialogic hermeneutics.[4] My book has tried to practice such a hermeneutics by placing the hope to understand before the wish for critique. I trust that confetti and flags have not been the result. The positive story I have told is not triumphal, not a return to Whiggish tales about the progress of liberalism. The formation of a changed conceptual horizon around the revaluation of mixture, after all, happens at a time when a powerful competitor, the Anglo-Saxon myth, has combined racial, linguistic, and political ingredients in a potent draught that would nourish ideas of English superiority well into the nineteenth century. In reconstructing a counterparadigm, I have told a story about an increase in the value that the English found in impurity, heterogeneity, and discontinuity, but not about its triumph.

And yet, because it authorizes greater liberty, diversity, equality, and cooperation, my counterparadigm might still look like it could soothe neoliberals who are anxious to reinsert at least some aspects of the English past into a narrative of progressive liberalization. That, too, seems ultimately unlikely. When mixture is in charge of such authorization, the liberal narrative cannot unfold. John Locke strikingly illustrates why this is so. Against the still-prominent association of Locke with the birth of liberal individuals and societies, I have argued that Locke uses mixture to reject the idea of a clearly bounded self that achieves privacy and autonomy by distancing the claims of communal and political obligation. If there are still defenders of Locke as the father of liberalism (or, more likely, critics who wish to take Locke down for such parentage), some rethinking may be required. In Locke, mixture is an expansive and integrating mode that can exert transformative powers over nature, society, selves, and territories. It is an active agent that performs not the protective drawing, but the transformative crossing of boundaries. Such activity not only makes selfhood a literally collective enterprise that is open to the other but also raises the prospect of a rather problematic biopolitics. The English, in fact, were well aware of this prospect and of its aggressive and violent implications.

Ancient Rome's policy of mixture with the conquered, for example, was familiar in the seventeenth century as one of the keys to imperial expansion and integration.[5] It is likely that this policy was in the back of William Petty's mind when he recommended in the 1670s the social and sexual mixture of the English with the Irish or when Robert Beverley wished in 1705 that there had been more intermarriage between the English and native populations of Virginia.[6] The policy was certainly on Francis Bacon's mind as he privately advised James I about the prospects of a union between England and Scotland, advice that was republished in 1706, when England was about to finalize its controversial union with Scotland. Bacon had cited the authority of Machiavelli, whose analysis of the "Growth of the Roman Empire" explained that the main reason for such growth was "that the State did so easily compound and incorporate with Strangers."[7]

Another example for aggressive uses of mixture's transformative crossings is the strident nationalism of Daniel Defoe. As we have seen, Defoe views English culture as the product of a long, violent history that has rendered it irreducibly mixed and impure and then turns around to present this fact as the source of national superiority. Defoe's ability to wed mixture and nationalism, in fact, is not unique. The United States might teach some useful lessons here, but so does the Caribbean. In studying the Asian diaspora in the Americas, the anthropologist Viranjini Munasinghe has shown that some Trinidadians construct their national identity in an aggressively exclusionary manner by rooting it in the ethnic and cultural mixtures they experienced in the past.[8] The Trinidadians who construct their national identity in this way resemble those late seventeenth- and early eighteenth-century Englishmen who, in trying to understand their past as a colony and their present as a trading nation, claimed that England was great because of its extensive mixtures with the Romans, Saxons, Danes, and French. Leaning on a distinction that Mikhail Bakhtin developed, we might say that seventeenth-century England and twentieth-century Trinidad present different examples of cultures in which the involuntary ethnic and cultural mixtures that produced them historically are consciously embraced and made to serve a positive and nationalistic program.[9]

*   *   *

The authorization of greater liberty, diversity, equality, and cooperation through mixture thus contains disconcerting tendencies, and some might say that these tendencies lurk also in science, whose knowledge of natural bodies rested on an enforced "sociability," as Nehemiah Grew saw it—on the experimental mandate to mix everything with everything. These tendencies trouble neoliberal desires, and they ultimately point to an even more basic contradiction between the civilizing narrative that mixture increasingly supports in the seventeenth and eighteenth centuries and the narratives of progressive liberalization that came into their own in the nineteenth and twentieth centuries. Because they assume that the crossing of boundaries is more productive than their drawing, and because they believe that impurity can be more powerful than purity, the writers I have studied in this book tell a very different story about the development of modern, enlightened societies.

To make mixture the path to a more civilized, cultivated, prosperous, and powerful nation questions our understanding—handed down by a long line of twentieth-century historians, anthropologists, and sociologists—that the process of modernization is animated by an ordering impulse that disciplines the heterogeneity and multiplicity of traditional societies. Such order, we have been told many times, is achieved by actions of classification and differentiation. Modernization separates that which was once joined or related, from different kinds of labor to public and private spheres, male and female, individual and society, economics and politics, nature and society, religion and state—the list is long. In this account, societies develop and modernize when they differentiate kinds, spheres, and functions. Assumptions like these explain, among other things, why historians of modern constitutionalism often see mixed government as an uncouth precursor to forms of government that clearly differentiate between judicial, executive, and legislative functions.[10] In contrast, my book has tried to take seriously the argument that, by mobilizing the ingredients of political power in the opposite direction, mixture offers an alternative path toward enlightened political bodies.

The idea that development expresses itself in increasing and rationalizing differentiations has formed a powerful and, today, still deeply intuitive archetype. It even affects the way many Westerners picture personal development. We tend to imagine that we develop by moving from a state in which our lives are embedded in material, familial, and social contexts to a state in which we differentiate ourselves from these contexts and become "our own person." Our modern liberty and individualism are paid for by a separation that is both painful and pleasurable. The story may be about loss or gain, decline or progress, or both, but this archetype is everywhere in our thinking, from our interpretations of man's expulsion from Eden, to the psychology of childhood development, to the transition from the concrete *Gemeinschaft* to the abstract *Gesellschaft*: in these areas and others, we like to think about development as a movement from a relatively undifferentiated to a relatively differentiated state. To be an adult, to be modern, to be enlightened is to learn distance and differentiation. As my book has started to show, different stories become possible once mixture is the narrative engine of development.

We have only recently begun to consider what would change if we told the story of enlightenment and modernization by invoking mixture. One of the most spirited attempts to correct our undue attachment to differentiation as a modernizing force belongs to Bruno Latour. In *We Have Never Been Modern* (1993), Latour resists the view that the modernization of Europe can be grasped as a process of increasing differentiation between society and nature, persons and things, human imagination and material causality.[11] He grants that this is what appears to have happened, but contends that such differentiations enable a contrary process, the production of mixtures or hybrids. For Latour, differentiation is a first step that is completed by the increased contact and crossover between the different spheres it establishes. This second step, however, has remained unacknowledged. The fatal flaw of the modern constitution, as Latour calls the template that governs the production of advanced knowledge, is that it is too invested in legitimizing itself through differentiation and purification to account openly for the mixtures it produces.

Convinced that the hermeneutics of suspicion has run its course, Latour offers an inviting revision. He contends that the point of increasing differentiation is to enable more and more complex mixtures. Mixture is thus central to the modernization of Western societies. Or is it? In the final analysis, Latour's brilliant book does both too much and too little: contending that we have never been modern is too willful a denial, and arguing that differentiation is the basis for mixture too respectful a concession to established modernization narratives. In Latour's story, mixture remains shadowy and secondary, constantly practiced but never fully legitimate. Because he presents mixture as depending on prior differentiation, Latour echoes the Aristotelian restrictions I discussed in Chapter 2. Thinkers such as Thomas White, Robert Boyle, and John Locke pointed in the opposite direction. Working against and around Aristotle toward a different modernity, they rejected the logical, historical, and cosmological primacy of differentiation. They insisted that mixture itself was fundamental and argued for its legitimacy and usefulness in the broad daylight of public debate. For these scientists and philosophers, mixture was not the unspoken secret of differentiation; it did not linger in the shadows of official culture.

Interventions such as Latour's or Anthony Giddens's (whose modernizing narrative moves from "disembedding" to "reembedding" practices and thus follows a similar logic) are still spellbound by the ordering impulses of modernization.[12] They constrain mixture from becoming a fully vested cause or ontological ground. In this way, the work of Latour and Giddens continues to reflect the limits that Claude Lévi-Strauss, Victor Turner, and Mary Douglas associated with the agency of hybrid and mixed cultural formations. Like these modernist anthropologists, Latour and Giddens assign mixture a function inside a dominant or preceding order that retains the upper hand.[13] Mixture is a product of that order.

If we turn from these at least residually modernist uses of mixture to its most influential postmodern use, we might expect that mixture would emerge from such a dependent position. More than any other current thinker, Homi Bhabha has made mixture or hybridity (his favored term) central to our attempts at understanding identity and agency in a postcolonial, globalizing world. Bhabha's influence reaches far and wide, but he, too, resists making mixture a cause of order. We can witness this resistance when Bhabha discusses the workings of "cultural hybridity" and its potential to carry us beyond the boundaries of the familiar and the known. We come into contact with cultural hybridity, he writes, when we pass "between fixed identifications," a passage he compares to the "liminal space" of a stairway. Yet "our intimations of exceeding the barrier or boundary—the very act of going beyond," Bhabha explains, "are unknowable, unrepresentable, without a return to the 'present' which, in the process of repetition, becomes disjunct and displaced."[14] The hybrid or mixed situation is captured here as an ambivalent space "between," a space that can give us only an intimation of a different reality. That intimation becomes more solid knowledge when we return to a position that is not suspended between others. It is the return to a less ambivalent sense of position that allows us to see that the world's order has been disturbed.

In Bhabha's account, mixture does not possess agency itself. It does not produce anything by itself and is instead defined as a kind of suspension between existing identifications. The effect of such equivocal suspension can be felt only with our return to the world of univocal identifications. Once we leave the liminal situation behind, we see that the order of the world is disjointed. Thus, while Bhabha sees mixture entirely positively and recognizes its operations as a global phenomenon, he, too, remains captivated by the status Aristotle assigned to it. Mixture has to remain eternally unsettled, ambivalent, and in-between. It must not settle down to anything or reach anything; it has to remain a process that can never result in a product. While it exists in relationship to order and has effects on this order, mixture is not itself an order or productive of one. Like Aristotle's mixture, Bhabha's hybridity continuously lingers in front of the gates that determine what the world counts as real and embodied. Such a hybridity remains paradoxically pure. It does not enter the business of creating identities, but chastely points to identity as a problem. It is a counter-discourse of order, the margin that unsettles the center. If for Aristotle the point of excluding mixture from agency was securing a hierarchical order, for Bhabha the point is preserving a heterotopia that can disturb order. In this way, Bhabha still echoes the general scheme of Turner's analysis of liminality. No matter how much he tries to associate mixed and hybrid formations with the creation of the new, Bhabha stays close to Turner's conception of the liminal as a temporary suspension.[15] Mixture is contained by the dominant order, whose stratifications precede and succeed it.

Bhabha's work is an especially influential example of our current fascination with the concept of mixture. Contemplating Bhabha through the lens of the early modern deployment of mixture reveals the extent to which, for him, mixture remains a non-place inside the world created by European modernization. Bhabha's fascination and ours, I suspect, finds its source here, in mixture's elusive otherness, in its out-of-place-ness. This is ironic because, at the same time, we also live in an increasingly less bounded world that makes the operations of mixture more and more routine and commonplace. As I emphasized in the opening pages of this book, mixed or hybrid formations are today far less strange than they were twenty years ago. By desiring mixture to be other, we are lengthening the shadow that has followed it for a long time. For most of its history, mixture has been construed as liminal or hidden, the other of European civilization, a secret or barely acknowledged wish, the signature of premodern ways, a transgressor, threat, or critic of all that appears stable, clear, and bounded. For many of us, mixture's ethical and political attractions would seem to depend on its inability to get involved in the production and reproduction of the world. But in a globalizing world of rapid technological innovation, such inability becomes recognizable as the product of wishful thinking, a perhaps already nostalgic desire for a pure hybridity, uncontaminated by the dense networks of people, things, and capital that make and remake our world.

The politics of mixture in early modern England, by contrast, is not nostalgic. It seeks to open the gate to a transformed future and shares ground with Antonio Negri's, Michael Hardt's, and Donna Haraway's belief in the utopian possibilities of a boundless world.[16] While they deploy mixture as a critical language against the essentializing tendencies of the Aristotelian tradition, the writers I have studied in this book recognize mixture as an epistemological and ontological reality. For them, mixture is a process that leads to a product whose identity cannot be defined by pointing to the sameness of essences, substances, or forms. Instead, they boldly argue that all things are irreducibly mixed and seek to understand identity as something that is produced by difference and discontinuity. Mixture is the most productive ground, as Locke points out, of human agency and the only path toward a better civilization. The tradition that Locke belongs to actively and consciously contests the construction of natural, political, and cultural order around ideas of purity, homogeneity, and continuity. This tradition sees no contradiction between mixture and order. On the contrary: it entrusts mixture with producing a superior order. The usefulness of analytic reduction may be acknowledged and a lingering attachment to the old certainties of essences and forms may be confessed, but these impulses do not dominate the texts I have studied. In these texts, mixture relates to purity and differentiation by active contradiction, not as their hidden, unconscious, or even conscious flipside.

What I am arguing, then, is that an impressive range of writers in seventeenth- and early eighteenth-century England promotes a paradigm of modernization that fundamentally contradicts the one that has been working for us over the past two hundred years or so but is today becoming less and less productive. In the hands of these writers, terms such as *liberty, diversity, equality,* and *cooperation* acquire meanings that do not fit this paradigm. Obviously, my book does not study the question of whether mixture did, in fact, propel the modernization of English society.[17] But by identifying a significant group of early modern thinkers who actively promoted mixture as a path to a better world, *Exquisite Mixture* proposes that differentiation may not be the founding or dominant mechanism in the creation of modern societies, individuals, and knowledges. In late seventeenth- and early eighteenth-century England, many thinkers see mixture as more promising than differentiation and as a clear alternative to it. The intellectual models for a different vision of order and modernization were thus available in considerable detail. But while my book has demonstrated the remarkable value mixture acquired in numerous fields of inquiry in early modern England, it will be the task of future studies to determine in full if the English elevation of mixture represents a different mode of modernization. And then we may be able to decide whether we need to see modernization as a much more heterogeneous force with extraordinary modal variability between and within different nations or even take differentiation altogether out of the toolbox we use to think about development.

In conclusion, it may be helpful to sketch some of the consequences that such a reorientation is likely to produce. The differentiations that modernization has claimed in order to define itself—between the ancient and the modern, magic and science, religion and reason, figurative and literal, to use a different set—would fall. They could no longer serve as criteria of modernization. Other criteria would have to be found. Because these differentiations have been used to describe spatial, temporal, and procedural dimensions, modernization would lose its ability to refer to a region (Europe), to a period (1500–1800), or to a single process. Instead, modernization would become a variable and perhaps pluralistic mode whose activities could be found in thirteenth-century America, in seventeenth-century England, and in twentieth-century India. Modernization would no longer divide human experience—not by imposing a totalizing historical time that promotes distinctions between archaic and modern, developed and underdeveloped societies, and not by grasping European civilization itself as the product of increasing differentiations. Perhaps modernization would lose its usefulness as a concept.

These changes in how modernization signifies have methodological implications. They would trouble, of course, narratives of development that prioritize increasing differentiation. But as a consequence, they would also undo, as Dipesh Chakrabarty has suggested, the hermeneutics of suspicion.[18] For this hermeneutics thrives in a divided world, a world so differentiated that its unity and the relationships between its parts become difficult to grasp. The most familiar and influential example of such a world picture is probably Marxism's, in which increasing differentiation causes increasing alienation, contradiction, and strife. The separation of man from his products and the emergence of classes and class conflict are the best-known examples of such effects. Through them, ideology is born, the need to weave a deceptive veil that hides the divisive operations of capitalism from ordinary human sight. It is here that the hermeneutics of suspicion has most frequently situated its operations, in the place where it can unmask the fabrications that paper over the divisions and conflicts of modern life.

This is a powerful place to be, yet it is also clear that the practitioner of hermeneutic suspicion privileges his or her "analytical relationships to the world" over his or her "lived relationships to the world."[19] In other words, the hermeneutics of suspicion helps the analyst to steel him- or herself against the fact that we are subject to transformation by the materials we are studying. The thoroughly suspicious reader carefully guards the alienation from the object he or she is investigating. Such a reader resists recognition in the object and makes distance, objectification, and distrust the inescapable framework of all inquiry, thus reproducing the very conditions he or she wishes to expose.

The early modern thinkers featured in this book would seem to recommend a different framework. By elevating the ontological and epistemological value of mixture, they prompt us to rethink the relationship between investigator and object, to revise our configuration of critical identity and agency. They ask us, I think, to accept the riskiness of open-ended contact with the objects we study and the genuine transformations that such contact can trigger. They encourage us to think about our activity as expansive and integrative and remind us that such an approach is more productive than one that revolves around analytic separation. Possessed of fewer qualms than we are today, they realize that expansion, integration, and liberty go together. Such recommendations are worth pondering. They may be uncomfortable, but they could put humanistic inquiry on a path on which our contact with the past could, once again, remake our world and our selves. What seems virtually certain, meanwhile, is that the hermeneutics of suspicion and the narrative of modernization it relies on have lost their way. In an increasingly boundless world, we have different questions about the past. The past speaks differently to us. We should not, suspiciously, close our ears.

NOTES

PREFACE

1. For Crèvecoeur's comment about racial and religious mixture, see *Letters from an American Farmer* (London, 1782), 62. For a more extensive discussion of racial mixture in America, see ibid., 48–52.

2. For a critical discussion of the distinction between metaphor and concept in *Begriffsgeschichte*, see Stefan Willer, "Metapher und Begriffsstutzigkeit," in *Begriffsgeschichte im Umbruch?* ed. Ernst Müller (Hamburg: Felix Meiner Verlag, 2005), 69–80. Hans Blumenberg has argued for the importance of the metaphorical to an intellectual history that extends into the realm of human experience: see his *Paradigmen zu einer Metaphorologie* (Frankfurt: Suhrkamp, 1998).

3. Ulrich Johannes Schneider, "Über das Stottern in Gedanken: Gegen die Begriffsgeschichte," *Archiv für Begriffsgeschichte* 7 (2010), 126 (my translation).

4. Samuel Johnson, *A Dictionary of the English Language* (Dublin, 1775), s.v. *decompound*.

5. See entry decompounded in *Oxford English Dictionary*.

INTRODUCTION

1. Homi Bhabha, *The Location of Culture* (London: Routledge, 2004); Donna Haraway, *Simians, Cyborgs, and Women: The Reinvention of Nature* (New York: Routledge, 1991); Antonio Negri and Michael Hardt, *Empire* (Cambridge, Mass.: Harvard University Press, 2000).

2. Perry Anderson, *The Origins of Postmodernity* (London: Verso, 2002), 93.

3. In his introduction to *Cultural Mobility: A Manifesto* (Cambridge: Cambridge University Press, 2010), Stephen Greenblatt argues for the need to recognize the dialectic of heterogeneity and homogeneity, of difference and sameness, of discontinuity and continuity, as fundamental to the articulation of cultural identity in all historical periods (1–23).

4. For an account of the Saxon political myth, see Samuel Kliger, *The Goths in England: A Study in Seventeenth- and Eighteenth-Century Thought* (Cambridge, Mass.:

Harvard University Press, 1952). See also Hugh A. MacDougall, *Racial Myth in English History: Trojans, Teutons, and Anglo-Saxons* (Hanover, N.H.: University Press of New England, 1982), 53–72; R. J. Smith, *The Gothic Bequest: Medieval Institutions in British Thought, 1688–1863* (Cambridge: Cambridge University Press, 1987); Colin Kidd, *British Identities Before Nationalism: Ethnicity and Nationhood in the Atlantic World, 1600–1800* (Cambridge: Cambridge University Press, 1999), 75–98.

5. For David Hume's description of the Saxon origins of English liberties, see *The History of England, from the Invasion of Julius Caesar to the Accession of Henry VII*, vol. 1 (London, 1762), 141–154. For Hume's description of William I's tyrannical rule, see ibid., 172–175. For an account of the Norman Yoke in seventeenth-century England, see Christopher Hill's classic *Puritanism and Revolution: Studies in Interpretation of the English Revolution in the Seventeenth Century* (1958; reprint, New York: St. Martin's Press, 1997), 46–111.

6. For an account of the difficulties church historians faced when they tried to integrate the Saxon period into the history of the reformed church, see Kidd, *British Identities Before Nationalism*, 99–109.

7. MacDougall, *Racial Myth in English History*, 35.

8. MacDougall, *Racial Myth in English History*, 37–40.

9. The story of the rise of linguistic Saxonism in seventeenth-century England has been comprehensively told by Richard Foster Jones, *The Triumph of the English Language* (Stanford, Calif.: Stanford University Press, 1953). For a more recent and comparative history of early modern ideas about language, see Peter Burke's *Languages and Communities in Early Modern Europe* (Cambridge: Cambridge University Press, 2004). Burke confirms that linguistic mixture was mostly viewed pejoratively in early modern Europe and that the seventeenth century, when the borrowing between different European languages peaked, was also the period when "European movements for linguistic purification really gathered force" (140). See more generally Burke's chapters "Mixing Languages" (111–140) and "Purifying Languages" (141–159).

10. Samuel Johnson, *A Dictionary of the English Language* (London, 1755), cir.

11. *Tacitus on Britain and Germany*, trans. H. Mattingly (Harmondsworth: Penguin, 1948), 4:103, cited in MacDougall, *Racial Myth in English History*, 43.

12. For an overview of the claims made by Camden and Verstegan, see MacDougall, *Racial Myth in English History*, 45–50.

13. John Hare, *St. Edward's Ghost; or, Anti-Normanisme* (1647), 34. Cited in MacDougall, *Racial Myth in English History*, 60. For a discussion of Hare and Whyte more generally, see ibid., 59–63.

14. Colin Kidd and Mary Floyd Wilson are both interested in the extent to which English identity was forged in the conscious exchange with various others, but both believe that the seventeenth century marked the rapid ascent of Anglo-Saxon ideology. Thus, Kidd argues that the "rich ethnic diversity" of the English was "a minor ingredient of English national identity" (*British Identities Before Nationalism*, 75–98). Kidd also outlines "eight broad strategies for dealing with [England's] chequered history of settle-

ment and invasion": the strategy I am about to present is not mentioned (*British Identities Before Nationalism*, 79–81). For Wilson's argument, see *English Ethnicity and Race in Early Modern Drama* (Cambridge: Cambridge University Press, 2003), 1–21. For a different revisionist history that highlights the interactions between essentialist fictions and the hybrid identities that the British empire fostered in the eighteenth century, see Kathleen Wilson, *The Island Race: Englishness, Empire, and Gender in the Eighteenth Century* (London: Routledge, 2003). Linda Colley's marvelous *Britons: Forging the Nation, 1707–1837* (1992; reprint, New Haven: Yale University Press, 2009) also emphasizes that the construction of British identity occurred relationally, in the engagement with various others. But in Colley's argument, this engagement with others is productive of identity by setting the British against the French, the Catholics, or the Indians. Colley thus demonstrates the constructedness of British identity, but the emergence of such identity from acts of differentiation contradicts the impulse I observe in many early eighteenth-century writers, who foreground a lack of differentiation from others as the source of English virtue.

15. I am not the first to observe the complexity that could attach to ideas of personal, racial, or cultural identity in eighteenth-century Britain. Others who have made this observation include: Howard Weinbrot, *Britannia's Issue: The Rise of British Literature from Dryden to Ossian* (Cambridge: Cambridge University Press, 1993); Clifford Siskin, *The Work of Writing: Literature and Social Change in Britain, 1700–1830* (Baltimore: Johns Hopkins University Press, 1998); Srinivas Aravamudan, *Tropicopolitans: Colonialism and Agency, 1688–1804* (Durham, N.C.: Duke University Press, 1999); Roxann Wheeler, *The Complexion of Race: Categories of Difference in Eighteenth-Century Culture* (Philadelphia: University of Pennsylvania Press, 2000); Dror Wahrman, *The Making of the Modern Self: Identity and Culture in Eighteenth-Century England* (New Haven, Conn.: Yale University Press, 2004); *A New Imperial History: Culture, Identity, and Modernity in Britain and the Empire, 1660–1840*, ed. Kathleen Wilson (Cambridge: Cambridge University Press, 2005); Daniel Carey, *Locke, Shaftesbury, and Hutcheson: Contesting Diversity in the Enlightenment and Beyond* (Cambridge: Cambridge University Press, 2006). I add to these studies by providing an intellectual history of mixture that cuts across several disciplines.

16. For Bailey's importance, see De Witt T. Starnes and Gertrude E. Noyes, *The English Dictionary from Cawdrey to Johnson* (Chapel Hill: University of North Carolina Press, 1946), 107. For the success and influence of de Rapin's history, see Philip Hicks, *Neoclassical Literature and English Culture* (Houndmills, Basingstoke: Macmillan, 1996), 146–150.

17. Bailey, *An Universal Etymological English Dictionary* (London, 1721), a1v–a2r. For de Rapin's statement on linguistic mixture and its beauties, see *The History of England*, vol. 2 (London, 1726), 208–210.

18. For Bailey's use of the term *mutation,* see *English Dictionary*, A4r, a1v.

19. Bailey notes in passing that the Saxons were such a great and potent nation because of "the Aggregation of many People under their Name and Service" (*English Dictionary*, A4v). While this does not argue for sexual mixture, it is clear that Bailey sees a multicultural composition as a cause of strength. De Rapin describes the native Britons

as "now consisting of a Mixture of Romans and other Foreigners" (*History of England* [London, 1725], vol. 1, 71) and Norman invaders as mixed from Norman and Danish ingredients (*History of England*, vol. 2, 216).

20. The quotations in this paragraph come from Edward Chamberlayne, *Anglia Notitia; or, The Present State of England* (London, 1669), 18–19. For Miege's borrowing of Chamberlayne's language on race, see *The New State of England Under Their Majesties K. William and Q. Mary* (London, 1691), AA2r; the comments on language are on AA6v–AA7r.

21. For an account of Moll's career, see Dennis Reinhartz, *The Cartographer and the Literati: Herman Moll and His Intellectual Circle* (Lewiston, N.Y.: Edwin Mellen Press, 1997). Compare Reinhartz's entry on Moll in *Oxford Dictionary of National Biography*.

22. Herman Moll, *A System of Geography* (London, 1701), 2.

23. Moll's combination of a discontinuous national history with an improving narrative about the blending of different national temperaments can also be found in other histories published around this time. See, for example, the anonymous *The History of England, Faithfully Extracted from Authentick Records*, vol. 1 (London, 1702), which associates the Norman conquest with an "Innovation in all things but Religion" that is in part based on the superior civility enabled by the temperate French climate: "the Normans having more of the Sun and Civility, by mixing with the *English*, begat more commodious Customs" (71). Laurence Echard's *The History of England* (London, 1707) echoes this account (135–136).

24. For an account of Salmon's work in the context of Augustan historiography, see Laird Okie, *Augustan Historical Writing: Histories of England in the English Enlightenment* (Lanham, Md.: University Press of America, 1991), 99–113.

25. Despite the acknowledgment of discontinuity and destruction, Salmon was proud of Britain's Roman heritage: see *Historical Collections: Relating the Originals, Conversions, and Revolutions of the Inhabitants of Great Britain to the Norman Conquest* (London, 1706), 142.

26. Salmon, *Historical Collections*, 430.

27. Salmon, *Historical Collections*, 439.

28. Okie notes that Salmon's Toryism was unusual in that it combined with "respect for and dispassionate interest in foreign cultures" (*Augustan Historical Writing*, 102). In 1749, Salmon wrote: "As I am a Citizen of the World, I look upon all Men as my Brethren, and have long endeavoured to set them right in their Notions of one another. I am extremely concerned to see almost every People representing the Inhabitants of distant Nations, as Barbarians, and treating them as such. For my Part, I have met with People as polite, ingenious and humane, whom we have been taught to look upon as Cannibals, as ever I conversed with in Europe" (*A New Geographical and Historical Grammar* [London, 1749], a1r). For Salmon's critique of the upper-class assumption that "Blood distinguishes them from their Brethren," see ibid., 199.

29. As Quentin Skinner has shown, the argument for historical discontinuity—especially around the Norman conquest—was not owned by royalists, absolutists, or

Tories. There was a significant tradition of political thought in seventeenth-century England that argued for the discontinuity of 1066 to make radical arguments about the nature of political power—without advocating absolutism. See Skinner's "History and Ideology in the English Revolution," *The Historical Journal* 8:2 (1965), 151–178. I believe that Defoe has to be considered part of this tradition.

30. Reinhartz, *The Cartographer and the Literati*, 84–89.

31. The description of Defoe's poem as an "unprecedented bestseller" comes from W. R. Owens, "Introduction," Defoe, *Satire, Fantasy, and Writings on the Supernatural*, vol.1, ed. W. R. Owens (London: Pickering and Chatto, 2003), 17. Within the first year of the poem's publication, ten editions appeared. By 1705, Defoe claimed that nine authorized editions and twelve piracies were in circulation. By 1750, around fifty editions and issues had appeared. For the publication history of *The True-Born Englishman*, see David Foxon, "Defoe: A Specimen of a Catalogue of English Verse, 1701–1750," *The Library*, 5th series, 20:4 (1965), 277–297. One example of the influence Defoe's poem exerts on today's debates is Lord Desai's response to Tory MP John Townend's remarks in 2001 that immigrants undermined Britain's homogeneous Anglo-Saxon culture. Lord Desai recommended *The True-Born Englishman* as a useful antidote to such racist politics. For Lord Desai's recommendation to Townend, see: http://news.bbc.co.uk/2/hi/uk_news/politics/1304770.stm (accessed 1/16/2011).

32. I quote Defoe's poem from Owens's edition: Defoe, *Satire, Fantasy, and Writings on the Supernatural*, 1:77–122, lines 167–174. Subsequent references to Defoe's poem appear in the text.

33. For the point that the English mixtures are too deep to be analyzed, see also these lines: "The Scot, Pict, Britain, Roman, Dane submit, / And with the English-Saxon all unite: / And these the Mixture have so close pursu'd / The very Name and Memory subdu'd" (Defoe, *The True-Born Englishman*, ll. 358–361).

34. Defoe does not use the phrase "mixed multitude" in *The True-Born Englishman*, but uses closely related language when he presents the "promiscuous Crowd" (l. 810) that the English became after the collapse of government in 1688. This promiscuous crowd is for Defoe the legitimate origin of new political institutions. The insight that political power and form spring from the multitude also informs Defoe's nuanced portrayal of mob and multitude in *A Hymn to the Mob* (1715), reprinted in: Defoe, *Satire, Fantasy, and Writings on the Supernatural*, 1:413–438.

35. Defoe made the comment on the relatively unmixed blood of the Irish, Welsh, and Scottish in the "Explanatory Preface" he added to *The True-Born Englishman* in 1701: see Defoe, *Satire, Fantasy, and Writings on the Supernatural*, 1:79.

36. Questioning *The True-Born Englishman*'s generic identity, one of Defoe's most prominent critics, William Pittis, noted that Defoe's poem was a "Libel which has stoln into the World, under the Name of a Satyr, and dispersed its Venom in a concealed manner": Pittis, *The True-Born Englishman: A Satyr, Answer'd, Paragraph by Paragraph* (London, 1701), 1. Compare the amusingly straight rebuttal Defoe's poem drew in the title of the anonymous *Englishmen No Bastards* (London, 1701).

37. Defoe, "Explanatory Preface," 79.

38. Defoe confirms this argument for the benefits of conquest in *An Essay Upon Projects* (London, 1697) when he suggests that England received "Civilizing and Method-izing" gifts when it was "Conquer'd by [Roman] Valour" (72).

39. For Kidd's comments about Defoe's poem, see *British Identities Before National-ism*, 76. Compare Colley's remarks on Defoe's poem in *Britons*, which similarly down-play its significance: 15–16.

40. Jonathan Israel, "General Introduction," *The Anglo-Dutch Moment: Essays on the Glorious Revolution and Its World Impact*, ed. Jonathan Israel (Cambridge: Cambridge University Press, 1991), 43.

41. Bailey endorses populousness as the source of wealth in *The Antiquities of London and Westminster* (London, 1722), 2. For a history of the argument for populousness that ties it to the debates about naturalization in eighteenth-century England, see Daniel Statt, *Foreigners and Englishmen: The Controversy over Immigration and Population, 1660–1760* (Newark: University of Delaware Press, 1995).

42. Defoe, "Explanatory Preface," 80.

43. Despite his cosmopolitanism and his belief that populousness was linked to prosperity, Salmon rejected the idea of a general naturalization. See his discussion of the naturalization bill in *The Life of Her Late Majesty Queen Anne*, vol. 2 (London, 1721), 104–108.

44. On Defoe's lifelong defense of active immigration policies, see Daniel Statt, "Daniel Defoe and Immigration," *Eighteenth-Century Studies* 24:3 (1991), 293–313.

45. In *Economic Thought and Ideology in Seventeenth-Century England* (Princeton, N.J.: Princeton University Press, 1978), Joyce Appleby discusses the influence of the Dutch example on English economic thought: 73–98.

46. For the influence of William Temple's *Observations Upon the United Provinces of the Netherlands* (London, 1673), see Istvan Hont's observations in "Free Trade and the Economic Limits to National Politics: Neo-Machiavellian Political Economy Reconsid-ered," in *The Economic Limits to Modern Politics*, ed. John Dunn (Cambridge: Cambridge University Press, 1990), 41–42. Temple also influenced histories concerned with empha-sizing the benefits of conquest and mixture (though he was split between a continuous and a discontinuous interpretation of the Norman conquest, Temple emphasized its benefits). This assessment of the Norman conquest influenced, for example, the anony-mous *The History of England, Faithfully Extracted from Authentick Records*, vol. 1, 70–71, which stressed the benefits of Norman civility "mixing" with the English. See also Salmon, *Historical Collections*, 413–429, for a lengthy quotation from Temple describing the Norman conquest.

47. For the quotations from Temple in this paragraph, see *Observations Upon the United Provinces of the Netherlands*, in *The Works of Sir William Temple* (London, 1731), vol. 1, 59–64. Compare Temple's comments about Rome, whose superior civilization was a direct result of the goods and knowledge flowing into Italy from its vast imperial hold-ings: *Upon the Gardens of Epicurus*, in *The Works of Sir William Temple*, 1:170–190.

48. Temple advocates a broad naturalization and toleration for England in *Of Popular Discontents*, in *The Works of Sir William Temple*, 1:264–267.

49. For a discussion of the naturalization bills in the 1690s, see Statt, *Foreigners and Englishmen*, 100. For an account of the sudden influx of German immigrants, see ibid., 121–141.

50. See Israel, "General Introduction," *The Anglo-Dutch Moment*, 20, for an account of William's initial vision for toleration.

51. Gordon J. Schochet, "From Persecution to 'Toleration'," in *Liberty Secured? Britain Before and After 1688*, ed. J. R. Jones (Stanford, Calif.: Stanford University Press, 1992), 152.

52. On the impact that the Toleration Act had on the church, see the discussion by John Morrill, "The Sensible Revolution," in *The Anglo-Dutch Moment*, 95–98.

53. Defoe's name for Sacheverell is quoted in Paula Backscheider, *Daniel Defoe: His Life* (Baltimore: Johns Hopkins University Press, 1989), 265. The quotation from Sacheverell can be found in his *The Political Union* (Oxford, 1702), 10.

54. Last two Sacheverell quotations from *The Political Union*, 48, 53.

55. Last three Sacheverell quotations from *The Perils of False Brethren* (London, 1709), 28–29, 44. See also the anonymous *An Answer to the Dissenters Pleas for Separation* (Cambridge, 1701) for another example of a conservative churchman worrying about toleration as dangerous religious mixture (13) and William Robertson, whose *Dissenters Self-Condemned* (London, 1710) accuses Jesuits and Dissenters "Of Granting Dispensations for incongruous Mixtures" (133). Robertson's tract responded specifically to the glowing preface Defoe had written to a reissued pamphlet by Thomas Delaune, one of the heroes of Dissenter resistance to Stuart persecution in the early 1680s.

56. In *English Advice to the Freeholders of England* (n.p., 1714), Atterbury criticizes the Whigs' "Schemes of Naturalization" (24) and equates "a general and unlimited comprehension" with "an equal Distribution of Places between Turks, Germans, and Infidels" (31).

57. Swift's critique of republican politics (two preceding quotations) can be found in *The Examiner* 21, December 28, 1710, reprinted in Swift, *The Examiner and Other Pieces Written in 1710–11*, ed. Herbert Davis (Oxford: Basil Blackwell, 1957), 48–49. Swift's association of toleration and naturalization with republican politics was not unreasonable. Caroline Robbins has shown that these two issues were central for eighteenth-century commonwealthmen: *The Eighteenth-Century Commonwealthman* (Cambridge, Mass.: Harvard University Press, 1959), 56–133. Swift's references to Toland in the *Examiner* can be found, for example, in *Examiner* 22, January 4, 1710 (*The Examiner and Other Pieces*, 55); *Examiner* 25, January 25, 1710 (*The Examiner and Other Pieces*, 71); and *Examiner* 39, May 3, 1711 (*The Examiner and Other Pieces*, 142). Swift's satire on the Calves Head Club is *T—l—d's Invitation to Dismal* (London, 1712).

58. Toland's positive view of Temple can be seen in *The Art of Governing by Partys* (London, 1701), where he twice refers approvingly to Temple's arguments (30, 137).

59. Atterbury, *English Advice to the Freeholders of England*, 24. Toland's critique of Atterbury is in *The State-Anatomy of Great Britain* (London, 1717), 16.

60. Toland, *The Description of Epsom* (London, 1711), 18.

61. Last three quotations in Toland, *Reasons for Naturalizing the Jews in Great Britain and Ireland* (London, 1714), 18–21.

62. In *The True-Born Englishman: a Satyr, Answer'd, Paragraph by Paragraph*, Pittis suggests that Toland was the author of Defoe's poem. He alludes to Toland's association with the Calves-Head Club (9), his Irish origins (2), his Catholic upbringing (3), and his atheism (23). He calls him "T____d" (49).

63. Quotations in this paragraph up to this footnote can be found in Toland, *The State-Anatomy of Great Britain* (London, 1717), 31.

64. Sacheverell makes his comments about fluctuation in *The Perils of False Brethren*, 30. Toland praises political trimmers as "Men of Peace and public Spirit" in *The Art of Governing by Partys*, 118. In *Memorial of the State of England* (London, 1705), Toland commends the Quakers for being "the exactest Trimmers in the Nation" (27).

65. Toland, *Tetradymus* (London, 1720), 184. Cited in Stephen H. Daniel, *John Toland: His Methods, Manners, and Mind* (Kingston and Montreal: McGill-Queens University Press), 143.

66. Last two quotations from Toland, *Memorial of the State of England*, 52, 48.

67. Examples of histories of William I that credit him with a civilizing influence include: William Temple, *An Introduction to the History of England* (London, 1695), esp. 308–318; James Tyrrell, *The General History of England* (London, 1704), vol. 2 (for the account of William I's reign, see B1r–E2v, and for Tyrrell's dedication to William III that explicitly links him to William I, see ibid., A1v–A2r); Echard, *The History of England*, 135–136. Echard's emphasis on the French civility that entered with William I was anticipated by the anonymous *The History of England: Faithfully Extracted from Authentick Records*, vol. 1, 70–71.

68. Charles Davenant, *The Political and Commercial Works*, vol. 1, (London, 1771), 88, cited in Hont, "Free Trade and the Economic Limits to National Politics," 68. Hont's discussion is helpful on the shift from politics as a domestic to an international concern in late seventeenth-century Britain.

69. David Armitage, *The Ideological Origins of the British Empire* (Cambridge: Cambridge University Press, 2000), 141.

70. Algernon Sidney recommends the mixing of the different "species" of government in *Discourses Concerning Government*, ed. Thomas G. West (Indianapolis: Liberty Fund, 1996), 31, 166. Toland edited Sidney's work in the 1690s. Toland endorses the "mixture of . . . kinds" in *State-Anatomy*, 9.

71. For Toland on mixed government, see, for example, *State-Anatomy*, 9; for Locke, see *Two Treatises of Government*, ed. Peter Laslett (Cambridge: Cambridge University Press, 1993), 406–411; for Swift, see *A Discourse of the Contests and Dissensions Between the Nobles and the Commons in Athens and Rome* (London, 1701), 5–9; for Atterbury, see *Sermons and Discourses on Several Subjects and Occasions* (London, 1761), vol. 1, 263–265; for Bolingbroke, see *A Dissertation Upon Parties* (Dublin, 1735), 158–159; for Walpole, see the discussion in Isaac Kramnick, *Bolingbroke and His Circle: The Politics of Nostalgia in the*

Age of Walpole (Ithaca, N.Y.: Cornell University Press, 1992), 124–127; for Addison, see *The Freeholder* (London, 1723), 291–292; for Hutcheson, see *A Short Introduction to Moral Philosophy* (Glasgow, 1747), 299–300; for Mandeville, see *Free Thoughts on Religion* (London, 1729), 331–342; for Pope, see *Essay on Man*, book iv, ll. 283–302 (*The Poems of Alexander Pope*, ed. John Butt [London: Routledge, 1989], 534); for Defoe, see *Jure Divino* (1706) in Owens and Furbank (eds.), Defoe, *Satire, Fantasy, and Writings on the Supernatural* 2:31–363: book xi, ll. 41–83 and ll. 209–230.

72. Swift, *A Discourse of the Contests and Dissensions*, 9.

73. J. G. A. Pocock, *The Ancient Constitution and the Feudal Law* (1957; reprint, Cambridge: Cambridge University Press, 1987), 173. For Pocock's discussion of Hale more generally, see 170–181.

74. Quotations in this paragraph from Matthew Hale, *The History of the Common Law of England* (1713; Chicago: University of Chicago Press, 1971), 39–43.

75. Hale's outlook was echoed by William Nicholson, whose *The English Historical Library* (London, 1699) polemicized against common lawyers of Coke's stamp and their contention that the ancient constitution had not been much affected by Roman, Saxon, Danish, and Norman invasions (iii–iv).

76. Daniel Defoe, *Jure Divino*, book x, l. 142.

77. De Rapin, *History*, 2:284–285. For de Rapin's assertion of a continuous ancient constitution, see *An Impartial History of Whig and Tory* (London, 1718), 1–2. For Salmon's critique of de Rapin, see "Mr. Salmon's Preface" in Salmon, *The History of Great Britain and Ireland* (London, 1725), A2r–A6r.

78. De Rapin, *History*, 2:276.

79. De Rapin, *History*, 2:283.

80. De Rapin's comments on England's mixed government can be found in *An Impartial History*, 1–2.

81. Swift, *A Serious and Useful Scheme to Make an Hospital for Incurables* (London, 1733), 13.

82. Swift, *A Proposal for Correcting, Improving, and Ascertaining the English Tongue* (London, 1712), 11. Swift's praise of the French influence distanced him from Samuel Johnson, who referred to Swift's work as his "pretty treatise on the English language," but saw no value in the French influence on English (Johnson, A *Dictionary of the English Language*, C2r). The Whig John Oldmixon, meanwhile, accused Swift (inaccurately) of wishing to make it "as Criminal to admit Foreign Words as Foreign Trades" (*Reflections on Dr. Swift's Letter . . . About the English Tongue* [London, 1712], 2).

83. Swift's comment on the genius of nations can be found in *A Discourse of the Contests and Dissensions*, 50. For Toland's comments on the changeability of nations and states, see *The Destiny of Rome* (London, 1718), 7–8.

84. I cite Swift's poem from *The Poems of Jonathan Swift*, ed. Harold Williams, vol. 1 (Oxford: Clarendon Press, 1958), 136–139.

85. Margaret Ann Doody, *The Daring Muse: Augustan Poetry Reconsidered* (Cambridge: Cambridge University Press, 1985), 56. For a post-hermeneutic, cross-generic

account of the influence mixture had on literary change in eighteenth-century Britain, see Siskin, *The Work of Writing*.

86. Alexander Pope, *The Dunciad* (1743), reprinted in *The Poems of Alexander Pope*, ed. John Butt (London: Routledge, 1989), 317–360. The quotations from Pope in the three preceding sentences are in book 1 of *The Dunciad*, ll. 38–42, 67–70, 274–277.

87. The assessment that the novel is a quintessentially modern genre is widely shared. I refer here specifically to Michael McKeon, "Introduction," *Theory of the Novel: A Historical Approach* (Baltimore: Johns Hopkins University Press, 2000), xv. Marthe Roberts has explored the illegitimacy of the novel in *Origins of the Novel*, trans. Sacha Rabinovitch (London: Harvester, 1980). For an account that argues the affinity of the eighteenth-century novel with illegitimate protagonists, see my "Illegitimacy and Social Observation: The Bastard in the Eighteenth-Century Novel," *ELH* 69 (2002), 133–166.

88. For Shaftesbury's suggestion that miscellaneous writing relies on patchwork and mixture, see *Characteristics of Men, Manners, Opinions, Times*, ed. Lawrence E. Klein (Cambridge: Cambridge University Press, 1999), 340–341. For his point about bastardy, see ibid., 339. Shaftesbury praises the restoration of English liberty in 1688 along with its promise for the arts, ibid., 97–100.

89. On Toland's relationship to Shaftesbury, see Robbins, *The Eighteenth-Century Commonwealthman*, 125–134, and Daniel, *John Toland*, 160–163.

90. Michael Seidel's *Satiric Inheritance: Rabelais to Sterne* (Princeton, N.J.: Princeton University Press, 1979) has helped me to think about satire's relationship to mixture in the early eighteenth century. I thank Deidre Lynch for referring me to this work.

91. David Fairer has urged us to recognize georgic poetry's "mixed economy." See his excellent essay "'Where Fuming Trees Refresh the Thirsty Air': The World of Eco-Georgic," *Studies in Eighteenth-Century Culture* 40 (2011), 201–218.

92. For Defoe's comments on the advantages derived from the social and sexual mixture of different classes (tradesmen and gentlemen), see *A Plan of the English Commerce* (London, 1728), 11–12, and *The Complete English Tradesman* (London, 1726), 311–313.

93. For Beverley's comments on intermarriage between English settlers and native Americans, see *The History and Present State of Virginia* (London, 1705), 25–26. Though he does not discuss mixture, David Armitage notes that British arguments for populousness and naturalization are related to the projection of empire abroad (*The Ideological Origins of the British Empire*, 125–145). For additional comments on mixture as a strategy of empire, see Chapters 4 and 5.

94. I differentiate myself here from Jonathan Israel, who narrowly associates a radical enlightenment with Spinoza and his European reception (*Radical Enlightenment: Philosophy and the Making of Modernity, 1650–1750* [Oxford: Oxford University Press, 2001]). Interestingly enough, one of the radical thinkers Israel discusses, Alberto Radicati, seeks support for his arguments by alluding to Boyle's chemistry: "That Matter always is a Mixture, is sufficiently known to the Chymists; who never have found, nor ever

can find a Body purely simple" (*A Philosophical Dissertation upon Death* [London, 1732], 6). My discussion of Boyle's chemistry in Chapter 2 shows that this is one of Boyle's most characteristic claims.

95. My argument for the politically liberating effects of naturalizing instability, disorder, and deformity sets this book apart from studies of the monstrous or disabled body. While the fascination with monstrosity in the early modern period has generated significant scholarly interest over the past twenty-five years or so, the monstrous body has been predominantly studied as an expression of deep-seated anxieties over the boundaries of the human (examples include *The Boundaries of Humanity: Humans, Animals, Machines*, ed. James Sheehan and Morton Sosna [Berkeley: University of California Press, 1991]; Dennis Todd, *Imagining Monsters: Miscreations of the Self in Eighteenth-Century England* [Chicago: University of Chicago Press, 1995]; Zakiya Hanafi, *The Monster in the Machine: Magic, Medicine, and the Marvelous in the Time of the Scientific Revolution* [Durham: Duke University Press, 2000]; Felicity Nussbaum, *The Limits of the Human: Fictions of Anomaly, Race, and Gender in the Long Eighteenth Century* [Cambridge: Cambridge University Press, 2003]). The political virtues of deformity and its constructive role in the process of modernization are not addressed in this literature. This holds also true for *Defects: Engendering the Modern Body*, ed. Helen Deutsch and Felicity Nussbaum (Ann Arbor: University of Michigan Press, 2000), one of the recent books that has brought disability studies into the early modern period. In their preface, the editors propose that the history of disability should be written as a gradual differentiation between the normal and the deformed body. My argument complicates this proposal. It shows that the boundary between form and deformity was rendered pervious in seventeenth-century science and politics and that the deformed body was normalized.

96. For Shapin's and Jacob's argument about the conservative drift of seventeenth-century science, religion, and politics, see, for example, Steven Shapin and Simon Schaffer, *Leviathan and the Air Pump* (Princeton, N.J.: Princeton University Press, 1985); Margaret and James Jacob, "The Anglican Origins of Modern Science: The Metaphysical Foundations of the Whig Constitution," *Isis* 71:2 (1980), 251–267. Other studies that follow this line of argumentation include: Carolyn Merchant, *The Death of Nature* (New York: Harper and Row, 1980); John Rogers, *The Matter of Revolution: Science, Poetry, and Politics in the Age of Milton* (Ithaca, N.Y.: Cornell University Press, 1996); and—despite his recognition of Boyle's "*nervous* glorification of the politics and aesthetics of order" (my emphasis)—Robert Markley, *Fallen Languages: Crises of Representation in Newtonian England, 1660–1740* (Ithaca, N.Y.: Cornell University Press, 1993), 100.

97. Barbara Shapiro, *Probability and Certainty in Seventeenth-Century England* (Princeton, N.J.: Princeton University Press, 1983); Richard Kroll, *The Material Word: Literate Culture in the Restoration and Early Eighteenth Century* (Baltimore: Johns Hopkins University Press, 1991).

98. Corinne Comstock Weston and Janelle Renfrow Greenberg, *Subjects and Sovereigns: The Grand Controversy over Legal Sovereignty in Stuart England* (Cambridge: Cambridge University Press, 1981).

99. The story of mixed government in the sixteenth and seventeenth centuries has been told by Zera Fink, *The Classical Republicans: An Essay in the Recovery of a Pattern of Thought in Seventeenth-Century England* (1945; reprint, Evanston, Ill.: Northwestern University Press, 1962); Corinne Comstock Weston, *English Constitutional Theory and the House of Lords, 156–1832* (London: Routledge, 1962); W. H. Greenleaf, *Order, Empiricism, and Politics: Two Traditions of Political Thought, 1500–1700* (London: Oxford University Press, 1964); Weston and Greenberg, *Subjects and Sovereigns*; Robert Eccleshall, *Order and Reason in Politics: Theories of Absolute and Limited Monarchy in Early Modern England* (Oxford: Oxford University Press, 1978); and Michael Mendle, *Dangerous Positions: Mixed Government, the Estates of the Realm, and the Answer to the XIX Propositions* (University: University of Alabama Press, 1985). Weston and Greenberg are especially helpful on the two revivals of mixed government in seventeenth-century England.

100. Pliny's passage on grafting is quoted in Francis Meres, *Wits Common Wealth, the Second Part* (London, 1634), 125.

CHAPTER 1. THE SCIENCE OF MIXTURE

1. The single best account of the scholastic debate about mixture is Anneliese Maier, *An der Grenze von Scholastik und Naturwissenschaft: Studien zur Naturphilosophie des 14. Jahrhunderts* (Essen: Essener Verlagsanstalt, 1943), 9–139. Compare E. J. Dijksterhuis's account, which summarizes Maier's findings: *The Mechanization of the World Picture* (Oxford: Clarendon Press, 1961), 200–209. See also Norma Emerton, *The Scientific Reinterpretation of Form* (Ithaca, N.Y.: Cornell University Press, 1984), 76–105, for another account of theories of mixture in the scholastic mold.

2. Revisionist historians of science have become aware that there is a significant relationship between the ancient debate about mixture and seventeenth-century science, but there is little recognition so far that the revaluation of mixture was closely related to the revival of classical atomism or that mixture's newly recognized causal capacities affected several fields of scientific inquiry. For an especially important example of a history of seventeenth-century science that engages the problem of mixture, see William Newman, *Atoms and Alchemy: Chymistry and the Experimental Origins of the Scientific Revolution* (Chicago: University of Chicago Press, 2006). Compare my comments on Newman's interpretation of Boyle below.

3. Galen, *Mixtures*, in *Selected Works*, trans. P. N. Singer (Oxford: Oxford University Press, 1997), 202.

4. Galen, *Mixtures*, 255, 261–263.

5. On balanced and unbalanced mixtures, see Galen, *Mixtures*, 206–208.

6. For an example of Galen's emphasis on the body's relationship to dietary and climatic environments, see Galen, *The Art of Medicine*, in *Selected Works*, 373–376.

7. Galen, *Mixtures*, 284.

8. Galen, *Mixtures*, 275.

9. The last two quotations are from Galen, *Mixtures*, 261.

10. For Galen's discussion of the soul or form in generation, see *The Construction of the Embryo*, in *Selected Works*, 200–201.

11. Aristotle, *De Generatione et Corruptione*, in *On Sophistical Refutations, On Coming-to-Be and Passing-Away, On the Cosmos*, Loeb Classical Library, ed. T. E. Page et al., trans. E. S. Forster (Cambridge, Mass.: Harvard University Press, 1955), 221. Subsequent references will appear in parentheses in the main text.

12. Aristotle's comments in *The Physics* link Anaxagoras explicitly to the position that all things were originally together and mixed. See Aristotle, *The Physics*, Loeb Classical Library, vol. 1, ed. T. E. Page et al., trans. Philip H. Wicksteed and Francis M. Cornford (London: William Heinemann, 1929), 43, 221–223.

13. Aristotle, *Meteorologica*, Loeb Classical Library, ed. T. E. Page et al., trans. H. D. P. Lee (London: William Heinemann, 1952), 293.

14. On the conflict between the physics of elemental mixture and the metaphysics of form in the middle ages, see Maier's account in *An der Grenze*, 9–139.

15. Daniel Sennert, *Epitome Naturalis Scientae* (1618), translated into English as *Thirteen Books of Philosophy* (London, 1659). I quote from the 1660 London edition: K1r. Compare the passage on I4r, where Sennert repeats his complaint about endowing the mixture of the four elements with generative capacity.

16. Sennert, *Thirteen Books of Natural Philosophy*, I2r.

17. I can offer three examples for commentaries on Aristotle that affirm that mixture is generative. Thomas Stanley's four-volume *The History of Philosophy* devotes a section to Aristotle. Stanley first states that "Mixtion is not generation," but almost immediately delivers an account of elemental mixture that claims that the mere heaping together of elements could "contemperate" them in such a way that a mixed body is created (*The History of Philosophy*, vol. 2 [London, 1656], HHH4r–HHH4v). Another example is Gideon Harvey, *Archelogia Philosophica Nova; or, New Principles of Philosophy* (London, 1663). Though Harvey prides himself on restoring the original meaning of Aristotle's text, he flatly asserts that elemental mixture is generative (*Archelogia Philosophica Nova*, RRR2v). A third example is Richard Blome's populist *The Gentleman's Recreation* (London, 1686). Blome distinguishes at first clearly between generation and alteration, but his qualification that "Alteration is as it were the way and Companion of Generation" undercuts a distinction dear to Aristotle (36). See my discussion of Kenelm Digby below, who also argues that Aristotle sees the mixture of elements as generative.

18. Jan Baptista van Helmont, *Ortus Medicinae* (Amsterdam, 1648), translated into English as *Oriatrike; or, Physick Refined* (London, 1662), 51.

19. It is very likely that Carpenter and Hakewill knew each other. They were born thirty-five miles apart in Devon, in Northleigh and Exeter, respectively. They both studied at Oxford and were elected fellows at Exeter College. Hakewill resigned his fellowship in 1611; Carpenter began his fellowship in 1607 (see the entries in *Oxford Dictionary of National Biography*). Hakewill referred to Carpenter's *Geographie Delineated* (Oxford, 1625) admiringly and at some length in the 1635 edition of his *An Apologie of the Povver*

and Prouidence of God in the Gouernment of the World (Oxford) and called him the "late Fellow of Exceter Colledge in Oxford" (CC5v). Both were friends with the mathematician Henry Briggs (for Carpenter's friendship with Briggs, see Christopher Hill, *Intellectual Origins of the English Revolution Revisited* [Oxford: Clarendon Press, 1997], 272; for Hakewill's friendship with Briggs, see *Apologie* [1635], in which he includes a letter by Briggs, whom he calls "my learned friend" [CC1r]). Carpenter shared a basic political orientation with Hakewill. Both extended their resistance to a blind acceptance of ancient authority in science to political authority. For an account that places Carpenter's work in the context of seventeenth-century science, see Richard Foster Jones, *Ancients and Moderns: A Study of the Rise of the Scientific Movement in Seventeenth-Century England* (1936; reprint, St. Louis, Mo.: Washington University Press, 1963), 62–71.

20. The most complete account of the debate about the decay of nature is Victor Harris's *All Coherence Gone* (Chicago: University of Chicago Press, 1949). See also the discussion of this debate in R. F. Jones, *Ancients and Moderns: A Study of the Background of the Battle of the Books* (St. Louis, Mo.: Washington University Studies, 1936), 23–42; Herschel Baker, *The Wars of Truth: Studies in the Decay of Christian Humanism in the Earlier Seventeenth Century* (Cambridge, Mass.: Harvard University Press, 1952), 65–89; Paul H. Kocher, *Science and Religion in Elizabethan England* (San Marino, Calif.: Huntington Library, 1953), 82–92. Since the 1950s, interest in this debate has been sparse.

21. William Bouwsma has emphasized that Calvin's aversion to mixture is a basic motif and disposition: *John Calvin: A Sixteenth-Century Portrait* (New York: Oxford University Press, 1988), 34–36 (I thank Hannibal Hamlin for drawing my attention to Bouwsma's book). In his commentaries on Jeremiah, Calvin anticipated Goodman's idea that our sins throw the elements into disarray, causing a universal state of mixture: "We throw heaven and earth into confusion by our sins. For were we in the right order as to our obedience to God, doubtless all the elements would be conformable, and we should thus observe in the world an angelic harmony. But as our lusts tumultuate against God; nay, as we stir up daily, and provoke him by our pride, perverseness, and obstinacy, it must needs be, that all things, above and below, should be in disorder . . . and that nothing should be unmixed and unstained in the world" (Calvin, *Commentaries on the Book of the Prophet Jeremiah*, vol. 1, trans. and ed. John Owen [Grand Rapids, Mich.: Eerdmans, 1950], 301).

22. Goodman, *The Fall of Man; or, The Corruption of Nature* (London, 1616), 18.

23. Goodman, *The Fall of Man*, 62.

24. Goodman uses the phrase "elements mixed and impure" twice in his exchanges with Hakewill. Hakewill appended these exchanges to the 1635 edition of *An Apologie of the Povver and Prouidence of God* (Oxford). For Goodman's use of "elements mixed and impure," see ibid., KKKK3r and SSSS4v.

25. All preceding quotations from Goodman, *The Fall of Man*, 19.

26. Goodman, *The Fall of Man*, 22–23.

27. Goodman, *The Fall of Man*, 18.

28. George Hakewill, *An Apologie of the Povver and Prouidence of God* (Oxford, 1627), 1. See Jones, *Ancients and Moderns: A Study of the Rise of the Scientific Movement in Seventeenth-Century England*, for an account of Hakewill's argument (22–40). Jones maintains that Hakewill's "influence upon subsequent phases of the conflict [between ancients and moderns] was second only to that of Bacon" (35).

29. Hakewill's and Goodman's self-positioning as Aristotelians who emphasize generation and corruption, respectively, can be observed in Hakewill, *An Apologie of the Povver and Prouidence of God* (1635), BBBB1r–BBBB2r.

30. Quotations in this paragraph (including blocked quotation) from Hakewill, *An Apologie of the Povver and Prouidence of God* (1630), 115. Subsequent page numbers in the main text refer to this edition.

31. Hakewill, *An Apologie of the Povver and Prouidence of God* (1635), BBBB3v.

32. For the idea that the elements can transform into each other, see Aristotle, *On the Heavens*, Loeb Classical Library, ed. T. E. Page, trans. W. K. C. Guthrie (Cambridge, Mass.: Harvard University Press, 1953), 319–321. Insofar as it supposes elemental changeability, the same argument also supports the thesis of decay.

33. Hakewill, *An Apologie of the Povver and Prouidence of God* (1635), DDDD2r.

34. Hakewill, *An Apologie of the Povver and Prouidence of God* (1635), CCCC3r.

35. Hakewill, *An Apologie of the Povver and Prouidence of God* (1635), GGGG5v.

36. For Goodman's absolutist politics, see his recommendation that "absolute government among the dumb creatures" provided a fitting model for human government. His ideal was "Monarchie. . . . the subjection . . . onely to one" (*The Fall of Man*, 100–101). For Hakewill's critique of older sons, see *An Apologie of the Povver and Prouidence of God* (1635), MMMM6r; for his critique of primogeniture, see ibid., BBBB4r–BBBB4v; for his argument on women, see ibid., BBBB4v; for his remark on custom, see ibid., B1v–B2r.

37. For the exchange around "mutinee," see Hakewill, *An Apologie of the Povver and Prouidence of God* (1635), MMMM6v. Compare Hill's assessment of Hakewill's politics in *Intellectual Origins*, 178–181.

38. Nathanael Carpenter, *Geographie Delineated* (Oxford, 1625), second book, 7–11. Subsequent references will appear in the main text and are to this second book. For an overview of the contents of *Geographie Delineated* that carefully notes the different authors Carpenter draws on, see J. N. L. Baker, "Nathanael Carpenter and English Geography in the Seventeenth Century," *Geographical Journal* 71:3 (1928), 261–271.

39. See my discussion of William Temple in Chapter 1.

40. Zera Fink points out that Bodin's theory "was much noticed in England" and mentions works by Thomas Nashe, Abraham Cowley, Thomas Wright, John Milton, and John Barclay: *The Classical Republicans: An Essay in the Recovery of a Pattern of Thought in Seventeenth-Century England* (1945; reprint, Evanston, Ill.: Northwestern University Press, 1962), 92–93.

41. For Galen's comment on the middle, see *Mixtures*, 218. For Bodin's inclusion of France in the middle region, see *Method for the Easy Comprehension of History*, trans. Beatrice Reynolds (New York: Octagon Books, 1966), 96.

42. Bodin, *Method*, 115, 126–127.

43. In *Geography Delineated*, Carpenter states that "all nations almost of the world since the beginning have suffered mixture" (second book, 276). For Bodin on the same point, see *Method*, 87.

44. For Bodin's stress on infinite variety in the middle, see *Method*, 91.

45. Aware of Bodin's and Carpenter's work, Hakewill doubted the ability of climate to control temperament and wit: *An Apologie of the Povver and Prouidence of God in the Gouernment of the World* (1635), A2v.

46. The passage that Carpenter echoes is in Bodin, *Method*, 144.

47. Carpenter's appropriation of Bodin's ideas signals that foreign bodies were not always seen as a threat to the body politic. This circumstance qualifies the "decisive epistemic shift" Gil Harris has argued was prompted by the challenge of Paracelsian medicine to Galenic assumptions in the sixteenth century (Jonathan Gil Harris, *Foreign Bodies and the Body Politic: Discourses of Social Pathology in Early Modern England* [Cambridge: Cambridge University Press, 1998], 16). In Harris's account, the Paracelsian conception of disease as transmitted by agents outside of the body was transferred to the body politic, which was no longer threatened by interior imbalances, but by foreign incursions. As Carpenter's claims show, the health of the body politic could depend on foreign intermixture.

48. Gervase Markham, *The English Husbandman* (London, 1613), F2v.

49. For another representation of grafting as mixture, see Rene Rapin, *Of Gardens*, trans. John Evelyn (London, 1672), 200–201.

50. For Markham's analysis of horse temperaments, see *Cauelarice; or, The English Horseman* (London, 1607), book 7, 1–4. For Markham's program of mixing races, see his third chapter, "Of the Mixture of these Former Races," Markham, *Cauelarice*, book 1, 17–20.

51. Markham, *Cauelarice*, book 1, 20.

52. The claims about African and Greek climates are in Markham, *Cauelarice*, book 7, 3–4. The statements on mixing English with Greek horses ("Turke") and African horses ("Barbarie") are in book 1, 19. In book 1, 12–13, Markham explains that "Turke" and "Barbarie" are the names for Greek and African horses, respectively.

53. For Bacon's comments on Africa, see *Sylua Syluarum: A Naturall History* (London, 1626), 123. Bacon flatly states that "we see that in living creatures, that have Male and Female, there is Copulation of severall Kindes; And so Compound Creatures; As the Mule that is generated betwixt the Horse and the Asse" (122).

54. Della Porta, *Natural Magic* (London, 1658), 33.

55. Della Porta, *Natural Magic*, 33.

56. In a fulsome twelve-page letter to Hakewill that responds to the expanded 1635 edition of the *Apologie*, Digby writes: "I have not in any language upon any particular subject, mett wth so large a body (and so well featured and composed a one) of naturall Philosophy, History, various erudition, wth Metaphysciall and Theologicall reflections, as in this piece of yours, wherein wth pregnant reasons drawne out of all these stores you

vindicate this worlde from the vulgarly receiued opinion of decay or deterioration." Digby notes "how seriously I have meditated upon the subiect of your book" and stresses his "earnest application of my minde to better my selfe by your booke": Digby to Hakewill, May 15, 1635. B. L. Harleian MSS 4153.

57. Joseph Needham, *A History of Embryology* (Cambridge: Cambridge University Press, 1934), sees Digby as a central force in the development of epigenesis. Needham was joined by Betty Jo Dobbs in this assessment ("Studies in the Natural Philosophy of Sir Kenelm Digby," *Ambix* 18:1 [1971], 3), but other students of generation have given Digby a less prominent place. Elizabeth Gasking's *Investigations into Generation, 1651–1828* (Baltimore: Johns Hopkins University Press, 1967) and Clara Pinto-Correia's *The Ovary of Eve: Egg and Sperm and Preformation* (Chicago: University of Chicago Press, 1997) do not mention Digby. Eve Keller, *Generating Bodies and Gendered Selves: The Rhetoric of Reproduction in Early Modern England* (Seattle: University of Washington Press, 2007) criticizes Digby for the failure of his mechanism to account adequately for development, complexity, and variety (143–144). For a helpful recent overview over the debates about epigenesis and preformation, see Linda van Speybroeck, Dani de Waele, and Gertrudis van de Vijver, "Theories in Early Embryology: Close Connections Between Epigenesis, Preformationism, and Self-Organization," *Annals of the New York Academy of Sciences* 981 (2002), 7–49. See also Michael Hagner, who examines the relationship between monstrous births and epigenesis in the eighteenth century: "Enlightened Monsters," in *The Sciences in Enlightened Europe*, ed. William Clark, Jan Golinski, and Simon Schaffer (Chicago: University of Chicago Press, 1999), 175–217.

58. Robert Hugh Kargon characterized Digby's philosophy as a "strange mélange" in *Atomism in England from Hariot to Newton* (Oxford: Clarendon Press, 1966), 72–73. Betty Jo Dobbs echoes Kargan's characterization of Digby's work when she describes it as a fruit of "that interim period when Aristotle was dethroned . . . and the Newtonian system was yet to emerge" ("Studies in the Natural Philosophy of Sir Kenelm Digby," 3). See also Stefania Tutino, *Thomas White and the Blackloists: Between Politics and Theology During the English Civil War* (Aldershot: Ashgate, 2008), who emphasizes "Digby's mix of Aristotelianism and new science" (143) without attending to the productive interaction between these two bodies of knowledge. My point is that the mélange or mixture of the old and the new is precisely what enabled Digby to move forward scientifically.

59. I quote here and throughout from the 1665 edition of Digby's *Two Treatises: Of Bodies and of Man's Soul* (London, 1665), 425. Subsequent references appear in the main text.

60. Digby's most concentrated use of mixture to describe processes of generation can be found in *Two Treatises*, 144–161.

61. Compare the "hourly mutation" Digby observes in chickens developing in the egg (*Two Treatises*, 275).

62. Harvey and Digby were acquaintances. Digby mentions Harvey's surprising observation regarding the absence of sperm in the womb after conception before this observation was published in Harvey's *Exercitationes de Generatione Animalium* (London,

1651) (Digby mentions Harvey's observation in the first edition of *Two Treatises* [Paris, 1644], 221). Harvey was actively working on generation in the 1630s, but Digby undertook his own experiments regarding the maturation of the chick in the egg (*Two Treatises* [1665], 275). They may have worked on similar issues during the same time. See the discussion in Geoffrey Keynes on the circumstances of Harvey's work on generation: *The Life of William Harvey* (Oxford: Clarendon Press, 1966), 329–359. Charles Webster has argued that Digby may have seen Harvey's treatise in manuscript form. See Webster, "Harvey's *De Generatione*: Its Origins and Relevance to the Theory of Circulation," *British Journal for the History of Science* 3:3 (1967), 262–274.

63. See my discussion of Harvey's immaterial conception in Chapter 4.

64. One sex may be dominant in the generation of one child, Digby concedes, but that doesn't mean this will be the case with the next child. Like Hakewill, Digby believes in the mutual repair that male and female seed can offer each other: *Two Treatises*, 280–281.

65. Quoted in Francis Meres, *Wits Common Wealth, the Second Part* (London, 1634), 125.

66. Boyle's biographer Michael Hunter sees Digby as exerting a "significant influence" on Boyle after 1654. See Hunter, *Boyle: Between God and Science* (New Haven, Conn.: Yale University Press, 2009), 105.

67. For a history of Parcelsus's influence on English medicine, see Allen Debus, *The English Paracelsians* (New York: Watts, 1966) and *The Chemical Philosophy: Paracelsian Science and Medicine in the Sixteenth and Seventeenth Centuries*, 2 vols. (New York: Science History Publications, 1977), which includes an account of the Helmontian reformulation of Paracelsus's chemical philosophy. For an excellent history of early medicine with instructive commentary on the Helmontian challenge to the establishment, see Andrew Wear, *Knowledge and Practice in English Medicine, 1550–1680* (Cambridge: Cambridge University Press, 2000), especially 353–433.

68. For Goodman's critique of the Paracelsians, see *The Fall of Man*, 18, 26. Paracelsus's follower Oswald Croll explained the Paracelsian cosmology by observing that "after the transgression and fall from unity to alterity, by the curse of God new Tinctures came in . . . by whose mixture . . . Impurity was joined to the pure roots, which was the predestination of diseases." "Nature therefore, as it is now," Croll continued, "gives us nothing that is pure in the world, but hath mixed all things with many impurities" (Croll, *Philosophy Reformed and Improved in Four Profound Tractates* [London, 1657]. The quoted material can be found on 95–96).

69. Croll, *Philosophy Reformed and Improved in Four Profound Tractates*, 97.

70. Croll, *Philosophy Reformed and Improved in Four Profound Tractates*, 93–94.

71. On van Helmont's epistemological program, see the discussion in Wear, *Knowledge and Practice in English Medicine*, 95–100.

72. For Boyle's relationship to chemical medicine, see Hunter, *Boyle: Between God and Science*, 160–163.

73. McGuire, "Boyle's Conception of Nature," *Journal of the History of Ideas* 33:4 (1972), 533.

74. Newman, *Atoms and Alchemy*, 223.

75. Newman, *Atoms and Alchemy*, 224.

76. Thomas Kuhn's classic article "Robert Boyle and Structural Chemistry," *Isis* 43:1 (1952), 12–36, gets Boyle's interest in transmutation right.

77. Eleutherius enlists Sennert in his defense of spagyric chemistry in Boyle, *The Sceptical Chymist; or, Chymico-Physical Doubts and Paradoxes Touching the Spagyrist's Principles* (London, 1661), K5r. Subsequent references to *The Sceptical Chymist* in the main text.

78. See *The Sceptical Chymist*, L7v, for an additional experiment that counters the paradigmatic status of Sennert's experiment, this time involving metals. Boyle concludes this experiment by saying that "it seems not always necessary, that the Bodies that are put together per minima, should each retain its own nature" (L8r).

79. For Boyle's acknowledgment that he borrows the term *decompound* from grammarians, see *The Sceptical Chymist*, E5v.

80. Boyle, *The Sceptical Chymist*, P3v.

81. Boyle, *The Sceptical Chymist*, P3v. Compare Boyle's comments in *A Free Inquiry into the Vulgarly Receiv'd Notion of Nature* (London, 1686), where he calls nature a "kind of compounded Accident" and explains that "there are far more [compounded Accidents] than, at the first mention of them, one would imagine" (264).

82. Thomas White, *Institutionum Peripateticarum* (London, 1647), published in English as *Peripateticall Institutions* (London, 1656), 79–80. White's work was self-consciously modeled on Digby's and was sometimes attributed to Digby (see the Royal Society obituary on Digby, which attributes White's book to him: Thomas Birch, *The History of the Royal Society of London*, vol. 2 [London, 1756], 82).

83. Boyle, *The Sceptical Chymist*, P4r–P4v. See also the following passage, in which Boyle explains his vision of the complexity of bodies in similar terms when he writes that he wishes to "distinguish the principles or more primitive, or simple Ingredients of mixt Bodies into three sorts, first Primary Concretions or Coalitions, next, Secondary mixts, and thirdly decompounded mixts, under which name I comprehend all sorts of mixt Bodys, that are of a more compounded Nature, than the primary, or Secondary ones newly mentioned" (Royal Society Boyle Papers, iv, fol. 41r, quoted in Antonio Clericuzio, *Elements, Principles, and Corpuscles: A Study of Atomism and Chemistry in the Seventeenth Century* [Dordrecht: Kluwer Academic, 2000], 123–124).

84. Boyle, *The Sceptical Chymist*, EE4v.

85. Boyle, "An Introduction to the History of Particular Qualities," in Boyle, *Tracts Written by the Honourable Robert Boyle* (Oxford, 1671), 21.

86. Boyle, *The Origine of Formes and Qualities* (Oxford, 1666), 102.

87. Boyle, *The Sceptical Chymist*, Y8v–Z1r. Boyle's critique of purification may mark a shift in his position. As Clericuzio has pointed out, Boyle's *Some Considerations Touching the Usefulnesse of Experimental Philosophy* (Oxford, 1663) contained passages that suggested

an affinity with the spagyrist program: see Clericuzio, "From van Helmont to Boyle: A Study of the Transmission of Helmontian Chemical and Medical Theories in Seventeenth-Century England," *British Journal for the History of Science* 26 (1993), 314.

88. Boyle, "An Introduction to the History of Particular Qualities," 12.

89. Boyle, "The Author's Proemial Discourse to the Reader," *Origine of Formes* (Oxford, 1667), B7v. Boyle mentions here the ten experiments that make up the practical section of his book. The vitriol experiment is one of these.

90. Last two quotations in Boyle, *The Origine of Formes and Qualities* (1666), 219. Subsequent references are from this edition and appear in the main text.

91. Compare Kuhn's essay and its emphasis on the centrality of transmutation in Boyle's natural philosophy: "Robert Boyle and Structural Chemistry," especially 21–24. I have learned much from Kuhn's discussion, but his conclusion—that Boyle's contribution to seventeenth-century science consisted of a "brilliant destructive criticism of naïve theories" (36)—forgets that transmutation was for Boyle a constructive force.

92. The primacy of fluidity over anatomy is emphasized in Boyle's *Some Considerations Touching the Usefulnesse of Experimental Naturall Philosophy*, first part, where Boyle writes: "Anatomy it self has not discover'd to us all the Wonders to be met with in a humane Body, nor will detect them, till Anatomists be skill'd in some other things over and above that of dexterously Dissecting: For it seems very probable, that the excellent contrivance of some parts will never be fully apprehended, without a competent knowledge of the Nature of those Juices that are to pass thorow them, and some of them receive their beginning or some alteration in them; And the nature of these Juices will scarce be exactly known, without some skill in divers parts of Physiology, and especially in Chymistry" (98). Compare also Boyle's *A Free Enquiry into the Vulgarly Receiv'd Notion of Nature*: "One great Cause of the common Mistakes about this Matter, is . . . That the Body of a Man is look'd upon, rather as a System of Parts, whereof Most are gross and consistent, and not a Few hard and solid too, than as, what indeed it is, a very compounded Engine; that, besides these Consistent Parts, does consist of the Blood, Chyle, Gall, and other Liquors; also more subtle Fluids, as Spirits and Air; all which Liquors and Fluids are almost incessantly and variously moving, and thereby put divers of the Solid Parts, as the Heart and Lungs, the Diaphragma, the Hands, Feet, &c. into frequent and differing Motions" (325–326). For a contrasting view, see Barbara Beigun Kaplan's *Divulging of Useful Truths in Physick: The Medical Agenda of Robert Boyle* (Baltimore: Johns Hopkins University Press, 1993), which considers Boyle as equally interested in the structure and the juices of the body (80).

93. Historians of science have acknowledged the influence of natural magic on seventeenth-century science, but without noting the importance of mixture. For an overview of natural magic's influence on seventeenth-century science, see John Henry, *The Scientific Revolution and the Origins of Modern Science*, second edition (Basingstoke: Palgrave, 2002), 54–67. For an overview of the debate about the place of the magical tradition in the history of science, see Brian Vickers, "Introduction," *Occult and Scientific Mentalities in the Renaissance*, ed. Brian Vickers (Cambridge: Cambridge University Press,

1984), 1–56. Digby signals his debt to natural magic not only in his broad acceptance of transgeneration or his infamous embrace of the weapon's salve (which could heal wounds by treating the weapon that caused them), but also in a chapter of *Two Treatises* that describes how all bodies can be generated from a mixture of the elements. There, he gamely invites his reader in a tone that is reminiscent of della Porta's: "let us now begin our mixture" (153).

94. Charles Webster, *From Paracelsus to Newton: Magic and the Making of Modern Science* (Cambridge: Cambridge University Press, 1982), 58.

95. Translated as Agrippa, *Three Books on Occult Philosophy* (London, 1650). I quote from this edition: 70.

96. Agrippa, *Three Books on Occult Philosophy*, 70–71.

97. Hakewill, *An Apologie of the Povver and Prouidence of God in the Gouernment of the World* (1635), B5r. Hakewill had Jonstonus's *Naturae Constantia* (Amsterdam, 1632) in mind. It was translated as *An History of the Constancy of Nature* (London, 1657).

98. Published in English as Jonstonus, *An History of the Wonderful Things of Nature* (London, 1657). I quote from this text.

99. Jonstonus, *An History of the Wonderful Things of Nature*, A2v.

100. For Boyle's transmutation of gold into silver, see *The Origine of Forms and Qualities* (1666), 349–378.

101. Previous two quotations from Boyle, *Some Considerations Touching the Vsefulness of Experimental Natural Philosophy*, first part, 20.

102. Published in English as della Porta, *Natural Magic* (London, 1658). I quote from this text.

103. Della Porta, *Natural Magic*, 23.

104. These four arguments can be found, respectively, in della Porta, *Natural Magic*, 36–37, 40, 46, 305.

105. Della Porta, *Natural Magic*, 33.

106. Della Porta, *Natural Magic*, 8.

107. Della Porta, *Natural Magic*, 61.

108. Last two quotations in Boyle, "The History of Fluidity and Firmness," in *Certain Physiological Essays* (London, 1669), 126–127.

109. "I do not believe all the Wonders, that Pliny, Aelian, Porta, and other writers of that stamp, relate of the Generation of Animals." These are simply "Romantic and Superficiall Narratives" (Boyle, *The Excellency of Theology Compar'd with Natural Philosophy*, [London, 1674], 49). For the quip about "notoriously fabulous writers," see Boyle, *An Essay About the Origine and Virtue of Gems* (London, 1672), A5v. For further skepticism, see the Boyle manuscript published in Boas, "Boyle's Method of Work: Promoting His Corpuscular Philosophy," *Notes and Records of the Royal Society of London* 41:2 (1987), 111–143. The comments on natural magic are on 130.

110. For a more general account of Boyle's complicated and intense relationship to magic, see Michael Hunter, "Alchemy, Magic, and Moralism in the Thought of Robert Boyle," *British Journal for the History of Science* 23:4 (1990), 387–410.

111. Boyle, *The Martyrdom of Theodora and Didymus* (London, 1687).

112. Boyle wrote an "Apology for Romances" (now lost): see Principe, "Newly Discovered Boyle Documents," *Notes and Records of the Royal Society of London* 49 (1995), 57. For the comparison of the book of nature to romance, see Boyle, *The Excellency of Theology Compar'd with Natural Philosophy*, 118–119.

113. Mentioning della Porta by name, Oldenburg wrote to Boyle in 1665 about an effort to publish a history of the Academy of Linceans. Oldenburg recognized the kinship between the Royal Society and the Academy and mused that it might be better not to let Thomas Sprat know about this history, since it might delay production of Sprat's *The History of the Royal Society* (London, 1667). Oldenburg to Boyle, October 31, 1665, in *The Correspondence of Henry Oldenburg*, vol. 2, ed. and trans. A. Rupert Hall and Marie Boas Hall (Madison: University of Wisconsin Press, 1966), 584–588.

114. Henry, *The Scientific Revolution and the Origins of Modern Science*, 59.

115. In 1669, Boyle noted that his beginnings as a scientist were tied to Bacon's text, whose method still served him as a model later in life. Explaining his approach to a correspondent, Boyle commented on the ten centuries that organized Bacon's experiments: "Many of the Particulars which we are now considering, were in my first Designe collected in order to a Continuation of the Lord Verulam's Sylva Sylvarum, or Natural History. And that my intended Centuries might resemble his, to which they were to be annex'd, it was requisite, that such kind of Experiments and Observations as we have been newly speaking of, should make up a considerable part of them" (Boyle, *Certain Physiological Essays*, 14). Boyle thus not only adopted Bacon's organizational form, but intended to "annex" his own centuries to Bacon's. He therefore perceived a significant continuity between the substance of his natural history and Bacon's and was apparently hoping to publish an edition that would join his own observations to Bacon's. Compare also Boyle, *Experimentae & Observationes Physicae* (London, 1691), A1r–A3v, where Boyle still invokes Bacon's *Sylua Syluarum* to justify his experimental practice.

116. Bacon, *Sylua Syluarum*, 29.

117. Last four quotations in Bacon, *Sylua Syluarum*, in this order: 33, 8, 30, 114.

118. On Bacon's acceptance of African fecundity, see my comments earlier in this chapter, in my discussion of Carpenter.

119. William Bouwsma, *The Waning of the Renaissance, 1550–1640* (New Haven, Conn.: Yale University Press, 2000), 50.

120. I have in mind Thomas Sprat's *History of the Royal Society* and Joseph Glanvill's *Plus Ultra* (London, 1668), both of which advertised the goals of the society.

121. Nehemiah Grew, *A Discourse Made Before the Royal Society, Decemb. 10, 1674 Concerning the Nature, Causes, and Power of Mixture* (London, 1675), and Grew, *Experiments in Consort of the Luctation Arising from the Affusion of Several Menstruums* (London, 1678). The former was theoretical, the latter practical. Both were included in Grew's *The Anatomy of Plants* (London, 1682).

122. Boyle's mentorship of Grew is described, for example, in Grew's dedication to Boyle in his fourth book in *The Anatomy of Plants* (AA4r).

123. Last three quotations from Grew, *A Discourse Made Before the Royal Society, Decemb. 10, 1674*, 29, 30, 75.

124. Grew, *A Discourse Made Before the Royal Society, Decemb. 10, 1674*, 58.

125. Grew, *A Discourse Made Before the Royal Society, Decemb. 10, 1674*, 74.

126. Grew, *A Discourse Made Before the Royal Society, Decemb. 10, 1674*, 57–58 and 50–51.

127. Grew, *The Anatomy of Plants*, E2r. Grew also thought that the behavior of bodies under mixture offered great promise for the production of more effective medicines whose ingredients mixture would "Mend, Exalt, Strengthen, and Ennoble" (ibid.). He turned these convictions into practice in what he considered an unprecedented "Systeme of Experiments" in which he mixed animal, vegetable, and mineral bodies and subjected them to "a multifarious Scrutiny" (*The Anatomy of Plants*, NN3v–NN4r). Reporting on these mixture experiments to the Royal Society in 1676, he expressed his hope to provide the model of a "Universal Survey" (ibid., NN4r) that could produce more effective medicines or more precise geological surveys (ibid., NN3v, OO4r). The Royal Society understood the experimental value of mixture as well. At the end of the 1670s, for instance, it systematically tried the qualities of compounds of gold and silver, lead and tin, tin and copper, tin and silver, silver and lead, silver and copper. Between January of 1679 and May of 1680, these experiments were conducted and reported on by Hooke (see the entries in Birch, *The History of the Royal Society of London*, vol. 4 [London, 1757]).

128. William Petty, *The Discourse Made before the Royal Society the 26. of November, 1674, Concerning the Use of Duplicate Proportion* (London, 1674), A5v.

129. The relevant passage on corpuscular hierarchy reads: "the motions of Corpuscles are compounded of the abovementioned motions of Atoms; and the motions of bigger and Tangible Bodies (viz. their qualities) are decompounded out of the Motions, Situation, Figure, and Magnitude of Corpuscles" (Petty, *Discourse . . . Concerning the Use of Duplicate Proportion*, 19–20).

130. Last two quotations taken from the first (unauthorized) edition of Petty's *Political Arithmetick*, which, under the title "England's Guide to Industry," was added at the end of Chamberlayne's *The Present State of England* (London, 1683): DD3r, DD4r. On transmutation as an important concept in Petty's political arithmetic, compare Ted McCormick, "Alchemy in the Political Arithmetic of Sir William Petty," *Studies in History and Philosophy of Science* 37 (2006), 290–307.

131. Last two quotations from Stubbe, *An Epistolary Discourse Concerning Phlebotomy* (London, 1671), 121.

132. Stubbe does not view "deep and subtle inquiries into Natural Philosophy" as harmful per se, but he asserts that those who engage in such inquiries aim to change medicine, religion, and education and thus threaten the political settlement. See Stubbe, *Legends, No Histories; or, a Specimen of some Animadversions upon The History of the Royal Society* (London, 1670), *2r–*2v. James Jacob has argued that Stubbes's monarchism does not break with his republican stance during the commonwealth, but represents a deflective action in a more restrictive political environment. See Jacob, *Henry Stubbe: Radical*

Protestantism and the Early Enlightenment (Cambridge: Cambridge University Press, 1983), 2–3.

133. Last three quotations from Stubbe, *An Epistolary Discourse Concerning Phlebotomy*, 121, 148, 146, respectively.

134. Quotations about the mixture and inseparability of the elements in Gott, *The Divine History of the Genesis of the World* (London, 1670), 139, 140. For an explicit critique of spagyrist principles, see ibid., 144.

135. Gott, *Divine History*, 139. In *The Planter's Plea; or, The Grounds of Plantation Examined* (London, 1630), John White suggests a parallel between the English, who God "first Civilized by the Romane Conquests, and mixture of their Colonies with us, that hee might bring in Religion afterwards" (11), and the new world, where the "heathen and brutish Nations" were acquainted by "mixture of some other people, with civility, to cause at length the glorious Gospell of Iesus Christ to shine out unto them" (15).

136. Gott, *Divine History*, 139.

137. The complexity of the natural philosophy that grew out of Gott's acceptance of mixture was not always a feature of his thinking. His utopian Puritan romance *Nova Solyma* (1648), by which Gott is today known to the few scholars engaged with his work, offered a clearer account of natural philosophy than his *Divine History* did twenty-two years later. In fact, mixture does not play a role in the earlier work, even when the creation of the world is discussed in some detail (see Gott, *Nova Solyma*, trans. Walter Begley [London: John Murray, 1902], 1:178–192; 2:9–22, 26–40).

138. Gott praises Bacon's "Naturall History" and says of Boyle: "all ought to believ whatsoever this Noble Person . . . has done, in all those manifold experiments" (*Divine History*, 13). The reference to the scale and order of nature is ibid., 147.

139. Gott, *Divine History*, 152.

140. For information on Elizabeth Gott's marriage, see the entry for Edmund Harvey in *Oxford Dictionary of National Biography*. For Gott's comments on Harrington's *Oceana*, see *Diary of Thomas Burton* (1828; reprint, New York: Johnson Reprint Corporation, 1974), vol. 3, 144.

141. Gott, *Divine History*, 127. Compare Gott's opening conceit, which singles out transmutation as a central issue in the mechanic philosophy. Gott compares the mechanist philosopher to the shop owner, who, "having only an Hercules of Wax in his shop, when one came to buy of him a Mercury, could presently turn his Beard into a Galerus, his Club into a Caduceus, and his Buskins into Talaria; and so he might as well have made thereof a Jupiter, Juno, Venus, Man, Beast, or Tree. . . . Thus our new Philosophers, not acknowledging all those several Primitive Natures which God in his Infinite Wisedom pleased to Create, like Etymologists, can derive one thing from another so far as scarcely to leav any Primitives" (*Divine History*, 5). Gott's playful conceit satirizes the transformation of Hercules into Mercury by suggesting a change of Hercules' blunt weapon of aggression into a caduceus (a wand worn by Mercury associated with healing) or Hercules' boots (buskins) into the winged sandals (talaria) that Mercury wore in Roman mythology. The world is wax in the hands of the mechanic philosopher, and man

can be kneaded into beast and tree. Everything may be made of everything, just like della Porta, Digby, and Boyle suggested.

142. Gott, *Divine History*, 142.

143. The discussion of the meadow and the colored powders is in Gott, *Divine History*, 130.

144. Gott, *Divine History*, 130.

145. The one acknowledgment of Gott's book I found comes from Richard Baxter, who praises Gott's "excellent Philosophy, (excepting the style and some few presumptions)": *A Treatise of Knowledge and Love Compared* (London, 1689), 167.

146. Newton's theory gained international notoriety during the first half of the 1670s and was itself influenced by Boyle, whose works Newton had studied extensively in the 1660s. On Newton's debt to Boyle, see Richard Westfall, "The Foundations of Newton's Philosophy of Nature," *British Journal for the History of Science* 1:2 (1962), 173 (fn.), and Westfall, "The Development of Newtons Theory of Color," *Isis* 53:3 (1962), 348. For Boyle's influence on Newton's color theory, see also Alan Shapiro, *Fits, Passions, and Paroxysms: Physics, Method, and Chemistry and Newton's Theories of Colored Bodies and Fits of Easy Reflection* (Cambridge: Cambridge University Press, 1993), 99–106. Casting himself in the role of the humble student, Newton thanked Boyle publicly in 1675 for comments the latter had made on one of his papers on light (see Birch, *The History of the Royal Society of London*, vol. 3 [London, 1757], 261). In this paper, Newton referenced two of Boyle's experiments in support of his argument (ibid., 252 and 254).

147. Isaac Newton, "A Letter of Mr. Isaac Newton . . . Containing His New Theory About Light and Colours," *Philosophical Transactions* 6 (1671), 3079.

148. Newton, "A Letter of Mr. Isaac Newton . . . Containing His New Theory About Light and Colours," 3081, 3083. Newton contradicted Descartes's theory of light already in the 1660s: see Westfall, "The Foundations of Newton's Philosophy of Nature," 177.

149. Newton, "A Letter of Mr. Isaac Newton . . . Containing His New Theory About Light and Colours," 3083.

150. Newton, "Mr. Isaac Newtons Answer to Some Considerations Upon His Doctrine of Light and Colors," *Philosophical Transactions* 7 (1672), 5097.

151. For Newton's use of the distinction between compounded and decompounded, see "An Extract of Mr. Isaac Newton's Letter, Written to the Publisher from Cambridge April 3. 1673," *Philosophical Transactions* 8 (1673), 6109–6110.

152. For Hooke's sentiments, see his letter to Oldenburg, February 15, 1671/2 (*The Correspondence of Isaac Newton*, vol. 1, ed. H. W. Turnbull [Cambridge: Cambridge University Press, 1959], 110). The second opinion belongs to James Gregory. See his letter to John Collins, April 9, 1672 (*Correspondence of Isaac Newton*, 1:120).

153. For the narrowing of Newton's argument, see Alan E. Shapiro, "The Evolving Structure of Newton's Theory of Light and Color," *Isis* 71:2 (1980), 223–228.

154. Newton to Oldenburg, December 7, 1675 (*Correspondence of Isaac Newton* 1:385).

155. As Shapiro notes, Newton was not able to prove the immutability of the rays: "The Evolving Structure of Newton's Theory of Light and Color," 215–216.

156. "It has been commonly observed," Newton said, "that when diversely colored powders are mixed together a new color emerges; yet if those powders are examined with microscopes, they all appear imbued with their proper colors. Consequently, their proper colors are not destroyed in a mixture of powders, but rather by mixing a new color is only derived. Clearly the same colors are produced from a mixture of prismatic colors as of powders. Thus a blue powder mixed with a yellow one produces green, and the same green is also produced from a mixture of rays imbued with blue and yellow. Consequently, it cannot be doubted but that new colors similarly arise from a combination of prismatic colors and are not made by assimilation but only by mixture." This statement comes from lectures Newton gave in the 1660s. Quoted in Shapiro, "The Evolving Structure of Newton's Theory of Light and Color," 228–229. Newton stuck to the comparison at least until 1694: see ibid., 233.

157. Newton, "Mr. Newton's Answer to the Foregoing Letter," *Philosophical Transactions* 8 (1673), 6091.

CHAPTER 2. THE POLITICS OF DEFORMITY

1. For an account of the decline of the analogy between the human and the political body, see W. H. Greenleaf, *Order, Empiricism, and Politics: Two Traditions of Political Thought, 1500–1700* (London: Oxford University Press, 1964). Greenleaf argues that such analogical thinking loses epistemological prestige in the seventeenth century and is replaced by empiricist comparison between different kinds of governments. I argue, by contrast, that the analogy between natural and political bodies remained an authoritative instrument of knowledge. The growing reputation of atomism, while it may have contributed to the decline of the comparison between the human body and the body politic, provided fresh incentives to think about political structures in terms that also applied to natural bodies.

2. For an illuminating early description of the multitude as a socially and geographically mixed beast characteristic of England's metropolis, see John Stow, *A Suruay of London* (London, 1598), 477–479. Stowe's account is unusually positive and stresses the political power of the multitude.

3. Adjectives taken from quotations in Christopher Hill, *Change and Continuity in Seventeenth-Century England* (Cambridge, Mass.: Harvard University Press, 1975), 183–201.

4. Horace, *A Poetical Translation of the Works of Horace* (London, 1747), vol. 4, 14. Shakespeare, *The Second Part of King Henry the Fourth*, ind. 18 (in *The Complete Works*, ed. Stephen Orgel and A. R. Braunmuller [Harmondsworth: Penguin, 2002], 1086).

5. For commentaries on the biblical multitude, see Thomas Wilson's sermon *David's Zeal for Zion* (London, 1641), which charged the "mixt multitude" with "lusting" that brought the Jews to reject manna (34). Henry Ainsworth, in *Annotations Upon the Five Books of Moses* (London, 1627), FFFF4v–FFFF5r, adds "mutinie" as the effect of the mixt

multitude's corruptions. Similar worries about the "mixt multitude" accompany John White's reflections on the men "of divers tempers" that are likely to follow the Puritan settlers into America (*The Planters Plea; or, the Grounds of Plantations Examined* [London, 1630], 81).

6. Richard Tuck has pointed to the rejection of mass politics in what he calls aristocratic republicanism: *Philosophy and Government, 1572–1671* (Cambridge: Cambridge University Press, 1993), 42.

7. For the point that the English tradition of mixed government did not rely on functional differentiation, but on cooperation among the kinds of government, see Quentin Skinner, *Hobbes and Republican Liberty* (Cambridge: Cambridge University Press, 2008), 60–63.

8. For Hobbes's argument that the idea of mixed government was responsible for the civil war, see *Leviathan*, ed. Edwin Curley (Indianapolis: Hacking, 1994), 115. For his comparison of mixed government to a monstrous body, see ibid., 217. On the vehicle of the comparison, see the reference to "The Two Inseparable Brothers" in Katherine Park and Lorraine Daston, "Unnatural Conceptions: The Study of Monsters in Sixteenth- and Seventeenth-Century France and England," *Past and Present* 92 (1981), 20–21.

9. Hobbes, *Leviathan*, 217.

10. Arnold Davidson has pointed out that monstrous births were often seen to result from an excess of matter: "The Horror of Monsters," in *The Boundaries of Humanity: Humans, Animals, Machines*, ed. James Sheehan and Morton Sosna (Berkeley: University of California Press, 1991), 48.

11. All quotations in this paragraph from: Thomas Hobbes, *The Elements of Law Natural and Politic*, ed. Ferdinand Tönnies (1889; reprint, London: Frank Cass, 1984), 124–125.

12. The idea that sovereignty was indivisible found broad acceptance across Europe after Jean Bodin published *Les Six Livres de la Republique* (Paris, 1577)—even in nations whose constitutional realities contradicted Bodin's theory. See Julian Franklin, "Sovereignty and the Mixed Constitution: Bodin and His Critics," in *The Cambridge History of Political Thought, 1450–1700*, ed. J. H. Burns (Cambridge: Cambridge University Press, 1991), 298–328.

13. Though he remains quiet about the political implications, Richard Kroll has emphasized mediation as a crucial figure of the atomist revival in seventeenth-century England. See *The Material Word: Literate Culture in the Restoration and the Early Eighteenth Century* (Baltimore: Johns Hopkins University Press, 1991), 62–64.

14. Quentin Skinner has argued that the Calvinist theory of revolution was largely derived from scholastic sources. See *The Foundations of Modern Political Thought*, vol. 2 (Cambridge: Cambridge University Press, 1978), 322–323. Compare Blair Worden's argument on the centrality of a sovereign, interventionist God in the justification of rebellion in the 1640s and beyond: "Providence and Politics in Cromwellian England," *Past and Present* 109 (1985), 55–99.

15. For a definition and concerted attack on "political atomism," see Charles Taylor, "Atomism," in *Powers, Possessions, and Freedom*, ed. Alkis Kontos (Toronto: University of Toronto Press, 1979), 39–62.

16. John Rogers equates atomism with liberalism in *The Matter of Revolution: Science, Poetry, and Politics in the Age of Milton* (Ithaca, N.Y.: Cornell University Press, 1996).

17. For Antonio Negri's and Michael Hardt's polemic against mediation, see *Empire* (Cambridge, Mass.: Harvard University Press, 2000), 78–79. Compare Negri, *The Savage Anomaly: The Power of Spinoza's Metaphysics and Politics*, trans. Michael Hardt (Minneapolis: University of Minnesota Press, 1991), 140–141.

18. Providing substantial discussions of both Digby and White, Stefania Tutino's *Thomas White and the Blackloists: Between Politics and Theology During the English Civil War* (Aldershot: Ashgate, 2008) has begun to change the neglect that has surrounded these figures. Her study is especially valuable because it analyzes the interactions between religious, political, and scientific concerns.

19. On Digby's friendship with Hobbes, see R. T. Peterson, *Sir Kenelm Digby: The Ornament of England, 1603–1665* (London: Jonathan Cape, 1965), 120–123.

20. Kenelm Digby, *A Discourse Concerning the Vegetation of Plants Spoken by Sir Kenelme Digby at Gresham College on the 23 of January, 1660* (London, 1661).

21. *Sr. Kenelme Digbyes Honour Maintained by a Most Couragious Combat* (London, 1641), A3r.

22. For an account of Digby's imprisonment, see Peterson, *Sir Kenelm Digby*, 156–164.

23. Digby, *Loose Fantasies*, ed. Vittorio Gabrieli (Rome: Edizione di Storia e Litteratura, 1968), 21.

24. Thomas Longueville, *The Life of Kenelm Digby* (London: Longmans, Green, and Co., 1896), 273.

25. For an account of Digby's friendship with Cromwell, see Peterson, *Sir Kenelm Digby*, 251–258. Tutino has emphasized Digby's political flexibility and opportunism, noting that his Catholicism "did not require a distinctive form of political government" (*Thomas White and the Blackloists*, 54).

26. Charles Webster, *The Great Instauration: Science, Medicine, and Reform, 1626–1660* (New York: Holmes and Meier, 1976). For Digby's plans to buy a laboratory for Hartlib's son, see Hartlib to Boyle (*The Correspondence of Robert Boyle*, ed. Michael Hunter, Antonio Clericuzio, Lawrence Principe, vol. 1 [London: Pickering and Chatto, 2001], 180).

27. Digby, *A Discoure Concerning the Vegetation of Plants*, 5–8.

28. Digby, *A Discourse Concerning the Vegetation of Plants*, 10–12.

29. Digby, *Two Treatises* (Paris, 1644). I refer here and throughout to the London edition of 1665: 217–218.

30. Digby reflected on the relationship between necessity and liberty in 1628, when he composed his autobiographical romance *Loose Fantasies* (first published in the nine-

teenth century). In the dialogue between Digby's alter ego Theagenes and an Indian magician he meets on his travels, Digby uses a disagreement over the influence of the stars to rehearse some of the concerns that were agitating Calvinists and Arminians at this time in England. The Indian begins the debate by claiming that "the heavens and stars govern this world . . . whose secret characters and influence but few, divinely inspired, can read in the true sense their Creator gave them." To Theagenes, this is not acceptable. "It seemeth to imply such a necessity in human actions as well as in other natural ones," he replies, "that it overthroweth quite the liberty of the will, which certainly is the only pre-eminence that man can glory in." The Indian insists initially that "one may consider an entire liberty together with a constrained necessity, which no way impeach or hinder one another." But he is quick to add that God's knowledge is the ultimate limit of such liberty. God's knowledge "is a law or prescript for the coming to pass of all things, be they either the actions of free agents, or future contingents, or the changes and vicissitudes of natural agents." Theagenes objects again. In "men's fortunes and future contingents . . . there concur so many several and different accidents to bring forth some one effect, that it cannot sink into me how a general cause . . . can extend itself to so many particulars" (Digby, *Loose Fantasies*, 75–77). After the Indian magician has called up the spirit of his beloved Stelliana, Theagenes seems to signal that he has now accepted his position, but Digby quickly adds fresh doubt (ibid., 83–87). Digby's narrative is fascinating in part because it wants to believe in the idealism of romance even as it articulates persistent doubts about its reliance on predetermination. See also Tutino, who emphasizes that Digby and White believed in the compatibility of atomism and free will: *Thomas White and the Blackloists*, 39.

31. Amusingly, Digby tried to outflank Hakewill's point that God's power expressed itself in the relative freedom of second causes by providing an account of the end of the world that, unlike Hakewill's, did not require God's immediate intervention (Digby to Hakewill, May 15, 1635. BL Harleian MSS 4153).

32. Digby, *Two Treatises*, 283.

33. For Digby's belief that the end of the world and the resurrection can be explained by natural causes, see his letter to Hakewill, May 15, 1635. The naturalness of resurrection is reasserted in *Observations upon Religio Medici* (London, 1643), 52. For Digby's belief in the natural causes of beatitude, see *Observations upon Religio Medici*, 60.

34. Hakewill charged Goodman with "disparagement to Gods providence" and then quoted Goodman's use of the divine clockmaker to defend the perfection of nature: "if a clocke or instrument of iron were made, which would daily want mending, would yee commend the workeman? but suppose this clocke should continue for many yeares, perfect and sound without reparation, then certainly the workeman should have his due praise and commendation: so is it in the frame of this world, which hath now continued for many thousand yeares, without alteration and change; &therefore therein Gods providence, power and protection doe more eminently appeare" (Hakewill, *An Apologie of the Povver and Prouidence of God* [Oxford, 1635], PPPP1r). Digby appropriates this interpretation of the analogy to support the idea that the end of the world will have a

natural cause and does not require God's immediate intervention: see Digby to Hakewill, May 15, 1635.

35. Digby's comparison between God and clockmaker reads in full: "He were an improvident Clockmaker, that should have cast his work so, as, when it were wound up and going, it would require the Masters hand at every hour, to make the Hammer strike the Bell" (*Two Treatises*, 283).

36. Last three quotations in Digby, *Two Treatises*, 289.

37. Digby, *A Conference with a Lady About Choice of Religion* (Paris, 1638), D5v. In different circumstances, when he debated Thomas Browne, Digby could make the opposite point: "in truth, there is no fortuitnesse or contingency of things, in respect of themselves, but onely in respect of us, that are ignorant of their certaine, and necessary causes" (*Observations Upon Religio Medici*, 28).

38. Hakewill, *An Apologie of the Povver and Prouidence of God* (1635), BBBB2v.

39. Hakewill calls the Catholic Church, among other things, the whore of Babylon in *An Answere to a Treatise Written by Dr. Carier* (London, 1616), 23–25.

40. Patrick Collinson, *The Elizabethan Puritan Movement* (Berkeley: University of California Press, 1967), 125.

41. William Perkins, *A Christian and Plaine Treatise of the Manner and Order of Predestination* (London, 1606), 77.

42. Perkins, *A Christian and Plaine Treatise*, 78–81.

43. Quotation from William Prynne, *The Church of Englands Old Antithesis to New Arminianisme* (London, 1629), 14. For William Twisse's appeal to the eleventh article of the Church of Ireland, see Twisse, *A Discovery of D. Jacksons Vanitie* (Amsterdam, 1631), 11.

44. Twisse, *A Discovery*, 7.

45. Arminius published his critique of Perkins in 1612: *Examen Modestum Libelli quem D. Gulielmus Perkinsius Edidit* (Leiden). For a nuanced account of Arminius's challenge to English Calvinism, see R. T. Kendall, *Calvin and English Calvinism to 1649* (Oxford: Oxford University Press, 1979), 141–150.

46. For Archbishop Abbot's comments, see Abbot to Sir Dudley Charleton, December 1618. Cited in Nicholas Tyacke, *Anti-Calvinists: The Rise of English Arminianism, c. 1590–1640* (Oxford: Clarendon Press, 1987), 91. The quotation from Arminius is in: *The Works of Arminius*, vol. 1 (1875), 564, cited in Kendall, *Calvin and English Calvinism*, 143.

47. Tyacke notes that supralapsarianism did not prevail in Dort: *Anti-Calvinists*, 96.

48. On Charles's 1628 declaration, see Kenneth Fincham and Peter Lake, "The Ecclesiastical Policies of James I and Charles I," in *The Early Stuart Church, 1603–1642*, ed. Kenneth Fincham (Stanford, Calif.: Stanford University Press, 1993), 30.

49. Three preceding quotations from: Thomas Jackson, *A Treatise of the Divine Essence and Attributes* (London, 1629), first part, 100; second part, 138; second part, 124.

50. These three points are in Jackson, *A Treatise of the Divine Essence*, second part, 117–124.

51. Jackson, *A Treatise of the Divine Essence*, first part, 101. For a parallel statement, see ibid., second part, 82.

52. Two last quotations in Jackson, *A Treatise of the Divine Essence*, first part, 127, 120.

53. For Carpenter's belief in a mediated relationship between first and second causes, see *Geographie Delineated* (Oxford, 1635), second book, 193–195.

54. Francis Oakeley has argued that Calvin reduced first and second causes to a single level, the *"potentia ordinata"*: "The Absolute and Ordained Power of God in Sixteenth- and Seventeenth-Century Theology," *Journal of the History of Ideas* 59:3 (1998), 450–459.

55. For Thomas Browne's argument about the underlying unity of Protestant and Catholic beliefs, see *Religio Medici* (London, 1642), 1–6.

56. Digby, *Observations upon Religio Medici*, 37.

57. Last two quotations from Digby, *Observations upon Religio Medici*, 104, 122.

58. The Arminian John Bramhall, whose politics I will discuss below, agreed with Digby's distrust of visionary knowledge: Bramhall, *A Defense of True Liberty from Antecedent and Extrinsecall Necessity* (London, 1655), 91, 126.

59. Browne, *Religio Medici*, 139.

60. Preceding quotations in Browne, *Religio Medici*, 33–37.

61. Preceding quotations in Digby, *Observations upon Religio Medici*, 17–18.

62. Two preceding quotations in Digby, *A Conference with a Lady*, 70, 67.

63. Digby, *A Discourse Concerning Infallibility in Religion* (Paris, 1652), 218–219.

64. Digby, *A Discourse Concerning Infallibility in Religion*, 217–218.

65. Digby, *A Discourse Concerning Infallibility in Religion*, 155–158.

66. Quotations in this paragraph from Digby, *Two Treatises*, 9–10.

67. For a (positive) definition of the multitude that involves these three groups, see Stow, *A Suruay of London*, 478–479.

68. For Hobbes's critique of collaborations between philosophers and the social multitude, see Hobbes, *Considerations upon the Reputation, Loyalty, Manners, and Religion of Thomas Hobbes of Malmesbury* (London, 1680), 52–55.

69. For Digby's judgment of Browne's passage as "affected," see *Observations upon Religio Medici*, 92.

70. Browne, *Religio Medici*, 113.

71. Michael Wilding has argued that Browne's passage acquired additional resonance because it appeared in the context of a particularly eventful period of mass political action in the early 1640s. Michael Wilding, *Dragon's Teeth: Literature in the English Revolution* (Oxford: Clarendon Press, 1987), 100–108.

72. Last two quotations from Browne, *Religio Medici*, 89–90.

73. Browne, *Religio Medici*, 24–25.

74. Quotations on language from Browne, "Of Languages, and Particularly of the Saxon Tongue," in Browne, *Certain Miscellany Tracts* (London, 1683), 134, 132, 139. See R. F. Jones, *The Triumph of the English Language* (Stanford, Calif.: Stanford University Press, 1953), for a survey of seventeenth-century arguments for the return of English to Saxon purity: 214–271. Browne's comment on spiritual purity underneath drossy exteriors

can be found in *Religio Medici*, 66, where Browne expresses his belief that spiritual principles can be "extract[ed] from the corpulency of bodies."

75. Aristotle's point that there are some good reasons why the multitude ought to be
in power is in *The Politics and the Constitution of Athens*, ed. Stephen Everson, trans. Benjamin Jowett and Jonathan Barnes (Cambridge: Cambridge University Press, 2008), 77.
The point about the multitude's superior judgment is in ibid., 77 and 86.

76. For Buchanan's argument about the multitude's superior judgment, see *De Jure
Regni* (n.p., 1680), 41–42.

77. White, *Institutionum Peripateticarum* (1647), published in English as *Peripateticall Institutions* (London, 1656). I quote from the English edition: 321.

78. White, *Peripateticall Institutions*, 320. I agree with Tutino's discussion of contingency and second causes in White's philosophy: *Thomas White and the Blackloists*, 40.

79. White, *Peripateticall Institutions*, 228–229. White also aligned the Catholic/
Arminian insistence on free will with Digby's philosophy in *Quæstio Theologica, quomodo,
Secundum Principia Peripatetices Digbeanæ* (Paris, 1652).

80. Last two quotations in White, *Peripateticall Institutions*, 318.

81. White firmly ties the creativity of second causes to the action of mixture. This is
perhaps most dramatically on display in White's description of how "more compounded
Bodies, and Plants" are generated (a discussion that echoes Digby's opinion that moisture
and earth produced "all thinges in perfection" in the beginning [Digby to Hakewill,
May 15, 1635] and his discussion of the generation of mixed bodies in *Two Treatises*, 144–
161). White's emphasis in the following on decompounded and demixed bodies anticipates Boyle's expansion of mixture's ontological reach: "'Tis plain . . . that, not only the
Elements are blended together to compound a singly-mix'd body; but also many mix'd
bodies are united into one more-compounded body: For, since, by the power of their
gravity, moist bodies (which we call Waters) run down from higher to lower places, and,
by their running, presse the bodies they meet, loos'ning partly their little particles in
passing by, and partly tearing them off along with them; the Water become thickned and
full of dregs, with many minutest bodies of divers bodies of divers natures. This Water if
it rest in any cavity of the Earth, those little bodies sink down in it; and, whether by heat
evaporating the humid parts of the water, or by cold binding them together, they coagu-
late, by their clamminesse, into one body appearing homogeneous through the littlenesse
of its parts: which, being imperceptible, are so equally mix'd in every the least sensible
bulk, that they show every where throughout the same uniforme nature. And, this is the
most simple generation of demix'd bodies" (White, *Peripateticall Institutions*, 79–80).

82. For Browne's comment on the instantaneity of creation, see *Religio Medici*, 67–
68. Arguing for a gradual creation, White writes: "God not instantaneously, but by a
congruous disposition of divers degrees brought up the world from its deepest possibility,
that is, its simplest and fewest principles, to its due perfection" (*Peripateticall Institutions*,
343).

83. Quotations in this paragraph in White, *Peripateticall Institutions*, 355–360.
White's creation story comes rather close to what Jonathan Israel has recently described

as the radical idea that "the creation of life, and mutation of life forms, [is] a process of natural evolution." Israel wants to credit Spinoza with the "first germ" of this idea, but White uses the mediated relationship between first and second causes to articulate this idea when Spinoza is but fifteen years old. See Jonathan Israel, *Radical Enlightenment: Philosophy and the Making of Modernity, 1650–1750* (Oxford: Oxford University Press, 2001), 251–252.

84. For White, the only thing that is not produced by second causes in God's creation is the "Rationall Soul," which does indeed depend on His direct intervention. See White, *Peripateticall Institutions*, 374.

85. Roger Coke, *A Survey of the Politicks of Mr. Thomas White, Thomas Hobbes, and Hugo Grotius* (London, 1662), E1v. John Maxwell had issued the same criticism in 1644 when he argued that the principle that the community is the seat of sovereignty "presupposeth the most excellent of Creatures, Men, to be like Cadmus off-spring, de terra nati, sprung out of the earth" (*Sacro-Sancta Regum Majestas; or, The Sacred and Royal Prerogative of Christian Kings* [Oxford, 1644], 111). See also Robert Filmer's association of equality with "terra nati": *Observations upon Aristotle's Politiques* (1652), reprinted in Filmer, *Patriarcha and Other Writings*, ed. J. P. Sommerville (Cambridge: Cambridge University Press, 1991), 253.

86. Thomas White, *The Grounds of Obedience and Government* (London, 1655), A3r–A3v.

87. Preceding two quotations in White, *The Grounds of Obedience and Government*, 161–162. Like Digby, White believed that "God proceeds according to the course of natural second causes. Nor must it be omitted that even in those miraculous Actions, God proceeds . . . according to Nature in general" (White, *Devotion and Reason* [Paris, 1661], 128).

88. White argues that we should not look into scripture to understand worldly events, but "into nature" (*The Grounds of Obedience and Government*, 161).

89. On the multitude's power to set up government, see White, *The Grounds of Obedience and Government*, 44–47. On the multitude's ability to remake government, see ibid., 120–124. The phrase "rationall multitude" can be found in ibid., 48.

90. For White's argument that man is naturally social and political, see *The Grounds of Obedience and Government*, 40–43. For the friendship between White and Hobbes, see Beverley C. Southgate, *Covetous of Truth: The Life and Work of Thomas White, 1593–1676* (Dordrecht: Kluwer, 1993), 8. Hobbes wrote an extensive response to White's *De Mundo Dialogi Tres* (Paris, 1642), recently translated as *Thomas White's De Mundo Examined*, ed. R. H. Popkin, trans. Harold Whitmore Jones (London: Bradford University Press, 1976).

91. Last three quotations in White, *The Grounds of Obedience and Government*, 125, 48, 143, respectively.

92. For the traditional Catholic belief in human life as based on equality and cooperation, see, for example, Thomas Aquinas, *Political Writings*, ed. and trans. R. W. Dyson (Cambridge: Cambridge University Press, 2002), 1–4. For Aquinas's position on the need for human coordination, see ibid., 5–6. Cf. the discussion of coordination in John

Finnis, *Aquinas: Moral, Political, and Legal Theory* (Oxford: Oxford University Press, 1998), 35–37.

93. For Aquinas's use of multitude, see Aquinas, *Political Writings*, 5–6 (Dyson translates "multitudo" as "community": see ibid., 6, fn. 17).

94. For an account of the scholastic integration of Aristotle's politics, see Quentin Skinner, *The Foundations of Modern Political Thought*, vol. 1 (Cambridge: Cambridge University Press, 1978), 49–68.

95. For an overview of the counter-reformationist Thomist and Jesuit political traditions in the sixteenth century, see Skinner, *The Foundations of Modern Political Thought*, 2:148–184.

96. For White's early exposure to Jesuit political argument, see Southgate, *Covetous of Truth*, 22–28.

97. Tuck, *Philosophy and Government*, 141.

98. On Suarez's argument about the right of the people to choose the forms of government, see J. P. Sommerville, *Politics and Ideology in England, 1603–1640* (London: Longman, 1986), 63. See also, for the same argument and a restatement of man's political and cooperative nature, Robert Bellarmine, *De Laicis; or, The Treatise on Civil Government*, trans. Kathleen E. Murphy (Westport, Conn.: Hyperion Press, 1993), 20–27, and Robert Persons, *A Conference About the Next Succession to the Crowne of Ingland* (Antwerp, 1595), 1–7.

99. For Molina's argument on a mediated relationship between first and second causes, see Anton C. Pegis, "Molina and Human Liberty," in *Jesuit Thinkers of the Renaissance*, ed. Gerard Smith (Milwaukee: Marquette University Press, 1939), 75–132. For Bellarmine's association of the argument for the rights of the multitude to choose the government with a mediated relationship between first and second causes, see *De Laicis*, 27.

100. Persons, *A Conference*, 17.

101. Bellarmine, *De Laicis*, 27.

102. Persons, *An Answere to the Fifth Part of Reports . . . by Syr Edward Cooke* (St. Omers, 1606), 26, quoted in: Thomas H. Clancy, *Papist Pamphleteers: The Allen-Persons Party and the Political Thought of the Counter-Reformation in England, 1572–1615* (Chicago: Loyola University Press, 1964), 93.

103. For Molina's influence on Gassendi, see Lisa Sarasohn, *Gassendi's Ethics: Freedom in a Mechanistic Universe* (Ithaca, N.Y.: Cornell University Press, 1996), 76–86.

104. For Gassendi's relationship to the Newcastle circle, see Kroll, *The Material Word*, 156–160. Robert Hugh Kargon notes that "during the 1640s, Digby was in close touch with members of Newcastle Circle": *Atomism in England from Hariot to Newton* (Oxford: Clarendon Press, 1966), 70.

105. Sarasohn, *Gassendi's Ethics*, 157.

106. For a history of Arminianism in England, see Tyacke's *Anti-Calvinists*.

107. Hugh Trevor-Roper, *Catholics, Anglicans, and Puritans: Seventeenth-Century Essays* (Chicago: University of Chicago Press, 1988), 97–99.

108. For Arminianism's association with republicanism in Holland, see Trevor-Roper, *Catholics, Anglicans, and Puritans*, 98. Compare Blair Worden, who argues that "to a man [republicans] rejected the Calvinist doctrine of predestination. . . . Seventeenth-century republicans are Armininans and Socinians": "The Revolution of 1688–9 and the English Republican Tradition," in *The Anglo-Dutch Moment*, ed. Jonathan Israel (Cambridge: Cambridge University Press, 1991), 252. Worden backs up this claim in more detail in "Classical Republicanism and the Puritan Revolution," *History and Imagination*, ed. Hugh Lloyd-Jones, Valerie Pearl, and Blair Worden (New York: Holmes and Meier, 1981), 195.

109. In the 1640s and 1650s, Milton became increasingly certain that Calvinist necessity was at odds with liberty. "We are not mere puppets," he argued against predestination in the 1650s, insisting that the freedom of man had not "the least shadow of necessity over it." John Milton, *Two Books of Investigations into Christian Doctrine* (in Milton, *Complete Prose Works*, vol. 6, ed. Maurice Kelley [New Haven, Conn.: Yale University Press, 1973], 186, 161). For Milton's Arminianism more generally, see ibid., 153–202.

110. Bramhall, *A Defense of True Liberty*, 197.

111. For Bramhall's identification of Hobbes's position with Calvinist necessity, see *A Defense of True Liberty*, 53, 76, 82–83, 134.

112. Bramhall, *A Defense of True Liberty*, 82.

113. For Bramhall's statement on the derivation of princely power from God, see *A Defense of True Liberty*, 104; for his statement about the superiority of law over princes, see ibid., 83; for his statement on the people's right to resist tyrannical law, see ibid., 100.

114. Bramhall, *A Defense of True Liberty*, 60.

115. For the reference to Buchanan and Bellarmine, see Bramhall, *The Serpent Salve; or, A Remedie for the Biting of an Aspe* [n.p., 1643], B1v.

116. For Bramhall's reference to the "Amphisbena," see *The Serpent Salve*, A1v. Bramhall expresses the mediated relationship between first and second cause as follows: "That Royalty and all lawfull Dominion considered in the abstract, is from God, no man can make any doubt, but he who will oppose the Apostle, the powers that be are ordeined of God; and God himselfe who saith, by me Kings raigne and Princes decree Justice. But the right and application of this Power and Interest in the concrete to this particular man, is many times from the grant and consent of the people. So God is the principall Agent, man the Instrumentall; God is the Root, the Fountain of Power; Man the Stream, the Bough by which it is derived; the essence of Power is always from God, the Existence sometimes from God, sometimes from Man" (*The Serpent Salve*, 6). Bramhall's reliance on the distinction between concrete and abstract also featured in William Bridge's definition of political power in *The Truth of the Times Vindicated* (London, 1643), 4–5. Bridge, like Persons, was adamant that political power belonged to the people.

117. For Bramhall's critique of Parker's emphasis on strength and power, see *Serpent Salve*, 200. For his concession of the people's ultimate authority, see *Serpent Salve*, 15. William Bridge showed how vulnerable Bramhall's concession was to a broader construction when he argued: "if the authority of ruling . . . returneth to [the people] to

see justice done in case there is no particular supreme Magistrate left to rule them the first subject seat and receptacle of ruling power must needs be in the people" (Bridge, *The Truth of the Times Vindicated*, 5–6, see also 7).

118. Bramhall, *Serpent Salve*, 17.

119. Bramhall, *Serpent Salve*, 36. For Bramhall's other agreements with Parker, see *Serpent Salve*, 88, 146–148.

120. Bramhall acknowledged the force of natural law when he noted that Parker's argument that the power of calling parliament ought to be shared between king and people is quite "seasonable" in the "first framing of a Monarchy," and only "sawcy and seditious" "when a Power is invested in the crown by law and lawfull custome" (Bramhall, *Serpent Salve*, 150).

121. For Bramhall's concession of natural law's ultimate superiority, see *Serpent Salve*, 138.

122. Bramhall, *Serpent Salve*, 97.

123. On the claim that legislative power is shared, see Bramhall, *Serpent Salve*, 82–82. For the argument on mixed government, see ibid., 89. For the argument on tyrannicide, see ibid., 10.

124. The anti-Arminianism of some of these writers can be seen in the following: Herle called for the burning of Arminian texts; Rutherford wrote a treatise against Arminianism; Bridge was temporarily suspended for preaching against Arminianism. See the entries for these figures in *Oxford Dictionary of National Biography*.

125. William Bridge's argument for the mediation of first and second causes is applied to the problem of the body politic in *The Truth of the Times Vindicated*, 4–6, 9 (Bridge uses the phrase "collation of power" [7], which was to play a prominent role in Maxwell's attack on the parliamentarians in *Sacro-Sancta Regum Majestas*). Herle's argument for the mediation of first and second causes can be found in *A Fuller Answer to a Treatise Written by Doctor Ferne* (London, 1642), 6, 23. For Rutherford's, Parker's, and Hunton's reliance on mediation, see the following pages of the main text. These parliamentary controversialists, Julian Franklin has emphasized, were not outspoken radicals who advocated rebellion or regicide (Franklin, *John Locke and the Theory of Sovereignty: Mixed Monarchy and the Right of Resistance in the Political Thought of the English Revolution* [Cambridge: Cambridge University Press, 1978], 22–52). But surely such advocacy is not the only measure of radicalism. I would count, for example, the recognition of the multitude as the cause of governmental forms and as a legitimate political agent, points that Franklin underplays. In part because he consistently moves in the conceptual world of constitutional law, Franklin doesn't see that the restraints these controversialists observed produced an important result: a vision of the body politic as a profoundly collective entity whose form was fluid and changeable.

126. Maxwell, *Sacro-Sancta Regum Majestas*, 7.

127. Rutherford quotes Molina approvingly on the mediation of political power through human agents in *Lex Rex* (London, 1644), 4, and Suarez and Bellarmine on the same: ibid., 5–6.

128. Bridge draws on Rutherford to support his argument for the sovereignty of the people in *Truth of the Times Vindicated*, 5. On the destruction of Jesuits, see Bridge, ibid., A2v. Bridge quotes Molina on the nature of political power in ibid., 11.

129. For Rutherford's reference to Durandus, see *Lex Rex*, 9. For Bridge's reference to Durandus, see *Truth of the Times Vindicated*, 4.

130. For Michael Mendle's point about Suarez's possible influence on Parker, see *Henry Parker and the Civil War: The Political Thought of the Public's Privado* (Cambridge: Cambridge University Press, 1995), 86 n. 44. Quotation in ibid., 86.

131. Mendle notes that Parker had access to Hooker's eighth book in *Henry Parker and the English Civil War*, 63.

132. Hooker, *Of the Laws of Ecclesiastical Politie* (London, 1666), 455. On Hooker's crypto-Catholicism, see Anthony Milton, *Catholic and Reformed: The Roman and Protestant Churches in English Protestant Thought, 1600–1640* (Cambridge: Cambridge University Press, 1995), 17, 69. For the notoriety of "*major singulis, universis minor*," see Mendle, *Henry Parker and the English Civil War*, 188. Mendle points out that, in *Considerations and Proposals in Order to the Regulation of the Press* (London, 1663), Roger L'Estrange singled out Parker's slogan as particularly pernicious.

133. Hobbes, *Leviathan*, 116.

134. Hooker, *Of the Laws of Ecclesiastical Politie*, 454.

135. For Maxwell's accusation that Parker's vision of shared, communal sovereignty found its ontological expression in the collective forces of atomism, see Maxwell, *Sacro-Sancta Regum Majestas*, 104. Maxwell's suggestion that atomism provided an appropriate ontology for Parker's politics may not have been unmotivated. Already in 1641, Parker had expressed admiration for Paolo Sarpi, whom he called the "learned Politician of the Popish religion." As Tuck notes, Sarpi "wrote extensively in support of the idea that everything in nature has come into being as a result of moving material objects interacting" (Parker's reference to Sarpi is in his *Discourse Concerning Puritans* [London, 1641], 19). I owe the identification of Parker's reference to Tuck (*Philosophy and Government*, 227), who also provides the description of Sarpi's philosophy (ibid., 98). Mendle has confirmed the influence of Sarpi in *Henry Parker and the English Civil War*, xiv. Compare also David Wooton's *Paolo Sarpi: Between Renaissance and Enlightenment* (Cambridge: Cambridge University Press, 1983), 13–20, which makes the case for Sarpi as a materialist.

136. Parker, *Jus Populi* (London, 1644), 3–4.

137. Last two quotations from Parker, *Of a Free Trade* (London, 1648), 6, 5.

138. Parker, *Jus Populi*, 8.

139. Parker, *Jus Populi*, 11. Echoing a point widely accepted among Catholic critics of the divine right of kings, Parker held that "the constitution of power in generall must be sever'd from the limitation of it to that and that form" (ibid., 4).

140. Parker, *Jus Populi*, 7.

141. The most concentrated expression of Maxwell's equation of social, sexual, familial, ontological, and political hierarchy can be found in *Sacro-Sancta Regum Majestas*, 80–97.

142. Parker, *Jus Populi*, 4.

143. Parker, *Jus Populi*, 5.

144. Parker, *Jus Populi*, 38. Parker had made the point about the mixture of equality and inequality in an earlier treatise with regard to father and son: *A Discourse Concerning Puritans*, 31. Herle had echoed it in *A Fuller Answer*, 5. Herle used this point to justify the coordination of power between king and parliament.

145. Parker, *Jus Populi*, 26.

146. Parker, *Observations upon some of His Majesties Late Answers and Expresses* (London, 1642), 14–15. For Persons's argument that mixed government was the structured reassertion of the original rights of multitude, see *A Conference*, 18–24. For Rutherford's embrace of mixed government, see *Lex Rex*, 211–213. For Bramhall's acceptance of Parker's argument regarding the management of the people's body, see *Serpent Salve*, 147–148.

147. Parker, *Jus Populi*, 13.

148. Last two quotations from Parker, *Jus Populi*, 51. "The forms of Government," Rutherford seconded, "are no more naturall, then politick Incorporations or Cities" (*Rex Lex*, 53).

149. Last two quotations from Parker, *The Contra-Replicant* (n.p., 1643), 7.

150. Filmer was appalled by the endless variety of forms of government Aristotle paraded in his *Politics*. See Filmer's *Observations*, 251–255. The result of the kind of thinking Parker reveals is to Filmer radical instability: "no man can say at any time that he is under any form of government, for in a shorter time than a word can be spoken, every government is begun and ended" (ibid., 255).

151. Last two quotations in Parker, *Contra-Replicant*, 6.

152. Last two quotations in Parker, *Contra-Replicant*, 8.

153. For Parker's use of temperance and balance, see, for example, *The True Portraiture of the Kings of England* (London, 1650), 2. One example of conservative uses of Galenic concepts for describing the body politic is Edward Forset's *A Comparative Discourse of the Bodies Natural and Politique* (London, 1606). Forset adopts the Aristotelian distinction between form and matter to describe the relationship between king and subject and then notes that the four "state-Elements" of aristocrats, scholars, farmers, and merchants have to find a "true and proportionable mixture" in the body politic. Mixture is here a "concord" that preserves social and political difference (38–39).

154. Parker, *Observations*, 1.

155. Last two quotations in Parker, *Jus Populi*, 13, 16–17, respectively. Interestingly enough, Parker uses this physical argument about political power to deny the formative influence of the Saxon, Danish, and Norman conquests. All that these conquerors achieved was derived from the English (ibid., 16–17).

156. Bridge, *The Truth of the Times Vindicated*, 5. Herne wrote that the "qualification of the [political] power is an efflux of the people's consent" (*A Fuller Answer*, 6).

157. Last two quotations in Parker, *Jus Populi*, 16.

158. Amusingly, Parker illustrates such networked causality and the preservative effects it has on the bearer of power with a scientific discussion of drunkenness, imposed

on him by his opponent Maxwell (*Sacro Sancta Regum Majestas*, 128). "Drunkenness," Parker points out, "proceeds not from wine immediately, but from other nearer causes. Wine heates the veines, annoyes the stomack with humors, and the brain with fumes, and these are the immediate causes of drunkennesse; the proper work of wine is heat, and so it ever has a heat as intense in it self, as that which it self causes elsewhere, and without the accession of other joynt causes, it cannot produce a greater degree of heat, in another thing then it reserves in it self" (*Jus Populi*, 16).

159. Three quotations from Parker in *A Discourse Concerning Puritans*, 45, 49; *Observations*, 15.

160. Rutherford, *Rex Lex*, 158.

161. Last two quotations from Parker in *Jus Populi*, 24, 11.

162. Parker, *Jus Populi*, 19.

163. Parker, *Observations*, 12–13.

164. Parker, *Observations*, 23.

165. Parker's recognition of the multitude as an active and legitimate political body can also be seen in his invocation of a reconciliation between king and nation in 1642. If the king kept his promise to name seditious members of parliament along with full evidence of their subversive plans, Parker argues, he would effect a complete reconciliation with the nation: "by the performance of this promise he shall not doe onely right to himselfe, but also to the whole kingdome, for the distracted multitude, being at last by this meanes undeceived, shall not onely prostrate themselves, and all their power presently at his feet, but for ever after remaine the more assured of his good, whether to publike liberties and Parliamentary Priviledges" (*Observations*, 31).

166. Tuck has pointed to the critique of multitude in the Tacitean tradition of republican thought he so brilliantly reconstructs and eventually calls "aristocratic republicanism" (*Philosophy and Government*, 42, 238). He remains quiet, however, about Parker's recognition of the rights of the multitude, presumably because this would weaken his argument that Parker works in the Tacitean mold. For Tuck's discussion of Parker, see *Philosophy and Government*, 227–234.

167. In *The Contra-Replicant*, Parker argues that royalists "seek to divide the coactive from the representative body of the people: they seek to divide between the two houses of Parliament: and they seek to divide between the head and the body of the Parliament. They perswade the multitude, that they have entrusted the Parliament only with their purses to give away subsidies, and replenish the Kings coffers; but not to settle their rights and franchises, and to make knowne the bounds of Prerogative, and restraine the unnatural encroachments or eruptions of the same" (16).

168. Such a physical understanding of power helps explain Parker's forceful arguments against the considerations of established law in emergencies. In the state of emergency, Parker argues, the "being" and not just the "well-being" of the commonwealth is at stake and therefore justifies letting "Reason of state" overrun "all particular formes and pacts." "Reason of state," Parker claims, "is more sublime and imperiall then Law" and has "a kind of dictatorian power" in situations of self-defense (*Contra-Replicant*, 19).

Because Parker explicitly attributes such right of self-defense to parliament, this passage provides the clearest indication that Parker advocates parliamentary absolutism. Yet Mendle himself notes that *Contra-Replicant*, the tract that contains this passage, was written at a moment when London seemed likely to fall to royalist forces. It is therefore understandably "impassioned," as Mendle recognizes, but it is not, as Mendle claims, the most "revealing" of Parker's tracts (Mendle, *Henry Parker and the Civil War*, xii–xiii). The positions aired in *The Contra-Replicant* do not nullify Parker's more philosophical statements on the nature of political power. I see congruity between the argument for the disregard of law in situations of emergency and Parker's physical notion of power. And I see good, urgent reasons why Parker would argue for parliament's dictatorial powers in 1643. The overall evidence suggests to me that Parker is arguing for parliamentary absolutism only in situations of national emergency.

169. Mendle, *Henry Parker and the Civil War*, 33–34. Mendle extends the view articulated by W. K. Jordan in *Men of Substance: A Study of the Thought of Two English Revolutionaries, Henry Parker and Henry Robinson* (Chicago: University of Chicago Press, 1942).

170. Rutherford argues for the naturalness of human political capacity in *Lex Rex* (2). See also Rutherford's account of Nero's fall as an example of how he sees the natural power of the people exert itself under government (*Lex Rex*, 45). Bridge argues that "the power of ruling and governing is naturall" in *The Truth of the Times Vindicated*, 5.

171. I disagree with Tuck's claim that Parker "eschewed any reliance on the notion of a mixed constitution" (*Philosophy and Government*, 232). Tuck narrowly associates mixed government with balance (238) and doesn't recognize (unlike Parker) its relationship with a physical, anti-constitutionalist idea of power. In other words, Tuck doesn't appreciate the anti-formal properties of mixture.

172. For the assertion of moderation against parliamentary sovereignty, see Hunton, *A Treatise of Monarchy* (London, 1643), 70. Compare also *A Vindication of the Treatise of Monarchy* (London, 1644), A2r–A2v.

173. For Hunton's emphasis on the semi-independence of second causes, see *Treatise of Monarchy*, 3–4, 54–55. For Hunton's emphasis on "con-causes" and "joint causes," see *Treatise of Monarchy*, 43. It is likely that his reliance on a mediatory metaphysics also informed what Webster has described as Hunton's interest in the science of his time (Webster, *The Great Instauration*, 237).

174. Hunton, *A Treatise of Monarchy*, 39.

175. Hunton, *A Treatise of Monarchy*, 41.

176. Hunton, *Vindication*, 39. Hunton was not always consistent in opposing mixture to limitation: see ibid.

177. The quotations in this paragraph come from Hunton, *Treatise of Monarchy*, 28–29.

178. Hunton, *Vindication*, 38.

179. Although Hunton had a keen interest in science, his debt to atomist philosophy is less clear: see Webster, *The Great Instauration*, 237.

180. Boyle's quip can be found in *Some Considerations Touching the Style of the Holy Scriptures* (London, 1663), 217.

181. Kroll, *The Material Word*, 85–115.

182. Boyle argues that occasional meditations can "contemplate not onely a Theological and a Moral, but also an Political, an Oeconomical, or even a Physical use" because of the ultimate unity of truth. "There is so perfect an harmony, and so near a kindred, betwixt Truths," Boyle contended, "that, in many cases, the one does either find out, or fairly hint, or else illustrate or confirm, the other" (Boyle, *Occasional Reflections Upon Several Subjects* [London, 1665], C4v–C5r).

183. Carolyn Merchant, *The Death of Nature: Women, Ecology, and the Scientific Revolution* (San Francisco, Calif.: Harper & Row, 1980); Margaret Jacob and James Jacob, "The Anglican Origins of Modern Science: The Metaphysical Foundations of the Whig Constitution," *Isis* 71:2 (1980), 251–267; Steven Shapin and Simon Schaffer, *Leviathan and the Air-Pump: Hobbes, Boyle, and the Experimental Life* (Princeton, N.J.: Princeton University Press, 1985); Rogers, *The Matter of Revolution.* That Boyle might not have been the politically conservative thinker these historians make him out to be is indicated by Malcolm Oster, "Virtue, Providence, and Political Neutralism: Boyle and Interregnum Politics," in *Robert Boyle Reconsidered*, ed. Michael Hunter (Cambridge: Cambridge University Press, 1994), 19–36. Oster finds recourse to socio-political explanations of Boyle's scientific theories "unwarranted" (32) but notes that Boyle displayed "sympathy towards the parliamentary regime [which] probably rested upon the conviction that virtue and personal industry would more easily flourish in a commonwealth than a monarchy" (29). Given Oster's critique of the Jacob thesis, it is ironic that this assessment echoes that of James Jacob, who arrives at a similar diagnosis for the early Boyle (but seems to imply that the restoration marked a conservative turning point; see Jacob's *Robert Boyle and the English Revolution: A Study in Social and Intellectual Change* [New York: Burt Franklin, 1977], 69–73).

184. Jacob and Jacob, "The Anglican Origins of Modern Science," 255.

185. John Henry, "Occult Qualities and the Experimental Philosophy: Active Principles in Pre-Newtonian Matter Theory," *History of Science* 24:4 (1986), 335–381. Opposed to a casual concourse as the engine of the world but in favor of Baconian science, Samuel Gott adopted the mediated relationship between first and second cause to argue in 1670 that "rude Matter . . . hath thus Naturally in itself Motion to Union, and also to Station" (*The Divine History of the Genesis of the World* [London, 1670], 149). Contemplating what makes matter move in 1672, John Wallis noted that it could either be "Percussion from some Body already in motion . . . Pulsion, from a contiguous Body beginning to move . . . or some Conatus or Endeavour of its own" ("An Extract of Letters from Dr. John Wallis to the Publisher, 1672," *Philosophical Transactions* 7 [1672], 5164). The high churchman Robert Midgley noted that God gave second causes a "power of acting" that he explained as "the Power which the Atoms have of moving themselves" (Midgley, *New Treatise of Natural Philosophy* [London, 1687], 18). For Digby and White, see my discussion earlier in this chapter.

186. One of the strange contradictions of Rogers's book is that it links vitalist radicalism to liberal individualism: *The Matter of Revolution*, 35–38.

187. Jan W. Wojcik has alerted us to Boyle's insistence on free will even as he accepts divine foresight; see his "The Theological Context of Boyle's *Things Above Reason*," in *Robert Boyle Reconsidered*, 150–151. Compare his discussion in *Robert Boyle and the Limits of Reason* (Cambridge: Cambridge University Press, 1997), 107–108. For Boyle's articulation of a mediatory metaphysics, see *The Origin of Formes and Qualities* (Oxford, 1666), 193–194. There is some indication that Boyle's position on second causes was not always consistent. In *The Christian Virtuoso* (London, 1690), for example, Boyle openly worries about deists and libertines and argues for a more routinely interventionist God (C7r–D3r). On this issue, see the debate between J. E. McGuire, "Boyle's Conception of Nature," *Journal of the History of Ideas* 33 (1972), 536, and Timothy Shanahan, "God and Nature in the Thought of Robert Boyle," *Journal of the History of Philosophy* 26 (1988), 556–559. But compare Rose-Mary Sargent's *The Diffident Naturalist: Robert Boyle and the Philosophy of Experiment* (Chicago: University of Chicago Press, 1995), 98–103, which offers the most coherent recent account of Boyle's mediatory metaphysics.

188. Boyle, *A Free Enquiry into the Vulgarly Receiv'd Notion of Nature* (London, 1686), 273–275.

189. Boyle, *A Free Enquiry*, 13.

190. For the list of these anomalies, see Boyle, *A Free Enquiry*, 288. For the rejection of anomalies as preternatural things, see *A Free Enquiry*, 260.

191. Boyle, *A Free Enquiry*, 264.

192. On Boyle's cooperation with the social multitude, see Sargent, *The Diffident Naturalist*, 149–158.

193. Richard Ashcraft, "Latitudinarianism and Toleration: Myth Versus Political History," in *Philosophy, Science, and Religion in England, 1640–1700*, ed. Richard Kroll, Richard Ashcraft, Perez Zarogin (Cambridge: Cambridge University Press, 1992), 163. Boyle himself uses the phrase "giddy Multitude" in a letter of March 2, 1651/2: quoted in Michael Hunter, *Robert Boyle, 1627–1691: Scrupulosity and Science* (Woodbridge, Eng.: Boydell Press, 2000), 54. The young Boyle believed that republics had distinct advantages in fostering virtue. "In Republicks," Boyle pointed out, "the way to honour & preferment lys more open to desert, which is a quickening Spur & a great incitement to Noble Spirits. . . . And second, the lesser Inequality of Men's Conditions in Commonwealths, renders these Heroick Spirits more conspicuous; which in Monarchys would be swallowed by the Glory of the King or Princes." Unpublished ms. quoted in Jacob, *Robert Boyle and the English Revolution*, 73.

194. Boyle, *Some Considerations Touching the Vsefulnesse of Experimentall Naturall Philosophy* (Oxford, 1663), part 1, 71.

195. In order of appearance, these formulations can be found in: *The Origine of Formes and Qualities* (Oxford, 1666), 191, 22, 37, and "An Introduction to the History of Particular Qualities," in Boyle, *Tracts* (Oxford, 1671): C3r, C4v.

196. Last two quotations from Boyle, *Certain Physiological Essays* (London, 1661), 31, 13. Compare ibid., 15, for additional contemplations of sentence length. See also Shapin's and Schaffer's comments on this passage: *Leviathan and the Air-Pump*, 63–64, and Hunter's comments on Boyle's increasingly convoluted writing style in *Robert Boyle, 1627–1691*, 34–35.

197. For a useful summary of the debate about seventeenth-century prose style, see Robert Markley, *Fallen Languages: Crises of Representation in Newtonian England*, 1660–1740 (Ithaca, N.Y.: Cornell University Press, 1993), 1–8.

198. On Boyle's invitation to Howe, see Wojcik, "The Theological Context of Boyle's *Things Above Reason*," 148–150.

199. John Howe, *The Reconcileableness of God's Prescience of the Sins of Men* (London, 1677), 87.

200. For Howe's position that the self-motion of second causes is the norm, see *Reconcileableness*, 133.

201. Thomas Danson, *De Causa Dei; or, A Vindication of the Common Doctrine of Protestant Divines, Concerning Predetermination* (London, 1678), 46–47.

202. Danson, *Causa Dei*, 12.

203. Last two quotations in Danson, *Causa Dei*, 121–122.

204. Andrew Marvell, *Remarks Upon a Late Disingenuous Discourse* (London, 1678), 61.

205. Boyle, *Origine of Formes and Qualities*, 92.

206. Boyle, *Origine of Formes and Qualities*, 6.

207. Boyle, *Origine of Formes and Qualities*, 93–95.

208. Boyle, *Origine of Formes and Qualities*, 72.

209. I do not use the word *metamorphosis* casually: Boyle himself uses it to describe experimental transmutation: *Origine of Formes and Qualities*, 401, 404, 420.

210. Boyle, *The Excellency of Theology* (London, 1674), 54.

211. Lucretius, *Of the Nature of Things*, trans. Anthony M. Esolen (Baltimore: Johns Hopkins University Press, 1995), Book 1, lines 144–145.

212. The story of the boat ride and the quotation are in Boyle, *Occasional Reflections*, EE2r–EE3r.

213. Quotations in this paragraph in Boyle, *Occasional Reflections*, EE3v–EE4r.

214. Tuck has shown that an emphasis on the divergence of interests is a common, but fairly new feature of the political debates in the 1640s. The emphasis belongs to a tradition that is sponsored by Tacitus's writings: see *Government and Philosophy*, 223.

215. For Lindamore's reference to the "vulgar," see Boyle, *Occasional Reflections*, EE5v.

216. Eugenius's statements can be found in Boyle, *Occasional Reflections*, EE4r.

217. For Eusebius's comments, see Boyle, *Occasional Reflections*, EE7r.

218. In *The Martyrdom of Theodora and Didymus* (London, 1687), Boyle deploys the generic resources of romance to defend the right to disobey laws that go against one's

conscience: 110–111. This defense was added when Boyle revised his original text for publication in 1687, perhaps in response to the specter of Catholicism, which was threatening to return under James II. Compare the reprint of the original version of *The Martyrdom of Theodora* in *The Works of Robert Boyle*, vol. 13, ed. Michael Hunter and Edward B. Davis (London: Pickering and Chatto, 2000), 3–41.

219. Boyle, *Certain Physiological Essays*, 177.

220. Boyle, *Certain Physiological Essays*, 177–178.

221. Purchas, *A Theatre of Politicall Flying-Insects* (London, 1657), 265, 278.

222. For a brief discussion of the tradition that associates bees with monarchy, see Claire Preston, *Thomas Browne and the Writing of Early Modern Science* (Cambridge: Cambridge University Press, 2005), 76–79. I thank Matt Augustine for drawing my attention to this text.

223. Samuel Hartlib, *The Reformed Common-wealth of Bees* (London, 1655), 54–55. Boyle was familiar with Hartlib's work: Boyle to Hartlib, September 14, 1655 (*The Correspondence of Robert Boyle*, vol. 1, 191).

224. For Hobbes's rejection of the status of bees as political animals, see, for example, *Elements of Law*, 102–103.

CHAPTER 3. LOCKE'S MIXED LIBERTY

1. For a full discussion of the history of mixed government in sixteenth- and seventeenth century England, see the studies by Zera Fink, *The Classical Republicans: An Essay in the Recovery of a Pattern of Thought in Seventeenth-Century England* (1945; reprint, Evanston, Ill.: Northwestern University Press, 1962); Corinne Comstock Weston, *English Constitutional Theory and the House of Lords, 1556–1832* (London: Routledge, 1962); W. H. Greenleaf, *Order, Empiricism, and Politics: Two Traditions of Political Thought, 1500–1700* (London: Oxford University Press, 1964); Weston and Janelle Renfrow Greenberg, *Subjects and Sovereigns: The Grand Controversy over Legal Sovereignty in Stuart England* (Cambridge: Cambridge University Press, 1981); Robert Eccleshall, *Order and Reason in Politics: Theories of Absolute and Limited Monarchy in Early Modern England* (Oxford: Oxford University Press, 1978); and Michael Mendle, *Dangerous Positions: Mixed Government, the Estates of the Realm, and the Answer to the XIX Propositions* (University: University of Alabama Press, 1985). See my remarks on this scholarship in Chapter 1.

2. For the beginning of Locke's friendship with Boyle, see Roger Woolhouse, *Locke: A Biography* (Cambridge: Cambridge University Press, 2007), 34.

3. For the Stuart attempt to expunge the language of shared sovereignty and for the return of mixed government during the exclusion crisis, see Weston and Greenberg, *Subjects and Sovereigns*, 149–221.

4. For a more detailed discussion of Monmouth's deployment by Whigs and Tories, see my "The Last Royal Bastard and the Multitude," *Journal of British Studies* 47:1 (2008), 53–76.

5. For Locke's involvement in meetings between Shaftesbury and Monmouth in the spring and summer before Monmouth's progress, see Ashcraft, *Revolutionary Politics and Locke's Two Treatises of Government* (Princeton, N.J.: Princeton University Press, 1986): "from mid-April to the end of May 1680, Locke was at Thanet House when Shaftesbury, Russell, and Monmouth were meeting virtually every night" (375 fn.) (cf. Maurice Cranston, *John Locke: A Biography* [London: Longmans, 1966], 194–195). Ashcraft also points out that in July 1680, "Shaftesbury and Monmouth retired to St. Giles to discuss political strategy, and Locke accompanied them" (Ashcraft, *Revolutionary Politics*, 86; cf. Cranston, *John Locke*, 195). That Locke drafted the instructions for the Oxford parliament is pointed out by John Dunn, *The Political Thought of John Locke: An Historical Account of the Two Treatises of Government* (Cambridge: Cambridge University Press, 1969), 55. For the argument that Locke provided funds for the Monmouth rebellion, see Ashcraft, *Revolutionary Politics*, 457–462.

6. For the link to Vernon, see Ashcraft, *Revolutionary Politics*, 375; for the connection to Dare, see ibid., where Ashcraft calls Dare "the leading English radical in Amsterdam" (411) and "chief financial conduit for Monmouth's Rebellion" (459). Dare's guardianship of the *Essay* is noted by Cranston in *John Locke*, 253. Locke deposited the manuscript as a precaution after he learned that the English government was trying to extradite him from Holland (Locke's name had appeared on a list of conspirators: Cranston, ibid.).

7. On the court reports about Locke's radical contacts in Holland, see Woolhouse, *Locke: A Biography*, 197–223. For Jean Le Clerk's comment on Locke's view of Monmouth, see Woolhouse, *Locke: A Biography*, 218. But compare Ashcraft's reading of Locke's letter to Edward Clarke (*Revolutionary Politics*, 414), which suggests that Locke's concern for Monmouth's political fortunes was more involved.

8. Monmouth's diary entry appears in James Welwood, *Memoirs of the Most Material Transactions in England for the Last Hundred Years* (London, 1700), 374. The original diary is lost. The entry is quoted and decoded in Ashcraft, *Revolutionary Politics*, 375. Ferguson and Locke were associated in other ways: some suspected that Ferguson's pamphlet *No Protestant Plot* (London, 1681) was authored by Locke (Woolhouse, *Locke: A Biography*, 174), and government spies reported about contacts between Ferguson and Locke during the latter's exile in Holland (ibid., 217).

9. Locke, *Drafts for the Essay Concerning Human Understanding*, ed. Peter H. Nidditch and G. A. J. Rogers (Oxford: Clarendon Press, 1990), 131. The draft passage recurs almost verbatim in the final version of *Essay* (quoted below).

10. Locke, *An Essay Concerning Human Understanding*, ed. Peter H. Nidditch (Oxford: Clarendon Press, 1991), 120.

11. See Laslett's discussion in Locke, *Two Treatises of Government*, ed. Peter Laslett (Cambridge: Cambridge University Press, 1993), 79–92.

12. Ruth Grant has been especially effective in showing that there is no contradiction, as Laslett claims, between natural law and Locke's argument against innate ideas: *John Locke's Liberalism* (Chicago: University of Chicago Press, 1987), 23–25 (cf. Tully's

discussion of Laslett in *A Discourse on Property: John Locke and His Adversaries* [Cambridge: Cambridge University Press, 1980], 7–8). For Ashcraft's argument about the relationship between Locke's politics and philosophy, see his *Locke's Two Treatises of Government* (London: Allen & Unwin, 1987), 13–59. For Albritton's argument, see "The Politics of Locke's Philosophy," *Political Studies* 24 (1976), 253–267.

13. One important exception to the dominance of Locke's political thought in the construction of a more unified view of his philosophy and politics is Neal Wood, *The Politics of Locke's Philosophy: A Social Study of An Essay Concerning Human Understanding* (Berkeley: University of California Press, 1983). Wood reads the *Essay* as promoting the attitudes, beliefs, and politics of the rising middle classes. My reading pursues a different direction. It follows the anti-liberal line of interpretation promoted by Dunn in *The Political Thought of John Locke*, by Tully in *A Discourse on Property*, and by Ashcraft in *Revolutionary Politics*.

14. Tully, *A Discourse on Property*, 110–118.

15. Tully, *A Discourse on Property*, 117.

16. Locke, *Two Treatises of Government*, 230–231. Subsequent references appear in the text.

17. Cf. *Two Treatises*, 258–259, where Locke employs a string of biblical figures to demonstrate how routinely the bible disregards rules of succession and inheritance, and ibid., 337, where Locke cites anthropological examples of elective kings.

18. In the second treatise, Locke approvingly quotes the biblical story of Jephta to show that bastards can be elected rulers (*Two Treatises*, 340). Jephta is a popular example among Whigs. See, for example, Elkanah Settle's *Absalom Senior* (London, 1682), which mentions the "mounting" of the "bastard Jephta" (21) to argue against divine right from Adam. See also Algernon Sidney, *Discourses Concerning Government*, ed. Thomas G. West (Indianapolis: Liberty Fund, 1996), 125, 228, 311–312, 502, 536. On these pages, Sidney uses Jephtah in Locke's sense: as an example that contradicts the divine right of kings and highlights the elective and conditional nature of kingship.

19. On culturally different practices of family and descent, see also Locke, *Two Treatises*, 310.

20. For the time of the composition of the first treatise, see John Marshall, *John Locke: Resistance, Religion, and Responsibility* (Cambridge: Cambridge University Press, 1994), 117.

21. Locke's journal entry is cited in Marshall, *John Locke*, 199. For Marshall's suggestion that Locke's meditations may have been prompted by Dryden's poem, see ibid., 199–200.

22. Robert Filmer, *Patriarcha and Other Writings*, ed. J. P. Sommerville (Cambridge: Cambridge University Press, 1991), 11. Cf. also the following passage: " 'God made all mankind of one man, that he might teach the world to be governed by a king, and not by a multitude' " (Filmer, *Patriarcha*, 14).

23. Filmer, *Patriarcha*, 5.

24. Locke, *An Essay Concerning Human Understanding*, 451. The quotation is from book three. In book two, Locke is more cautious about generation: 325.

25. On royalist attacks that denigrated Monmouth for his mixed origins, see my "The Last Royal Bastard and the Multitude," 56–64.

26. Dryden, *Absalom and Achitophel*, lines 367–370 (*John Dryden: Selected Poems*, ed. Steven N. Zwicker and David Bywaters [London: Penguin, 2001]).

27. Feminist critics—most famously Carol Pateman in *The Sexual Contract* (Stanford, Calif.: Stanford University Press, 1988)—have argued that Locke's claims for gender equality are undermined by persistent assertions of inequality. For a thorough discussion of the ambiguities in Locke's account of gender, see Jeremy Waldron, *God, Locke, and Equality: Christian Foundations in Locke's Political Thought* (Cambridge: Cambridge University Press, 2002), 21–43. Waldron also argues that Locke rejected the naturalistic fallacy: ibid., 69–71.

28. Giambattista della Porta, *Natural Magic* (London, 1658), 40.

29. Anon., *Grimalkin* (London, 1681), 1.

30. *Grimalkin* rejected the succession of a bastard by pointing out that such an idea implied a radical equality: "all the beasts are equal, and . . . Nature having left us no exact scale of Creatures, it could be none of her Intendment, that any one should have Rule or Sovereignty more than another" (*Grimalkin*, 7).

31. The debate about Locke's position on species falls, roughly, into two camps. Those who argue that Locke ultimately believed in objectively existing species and those who argue that Locke lacked such a belief. To the former camp belong, for example, J. L. Mackie, *Problems from Locke* (Oxford: Clarendon Press, 1976), 85–88; Peter Alexander, *Ideas, Qualities, and Corpuscles: Locke and Boyle on the External World* (Cambridge: Cambridge University Press, 1985), 277–278; Peter Anstey, *John Locke and Natural Philosophy* (Oxford: Oxford University Press, 2011), 204–218. Those who argue that Locke did not believe in objectively existing species include: Michael Ayers, *Locke: Epistemology and Ontology*, vol. 2 (London: Routledge, 1991), 67–68; Susanna Goodin, "Locke and Leibniz and the Debate over Species," in *New Essays on the Rationalists*, ed. Rocco Gennaro and Charles Huenemann (New York: Oxford University Press, 1999), 163–176; David Stamos, *The Species Problem: Biological Species, Ontology, and the Metaphysics of Biology* (Lanham, Md.: Lexington Books, 2003), 41–45. I side with the latter camp, but provide a more specific set of motivations for why Locke winds up arguing so vehemently against species boundaries in book three of the *Essay*.

32. Preceding two quotations are in Locke, *Drafts for the Essay*, 190–191.

33. Locke suggests that species distinctions are culturally contingent in *Drafts for the Essay*, 192.

34. For Locke's acknowledgment that simple mixture could be generative, see his essay "Morbus," transcribed by Jonathan Walmsley in "Morbus—Locke's Early Essay on Disease," *Early Science and Medicine* 5:4 (2000), 366–393. The quotation from Locke is on page 390. Walmsley emphasizes that Locke was not immediately an adherent of

the mechanical philosophy, but he rather overplays this argument when he insists that Locke's note on the powers of "bare mistion" could not refer to Boyle's *Origine of Formes and Qualities*, which, as we saw in the second chapter, is filled with examples of the transformative powers of simple mixture. For a more balanced discussion of this issue that emphasizes Locke's eclecticism, see J. R. Milton, "Locke, Medicine, and the Mechanical Philosophy," *British Journal for the History of Philosophy* 9:2 (2001), 221–243.

35. Previous three quotations in Locke's Journal, September 19, 1676, reprinted in Kenneth Dewhurst, *John Locke: Physician and Philosopher* (London: The Wellcome Historical Medical Library, 1963), 74.

36. Previous three quotations in Locke's Journal, November 19, 1677, reprinted in *An Early Draft of Locke's Essay*, ed. R. I. Aaron and Jocelyn Gibb (Oxford: Clarendon Press, 1936), 99.

37. Locke's Journal, May 16, 1678, reprinted in Dewhurst, *John Locke: Physician and Philosopher*, 121.

38. Locke sent the completed book three to Edward Clarke in 1686. Letter from Edward Clarke to Locke, October 16, 1686, *The Correspondence of John Locke*, vol. 3, ed. E. S. De Beer (Oxford: Clarendon, 1978), 51.

39. *Grimalkin*, 4.

40. Locke, *Essay*, 451–452. Subsequent references will appear in the main text.

41. See also the following comment on species from the *Essay*: "That which, I think, very much disposes Men to substitute their names for the real Essences of Species, is the supposition . . . that Nature works regularly in the Production of Things, and sets the Boundaries to each of those Species. . . . Whereas any one who observes their different Qualities can hardly doubt, that many of the Individuals, called by the same name, are, in their internal constitution, as different one from another, as several of those which are ranked under specifick Names" (501–502).

42. Locke recognizes the kinship of form, essence, and species in *Essay*, 440–441, 452, 475.

43. For the phrase "improbable stories," see J. L. Mackie, *Problems from Locke* (Oxford: Clarendon Press, 1976), 88. See note 31 for examples of philosophers who argue for and against Locke's belief in objectively existing species.

44. Algernon Sidney recommends the mixing of the different "species" of government in *Discourses Concerning Government*, 31, 166. Waldron does not recognize that Locke's argument on species questions social, sexual, and political hierarchies. For him, it presents an obstacle to Locke's argument for equality. See Waldron, *God, Locke, and Equality*, 44–82.

45. In later years, as Anstey shows, Locke was more willing to accept the ontological stability of species: *Locke and Natural Philosophy*, 205.

46. Bolingbroke, *The Works of Lord Bolingbroke*, vol. 4 (Philadelphia, 1841), 363, cited in Isaac Kramnick, *Bolingbroke and His Circle: The Politics of Nostalgia in the Age of Walpole* (Ithaca, N.Y.: Cornell University Press, 1992), 102.

47. Bolingbroke criticizes, for example, Locke's belief that mixed modes, for all their problems, signify human liberty (Bolingbroke, *The Philosophical Works*, vol. 1 [London, 1754], 89, 95). See my discussion of Locke's mixed modes below.

48. Cf. Locke's reassurances about the regularity of nature's productions in *Essay*, 415.

49. Boyle, *A Free Enquiry into the Vulgarly Receiv'd Notion of Nature* (London, 1686), 79–80.

50. I take the phrase "developmental plasticity" from Scott F. Gilbert's "The Genome in its Ecological Context: Philosophical Perspectives on Interspecies Epigenesis," *Annals of the New York Academy of Sciences* 981 (2002), 202–218.

51. This trajectory fits Locke's increasing liberalization in religion, philosophy, and politics. On this topic, see Woolhouse, *Locke: A Biography*, 83–84, 105, 235.

52. In Locke's 1671 draft, he uses "complex ideas" (see, for example, Locke, *Drafts for the Essay*, 83).

53. Locke, *An Early Draft of Locke's Essay*, 112.

54. On Locke's struggle with the distinction between simple and mixed modes, see R. I. Aaron, *John Locke* (Oxford: Clarendon Press, 1971), 66–67. Aaron cites a passage from draft C that features the term *mixed modes* (ibid., 66).

55. On Locke's finishing of book three in 1686, see Aaron, *John Locke*, 54.

56. On Locke's mental atomism, see M. A. Stewart, "Locke's Mental Atomism and the Classification of Ideas," parts 1 and 2, *Locke Newsletter*, 1979 and 1980, 53–82 and 25–62, respectively. Stewart argues that Locke literally thinks about ideas as atoms. Michael Ayers's "Locke's Logical Atomism," in *Rationalism, Empiricism and Idealism: British Academy Lectures on the History of Philosophy*, ed. Anthony Kenny (Oxford: Clarendon Press, 1986), 6–22, has criticized this approach. I believe Locke is using atomism as a model for thinking through issues of human understanding without deciding the question of the atomic nature of ideas.

57. Cf. Locke, *Essay*, 292, 478, for other instances of Locke using *compounded* and *decompounded* with regard to mixed modes.

58. Compare also the related notion of a "precise Collection" that Locke uses (*Essay*, 387). The notion of a "perfect" or "precise collection" is already present in the early drafts of the *Essay* (Locke, *Drafts for the Essay*, 171, 184). "Precise multitude" is not featured in the drafts, and its appearance in later drafts might be another manifestation of Boyle's influence or a trace of the political situation Locke worked in.

59. Locke happily articulates the utopian promise of mixed modes in the field of morality, where their ability to reconcile many and one promises a precision and lucidity that could make morality "capable of Demonstration, as well as Mathematicks" (*Essay*, 516). In the field of politics, Locke refrains from indulging such sanguine prospects. His exile and the political situation at home probably made this difficult.

60. In addition to my discussion of Filmer in this chapter, see my discussion in Chapter 3 of the uses absolutists and royalists made of Aristotelian assumptions.

61. Locke, *Two Treatises*, 268. Subsequent references in the main text.

62. David Hume's comments are in *A Treatise of Human Nature*, ed. L. A. Selby-Bigge (Oxford: Clarendon Press, 1990), 505 (fn.); Laurence Sterne's in *The Life and Opinions of Tristram Shandy, Gentleman*, ed. Melvyn New and Joan New (London: Penguin, 1997), 181.

63. An incomplete list of those philosophers who either rewrite Locke's language of mixture or dismiss it includes: Robert Nozick, *Anarchy, State, and Utopia* (New York: Basic Books, 1974), 174–177; Jeremy Waldron, *The Right to Private Property* (Oxford: Clarendon Press, 1988), 184–191; John Simmons, *The Lockean Theory of Rights* (Princeton, N.J.: Princeton University Press, 1992), 273–274; Gopal Sreenivasan, *The Limits of Lockean Rights in Property* (New York: Oxford University Press, 1995), 59–94; Matthew Kramer, *John Locke and the Origins of Private Property* (Cambridge: Cambridge University Press, 1997), 144–150; Stephen Buckle, *Natural Law and the Theory of Property*, 152. The philosopher who has come closest to accepting mixture is probably Karl Olivecrona, who notes that Locke sees property as an extension of personality: "Locke's Theory of Appropriation," *Philosophical Quarterly* 24 (1974), 220–234 (compare Waldron, *The Right to Private Property*, 195–196, for a critique of Olivecrona's account). The philosophical literature on Locke's argument on property is immense. For a helpful overview, see the extensive bibliography in Kramer, *John Locke and the Origins of Private Property*, 319–345. For a helpful overview of the most important arguments against the validity of mixture as the means of creating private property, see Simmons, *The Lockean Theory of Rights*, 266–270.

64. Simmons has offered a highly sophisticated defense of Lockean mixture, but even he backs off from a literal understanding of the term: *The Lockean Theory of Rights*, 274.

65. Michael Ayers, "Locke's Logical Atomism," 8.

66. Aristotle, *Generation of Animals*, ed. G. P. Goold, trans. A. L. Peck (Cambridge, Mass.: Harvard University Press, 1990), 117 (short quotation), 119–121 (block quotation).

67. Dewhurst notes that Locke started making "long extracts" from Harvey's *Exercitations* in 1658: *John Locke: Physician and Philosopher*, 27.

68. For Harvey's embrace of Aristotle's belief in an immaterial cause of generation, see *Anatomical Exercitations Concerning the Generation of Living Creatures* (London, 1653), NN4r–NN5r. "The form, or species which is without matter," Harvey argued, "is the principal cause" (ibid., NN5r).

69. Harvey, *Anatomical Exercitations*, NN6r.

70. Last two quotations in Harvey, *Anatomical Exercitations*, MM8v and MM8r, respectively.

71. For Harvey's use of "workmanship," see, for example, *Anatomical Exercitations*, MM8r–MM8v.

72. While Locke departed from Harvey's maker's theory, he also may have learned something from Harvey's somewhat contradictory suggestion, thrown out at the very end of his treatise, that generation may perhaps have something to do with "mixt Workmanship" (NN6r).

73. I am offering here a more substantial reading of this passage than I was able to develop in *Eighteenth-Century Fiction and the Law of Property* (Cambridge: Cambridge University Press, 2002), 59–60.

74. Cf. Tully's argument, which points out that Locke's extension of property rights responds to a conceptual problem encountered by Grotius and Pufendorf: *A Discourse on Property*, 104–105.

75. Buckle, *Natural Law and the Theory of Property*, 172–173.

76. For Buckle's failure to see the importance of mixture, see *Natural Law and the Theory of Property*, 152.

77. Gordon Schochet has noted Locke's investment in constructing an easy transition from the state of nature to the state of society: *Patriarchalism in Political Thought* (New York: Basic Books, 1975), 255.

78. See my *Eighteenth-Century Fiction and the Law of Property* (Cambridge: Cambridge University Press, 2002), 32–62.

79. For the English reliance on the language of plantation, see Patricia Seed, *Ceremonies of Possession in Europe's Conquest of the New World* (Cambridge: Cambridge University Press, 1995).

80. Tully raises some problems for his argument when he claims, on the one hand, that there is no continuity of property as we move from the state of nature to the state of society (*A Discourse on Property*, 98–99, 124) and emphasizes, on the other, how similar the state of nature is to the state of society (ibid., 157–176). Without the persistence of natural rights into society, Locke's project of guaranteeing inalienable political rights has to falter.

81. When Locke discusses the unequal relationship between parent and child in *Two Treatises*, he notes—echoing arguments already prominent in the political debates of the 1640s—that such inequality "consists with . . . Equality" (304). "Natural Freedom and Subjection to Parents may consist together and are founded on the same Principle" (ibid., 308).

82. Locke quotes Filmer here: *Two Treatises*, 200. Locke returns to this passage in ibid., 216.

83. I am connecting here two paragraphs. The connection strikes me as legitimate since Locke's subject ("the people," paragraph 220) is the same agent as the "confused multitude" (paragraph 219). Locke rebuts Filmer's emphasis on singularity at every turn of *Two Treatises*. From the "plural number" to which God gave dominion in the beginning of the world (ibid., 161), to the "community [God] granted to Noah and his Sons" (ibid., 163) and the dispersion of Babel (ibid., 245–250), Locke unfailingly resists Filmer's interpretation of these moments as so many instances in which singularity wins out over multiplicity.

84. My discussion adds a physical dimension to Julian Franklin's account of Lockean dissolution, which addresses the issue from the standpoint of constitutional theory: see *John Locke and the Theory of Sovereignty: Mixed Monarchy and the Right of Resistance in the Political Thought of the English Revolution* (Cambridge: Cambridge University Press, 1978), 87–126.

85. The image of a degeneration to a beastly state recurs in *Two Treatises* on 273, 274, 279, 327 (where the people are being "degraded from the common state of rational Creatures" by an absolute king), and 389. Ashcraft's comments on the image of the wild beast can be found in *Revolutionary Politics*, 401.

86. See preceding note for a series of references that illustrate these possibilities.

87. Like Boyle, Locke privileged the juices of the body over anatomy. Anatomical knowledge, he thought, was far less useful in the curing of disease than a knowledge of the juices of the body (on this, see Locke's manuscript "Anatomia," cited in Patrick Romanell, *John Locke and Medicine: A New Key to Locke* [Buffalo, N.Y.: Prometheus Books, 1984], 111–112). This preference should be understood in a political light as well, for anatomy readily supports a view of the body as subordinated and functionally differentiated, whereas the interaction of juices is easily aligned with cooperation and mixture.

88. Phillip Hunton, *A Vindication of the Treatise of Monarchy* (London, 1644), 39.

89. Locke's essay on general naturalization has been reprinted in David Resnick, "John Locke and the Problem of Naturalization," *Review of Politics* 49:3 (1987), 385–388. The quotation can be found on 388.

90. Samuel Clarke, *Third Defense of an Argument . . . to Prove the Immateriality and Natural Immortality of the Soul* (London, 1708), 64–66. Thanks to David Fairer for directing me to this passage.

91. Locke, *Essay*, 331. Subsequent references in the main text.

92. Charles Taylor, *Sources of the Self: The Making of the Modern Identity* (Cambridge, Mass.: Harvard University Press, 1989), 160–165. Jerrold Seigel has criticized Taylor's account along lines similar to mine (*The Idea of the Self: Thought and Experience in Western Europe Since the Seventeenth Century* [Cambridge: Cambridge University Press, 2005], 92–93). The argument I am offering here is, in general outlook and direction, related to Seigel's, which also recognizes the connection between Locke's argument on identity and his account of the self in the state of nature (105–108).

93. I argue here against Edwin McCann, who claims that those who have accused "Locke of supposing that a person might seem to remember an experience that she never had" have simply misread the chapter (McCann, "Cartesian Selves and Lockean Substances," *The Monist* 69:3 [1986], 473). I don't believe that this claim constitutes a misreading, and would like to add—against the arguments made by Antony Flew and Henry Allison— that Locke is not confused. Locke strikes me in this case as consistent. For Flew's and Allison's arguments that Locke's account of identity is confused, see, respectively, "Locke and the Problem of Personal Identity," *Philosophy* 26 (1951), 53–68, and "Locke's Theory of Personal Identity: A Re-examination," *Journal of the History of Ideas* 27 (1966), 41–58.

94. Ayers, "Locke's Logical Atomism," 8.

95. Derek Parfit, "Personal Identity," *Philosophical Review* 80 (1971), 10–11. Thanks to Mark Rollins for referring me to Parfit's work.

96. I am slightly overstating the parallel between physical and personal identity. The identity of the man has greater stability than the identity of the person, and the continuity of life is a more sturdy condition than the continuity of consciousness (which isn't

that continuous, after all). Still, the process that underlies both these connected identities is very similar.

CONCLUSION

1. Sankar Muthu, *Enlightenment Against Empire* (Princeton, N.J.: Princeton University Press, 2003); Stephen Eric Bronner, *Reclaiming the Enlightenment: Towards a Politics of Radical Engagement* (New York: Columbia University Press, 2004); Jennifer Pitts, *A Turn to Empire: The Rise of Imperial Liberalism in Britain and France* (Princeton, N.J.: Princeton University Press, 2005); *The Postcolonial Enlightenment: Eighteenth-Century Colonialism and Postcolonial Theory*, ed. Daniel Carey and Lynn Festa (Oxford: Oxford University Press, 2009). *This Is Enlightenment*, ed. Clifford Siskin and William Warner (Chicago: University of Chicago Press, 2010), provides an even more recent attempt to reorient our histories of enlightenment.

2. For Foucault's tendency to present the premodern world as admirably heterogeneous, see, for example, *Discipline and Punish: The Birth of the Prison* (New York: Vintage Books, 1995), trans. Alan Sheridan, 141–148; and *The History of Sexuality*, vol. 1, trans. Robert Hurley (New York: Vintage Books, 1990), 31–32. Though less disposed than Foucault to contemplate the premodern world with appreciative affection, Giorgio Agamben is currently extending the paranoid interpretation of enlightenment. See, for example, *Homo Sacer: Sovereign Power and Bare Life*, trans. Daniel Heller-Roazen (Stanford, Calif.: Stanford University Press, 1998).

3. Lorraine Daston and Katharine Park's elegiac *Wonders and the Order of Nature, 1150–1750* (New York: Zone Books, 1998) exemplifies the tendency to see the normalization of the deformed and the monstrous as a loss.

4. In the field of literary studies, Rita Felski has made a persuasive case against the hermeneutics of suspicion. See her *Uses of Literature* (Oxford: Blackwell, 2008), 1–22. I thank David Brewer for referring me to Felski's book.

5. In addition to Bacon, whom I mention in the main text, I can give two examples that show the familiarity of seventeenth-century Englishmen with the Roman practice of mixture. In *The Planter's Plea; or, The Grounds of Plantation Examined* (London, 1630), John White emphasizes the benefits of social mixture. He suggests a parallel between the English, whom God "first Civilized by the Romane Conquests, and mixture of their Colonies with us, that hee might bring in Religion afterwards" (11) and the new world, where the "heathen and brutish Nations" were acquainted by "mixture of some other people, with civility, to cause at length the glorious Gospell of Iesus Christ to shine out unto them" (15). In *The Modern States-Man* (London, 1653), George Withers attributes Rome's greatness in part to its aggressive sexual mixture with others (53–54).

6. For William Petty's statements on mixture between the English and Irish, see Chapter 2; for Beverley's reference to intermarriage between English and American populations, see Chapter 1.

7. Francis Bacon, *Reasons for an Union Between the Kingdoms of England and Scotland* (London, 1706), 7. Bacon commends Roman policy also in these terms: "they were so liberal of their Naturalization, as in effect they made perpetual Mixtures" (7). Not surprisingly, he is also in favor of mixing languages, which he views as "enriching" (9).

8. Viranjini Munasinghe, "Nationalism in Hybrid Spaces: The Production of Impurity Out of Purity," *American Ethnologist* 29:3 (2002), 663–692.

9. Mikhail Bakhtin, *The Dialogic Imagination*, trans. Caryl Emerson and Michael Holquist (Austin: University of Texas Press, 1981), 358–359.

10. M. J. C. Vile, *Constitutionalism and the Separation of Powers* (Oxford: Clarendon Press, 1967), and W. B. Gwyn, *The Meaning of the Separation of Powers: An Analysis of the Doctrine from Its Origin to the Adoption of the United States Constitution* (New Orleans: Tulane University Press, 1965), acknowledge the importance of mixed government, but present it as an old or "classical" idea that is not central to the development of modern governmental forms and is displaced or absorbed by the concept of separate powers. A different and equally problematic elision of mixed government can be seen in Scott Gordon's *Controlling the State: Constitutionalism from Ancient Athens to Today* (Cambridge, Mass.: Harvard University Press, 1999). Gordon argues that the separation of powers doctrine emerges in the mid-seventeenth century, through the debates on mixed government (258). However probable or improbable this is, Gordon ignores the fact that in the English tradition of mixed government, good government depends on the combination of the different branches of political power.

11. Bruno Latour, *We Have Never Been Modern*, trans. Catherine Porter (Cambridge, Mass.: Harvard University Press, 1995).

12. Anthony Giddens, *The Consequences of Modernity* (Stanford, Calif.: Stanford University Press, 1992).

13. On the tendency in modernist anthropology to frame mixture by giving it a discrete function within a dominant order, see the helpful summary by Pnina Werbner, "Introduction: The Dialectics of Cultural Hybridity," in *Debating Cultural Hybridity: Multi-Cultural Identities and the Politics of Anti-Racism*, ed. Pnina Werbner and Tariq Modood (London: Zed Books, 2000), 1–4.

14. All quotations in this paragraph from Homi Bhabha, *The Location of Culture* (London: Routledge, 2004), 5–6.

15. For Bhabha's engagement with the problem of newness, see *The Location of Culture*, 303–337. For Turner's work on liminality, see, for example, *The Ritual Process: Structure and Anti-Structure* (New York: de Gruyter, 1995).

16. The most influential articulation of Donna Haraway's belief in the utopian possibilities of the hybrid is her essay "Manifesto for Cyborgs: Science, Technology, and Socialist Feminism in the 1980s," which was first published in *Socialist Review* 80 (1985), 65–108. For Antonio Negri and Michael Hardt's articulation of the utopian potential of a boundless world, see *Empire* (Cambridge, Mass.: Harvard University Press, 2001).

17. One of the books that has begun to examine how the encounter with cultural and ethnic difference shaped a more complex British identity in the eighteenth century is

A New Imperial History: Culture, Identity, and Modernity in Britain and the Empire, 1660–1840, ed. Kathleen Wilson (Cambridge: Cambridge University Press, 2005). For a more wide-ranging account of how the encounter with ethnic and cultural difference helped shape early modern culture, see also *The Historical Practice of Diversity: Transcultural Interactions from the Early Modern Mediterranean to the Postcolonial World*, ed. Dirk Hoerder, Christiane Harzig, and Adrian Shubert (New York: Berghahn Books, 2003).

18. Dipesh Chakrabarty, *Provincializing Europe: Postcolonial Thought and Historical Difference* (Princeton, N.J.: Princeton University Press, 2000).

19. Chakrabarty, *Provincializing Europe*, 239. Chakrabarty draws here on the existentialist philosophy of thinkers such as Heidegger and Hans-Georg Gadamer to revise the Marxist vision of historical time and the totalizing account of modernization it enables.

BIBLIOGRAPHY

PRIMARY SOURCES

Addison, Joseph. *The Freeholder*. London, 1723.

Agrippa, Heinrich Cornelius. *Three Books on Occult Philosophy*. London, 1650.

Ainsworth, Henry. *Annotations Upon the Five Books of Moses*. London, 1627.

An Answer to the Dissenters Pleas for Separation. Cambridge, 1701.

Aquinas, Thomas. *Political Writings*. Edited and translated by R. W. Dyson. Cambridge: Cambridge University Press, 2002.

Aristotle. *On Sophistical Refutations: On Coming-to-Be and Passing-Away*. Edited by T. E. Page et al. Translated by E. S. Forster. Cambridge, Mass.: Harvard University Press, 1955.

——. *Generation of Animals*. Edited by G. P. Goold. Translated by A. L. Peck. Cambridge, Mass.: Harvard University Press, 1990.

——. *Meteorologica*. Edited by T. E. Page et al. Translated by H. D. P. Lee. London: William Heinemann, 1952.

——. *On the Heavens*. Edited by T. E. Page. Translated by W. K. C. Guthrie. Cambridge, Mass.: Harvard University Press, 1953.

——. *The Physics*. 2 vols. Edited by T. E. Page et al. Translated by Philip H. Wicksteed and Francis M. Cornford. London: William Heinemann, 1929.

——. *The Politics and the Constitution of Athens*. Edited by Stephen Everson. Translated by Benjamin Jowett and Jonathan Barnes. Cambridge: Cambridge University Press, 2008.

Arminius, Jakobus. *Examen Modestum Libelli quem D. Gulielmus Perkinsius Edidit*. Leiden, 1612.

Atterbury, Francis. *English Advice to the Freeholders of England*. N.p., 1714.

——. *Sermons and Discourses on Several Subjects and Occasions*. 4 vols. London, 1761.

Bacon, Francis. *Sylua Syluarum: A Naturall History*. London, 1626.

——. *Reasons for an Union Between the Kingdoms of England and Scotland*. London, 1706.

Bailey, Nathan. *An Universal Etymological English Dictionary*. London, 1721.

——. *The Antiquities of London and Westminster*. London, 1722.

Baxter, Richard. *A Treatise of Knowledge and Love Compared*. London, 1689.

Bellarmine, Robert. *De Laicis; or, The Treatise on Civil Government.* Translated by Kathleen E. Murphy. Westport, Conn.: Hyperion Press, 1993.

Beverley, Robert. *The History and Present State of Virginia.* London, 1705.

Birch, Thomas. *The History of the Royal Society of London.* 4 vols. London, 1756–1757.

Blome, Richard. *The Gentleman's Recreation.* London, 1686.

Bodin, Jean. *Les Six Livres de la Republique.* Paris, 1577.

———. *Method for the Easy Comprehension of History.* Translated by Beatrice Reynolds. New York: Octagon Books, 1966.

Bolingbroke, Henry. *A Dissertation Upon Parties.* Dublin, 1735.

———. *The Philosophical Works.* 5 vols. London, 1754.

Boyle, Robert. *The Sceptical Chymist; or, Chymico-Physical Doubts & Paradoxes Touching the Spagyrist's Principles.* London, 1661.

———. *Certain Physiological Essays.* London, 1661.

———. *Some Considerations Touching the Style of the Holy Scriptures.* London, 1663.

———. *Some Considerations Touching the Vsefulness of Experimental Natural Philosophy.* Oxford, 1663.

———. *New Experiments and Observations Touching Cold.* London, 1665.

———. *Occasional Reflections Upon Several Subjects.* London, 1665.

———. *The Origine of Formes and Qualities.* Oxford, 1666.

———. *Certain Physiological Essays.* London, 1669.

———. *Tracts Written by the Honourable Robert Boyle.* Oxford, 1671.

———. *An Essay About the Origine and Virtue of Gems.* London, 1672.

———. *The Excellency of Theology Compar'd with Natural Philosophy.* London, 1674.

———. *Free Inquiry into the Vulgarly Receiv'd Notions of Nature.* London, 1686.

———. *The Martyrdom of Theodora and Didymus.* London, 1687.

———. *The Christian Virtuoso.* London, 1690.

———. *Experimentae & Observationes Physicae.* London, 1691.

———. *The Works of Robert Boyle.* 14 vols. Edited by Michael Hunter and Edward B. Davis. London: Pickering and Chatto, 2000.

———. *The Correspondence of Robert Boyle.* 6 vols. Edited by Michael Hunter, Antonio Clericuzio, and Lawrence Principe. London: Pickering and Chatto, 2001.

Bramhall, John. *The Serpent Salve; or, A Remedie for the Biting of an Aspe.* N.p., 1643.

———. *A Defense of True Liberty from Ante-cedent and Extrinsecall Necessity.* London, 1655.

Bridge, William. *The Truth of the Times Vindicated.* London, 1643.

Browne, Thomas. *Religio Medici.* London, 1642.

———. *Certain Miscellany Tracts.* London, 1683.

Buchanan, George. *De Jure Regni.* N.p., 1680.

Burton, Thomas. *Diary of Thomas Burton.* 4 vols. 1828; reprint, New York: Johnson Reprint Corporation, 1974.

Calvin, Jean. *Commentaries on the Book of the Prophet Jeremiah.* 5 vols. Translated and edited by John Owen. Grand Rapids, Mich.: Eerdmans, 1950.

Carpenter, Nathanael. *Geographie Delineated.* Oxford, 1625.

Clarke, Samuel. *Third Defense of an Argument . . . to Prove the Immateriality and Natural Immortality of the Soul.* London, 1708.

Chamberlayne, Edward. *Anglia Notitia; or, The Present State of England.* London, 1669.

Coke, Roger. *A Survey of the Politicks of Mr. Thomas White, Thomas Hobbes, and Hugo Grotius.* London, 1662.

Croll, Oswald. *Philosophy Reformed & Improved in Four Profound Tractates.* London, 1657.

Danson, Thomas. *De Causa Dei; or, A Vindication of the Common Doctrine of Protestant Divines, Concerning Predetermination.* London, 1678.

De Crèvecoeur, Jean. *Letters from an American Farmer.* London, 1782.

Defoe, Daniel. *An Essay Upon Projects.* London, 1697.

———. *The Complete English Tradesman.* London, 1726.

———. *A Plan of the English Commerce.* London, 1728.

———. *Satire, Fantasy and Writings on the Supernatural.* 8 vols. Edited by W. R. Owens and P. N. Furbank. London: Pickering and Chatto, 2003.

Digby, Kenelm. "Digby to Hakewill." May 15, 1635. B. L. Harleian MSS 4153.

———. *A Conference with a Lady About Choice of Religion.* Paris, 1638.

———. *Observations upon Religio Medici.* London, 1643.

———. *A Discourse Concerning Infallibility in Religion.* Paris, 1652.

———. *A Discourse Concerning the Vegetation of Plants Spoken by Sir Kenelme Digby at Gresham College on the 23 of January, 1660.* London, 1661.

———. *Two Treatises: Of Bodies and of Man's Soul.* London, 1665.

———. *Loose Fantasies.* Edited by Vittorio Gabrieli. Roma: Edizione di Storia e Litteratura, 1968.

Dryden, John. *Selected Poems.* Edited by Steven N. Zwicker and David Bywaters. London: Penguin, 2001.

Echard, Laurence. *The History of England.* London, 1707.

Englishmen No Bastards. London, 1701.

Ferguson, Robert. *No Protestant Plot.* London, 1681.

Filmer, Robert. *Patriarcha and Other Writings.* Edited by Johann P. Sommerville. Cambridge: Cambridge University Press, 1991.

Forset, Edward. *A Comparative Discourse of the Bodies Natural and Politique.* London, 1606.

Galen. *Selected Works.* Translated by P. N. Singer. Oxford: Oxford University Press, 1997.

Glanvill, Joseph. *Plus Ultra.* London, 1668.

Goodman, Godfrey. *The Fall of Man; or, The Corruption of Nature.* London, 1616.

Gott, Samuel. *Nova Solyma.* 2 vols. Translated by Walter Begley. 1648; reprint, London: John Murray, 1902.

———. *The Divine History of the Genesis of the World.* London, 1670.

Grew, Nehemiah. *A Discourse Made Before the Royal Society, Decemb. 10, 1674 Concerning the Nature, Causes, and Power of Mixture.* London, 1675.

———. *Experiments in Consort of the Luctation Arising from the Affusion of Several Men-struums.* London, 1678.

———. *The Anatomy of Plants.* London, 1682.

Grimalkin: or, the Rebel-Cat. London, 1681.

Hakewill, George. *An Answere to a Treatise Written by Dr. Carier.* London, 1616.

———. *An Apologie of the Povver and Prouidence of God in the Gouerment of the World.* Oxford, 1627, 1630, 1635.

Hale, Matthew. *The History of the Common Law of England.* 1713; reprint, Chicago: University of Chicago Press, 1971.

Hartlib, Samuel. *The Reformed Common-wealth of Bees.* London, 1655.

Harvey, Gideon. *Archelogia Philosophica Nova; or, New Principles of Philosophy.* London, 1663.

Harvey, William. *Anatomical Exercitations Concerning the Generation of Living Creatures.* London, 1653.

Helmont, Jan Baptista van. *Oriatrike; or, Physick Refined.* London, 1662.

Herle, Charles. *A Fuller Answer to a Treatise Written by Doctor Ferne.* London, 1642.

The History of England, Faithfully Extracted from Authentick Records. 2 vols. London, 1702.

Hobbes, Thomas. *Considerations upon the Reputation, Loyalty, Manners, and Religion of Thomas Hobbes of Malmesbury.* London, 1680.

———. *Thomas White's De Mundo Examined.* Edited by R. H. Popkin. Translated by Harold Whitmore Jones. London: Bradford University Press, 1976.

———. *The Elements of Law Natural and Politic.* Edited by Ferdinand Tönnies. 1889; reprint, London: Frank Cass, 1984.

———. *Leviathan.* Edited by Edwin Curley. Indianapolis: Hacking, 1994.

Hooker, Richard. *Of the Laws of Ecclesiastical Politie.* London, 1666.

Horace. *A Poetical Translation of the Works of Horace.* 4 vols. London, 1747.

Howe, John. *The Reconcileableness of God's Prescience of the Sins of Men.* London, 1677.

Hume, David. *The History of England, from the Invasion of Julius Caesar to the Accession of Henry VII.* 2 vols. London, 1762.

———. *A Treatise of Human Nature.* Edited by L. A. Selby-Bigge. Oxford: Clarendon Press, 1990.

Hunton, Phillip. *A Treatise of Monarchy.* London, 1643.

———. *A Vindication of the Treatise of Monarchy.* London, 1644.

Jackson, Thomas. *A Treatise of the Divine Essence and Attributes.* London, 1629.

Johnson, Samuel. *A Dictionary of the English Language.* London, 1755, and Dublin, 1775.

Jonstonus, Joannes. *An History of the Constancy of Nature.* London, 1657.

———. *An History of the Wonderful Things of Nature.* London, 1657.

L'Estrange, Roger. *Considerations and Proposals in Order to the Regulation of the Press.* London, 1663.

Locke, John. *An Early Draft of Locke's Essay.* Edited by R. I. Aaron and Jocelyn Gibb. Oxford: Clarendon Press, 1936.

————. *The Correspondence of John Locke.* 8 vols. Edited by E. S. De Beer. Oxford: Clarendon, 1976–1989.

————. *Drafts for the Essay Concerning Human Understanding.* Edited by Peter H. Nidditch and G. A. J. Rogers. Oxford: Clarendon Press, 1990.

————. *An Essay Concerning Human Understanding.* Edited by Peter H. Nidditch. Oxford: Clarendon Press, 1991.

————. *Two Treatises of Government.* Edited by Peter Laslett. Cambridge: Cambridge University Press, 1993.

Lucretius. *Of the Nature of Things.* Translated by Anthony M. Esolen. Baltimore: Johns Hopkins University Press, 1995.

Mandeville, Bernard. *Free Thoughts on Religion.* London, 1729.

Markham, Gervase. *Cauelarice; or, The English Horseman.* London, 1607.

————. *The English Husbandman.* London, 1613.

Marvell, Andrew. *Remarks Upon a Late Disingenuous Discourse.* London, 1678.

Maxwell, John. *Sacro-Sancta Regum Majestus; or, The Sacred and Royal Prerogative of Christian Kings.* Oxford, 1644.

Meres, Frances. *Wits Common Wealth, the Second Part.* London, 1634.

Midgley, Robert. *New Treatise of Natural Philosophy.* London, 1687.

Miege, Guy. *The New State of England Under Their Majesties K. William and Q. Mary.* London, 1691.

Milton, John. *Complete Prose Works.* 8 vols. Edited by Don M. Wolfe. New Haven, Conn.: Yale University Press, 1953–1982.

Moll, Herman. *A System of Geography.* London, 1701.

Newton, Isaac. "A Letter of Mr. Isaac Newton . . . Containing His New Theory About Light and Colours." *Philosophical Transactions* 6 (1671): 3075–3087.

————. "Mr. Isaac Newtons Answer to Some Considerations Upon His Doctrine of Light and Colors." *Philosophical Transactions* 7 (1672): 5084–5103.

————. "An Extract of Mr. Isaac Newton's Letter, Written to the Publisher from Cambridge April 3. 1673." *Philosophical Transactions* 8 (1673): 6109–6110.

————. "Mr. Newton's Answer to the Foregoing Letter." *Philosophical Transactions* 8 (1673): 6091.

————. *The Correspondence of Isaac Newton.* 7 vols. Edited by H. W. Turnbull. Cambridge: Cambridge University Press, 1959–1977.

Nicholson, William. *The English Historical Library.* London, 1699.

Oldenburg, Henry. *The Correspondence of Henry Oldenburg.* 13 vols. Edited and translated by A. Rupert Hall and Marie Boas Hall. Madison: University of Wisconsin Press, 1965–1986.

Oldmixon, John. *Reflections on Dr. Swift's Letter . . . About the English Tongue.* London, 1712.

Parker, Henry. *A Discourse Concerning Puritans.* London, 1641.

————. *Observations upon some of His Majesties Late Answers and Expresses.* London, 1642.

————. *The Contra-Replicant.* N.p., 1643.

———. *Jus Populi*. London, 1644.

———. *Of a Free Trade*. London, 1648.

———. *The True Portraiture of the Kings of England*. London, 1650.

Perkins, William. *A Christian and Plaine Treatise of the Manner and Order of Predestination*. London, 1606.

Persons, Robert. *A Conference About the Next Succession to the Crowne of Ingland*. Antwerp, 1595.

Petty, William. *The Discourse Made Before the Royal Society the 26. of November, 1674, Concerning the Use of Duplicate Proportion*. London, 1674.

———. "England's Guide to Industry." In Edward Chamberlayne, *The Present State of England*, Aa1r–Ee2v. London, 1683.

Pittis, William. *The True-Born Englishman: A Satyr, Answer'd, Paragraph by Paragraph*. London, 1701.

Pope, Alexander. *The Poems of Alexander Pope*. Edited by John Butt. London: Routledge, 1989.

Porta, Giambattista della. *Natural Magic*. London, 1658.

Prynne, William. *The Church of Englands Old Antithesis to New Arminianisme*. London, 1629.

Purchas, Samuel. *A Theatre of Politicall Flying-Insects*. London, 1657.

Radicati, Alberto. *A Philosophical Dissertation Upon Death*. London, 1732.

Rapin de Thoyras, M. (Paul). *An Impartial History of Whig and Tory*. London, 1718.

———. *The History of England*. 14 vols. London, 1725–1731.

Rapin, Rene. *Of Gardens*. Translated by John Evelyn. London, 1672.

Robertson, William. *Dissenters Self-Condemned*. London, 1710.

Rutherford, Samuel. *Lex Rex*. London, 1644.

Sacheverell, Henry. *The Political Union*. Oxford, 1702.

———. *The Perils of False Brethren*. London, 1709.

Salmon, Thomas. *Historical Collections: Relating the Originals, Conversions, and Revolutions of the Inhabitants of Great Britain to the Norman Conquest*. London, 1706.

———. *The Life of Her Late Majesty Queen Anne*. 2 vols. London, 1721.

———. *The History of Great Britain and Ireland*. London, 1725.

———. *Modern History: The Present State of All Nations*. 26 vols. London, 1727–1735.

———. *A New Geographical and Historical Grammar*. London, 1749.

Sennert, Daniel. *Thirteen Books of Philosophy*. London, 1660.

Settle, Elkanah. *Absalom Senior*. London, 1682.

Shaftesbury, Anthony Ashley Cooper, Earl of. *Characteristics of Men, Manners, Opinions, Times*. Edited by Lawrence E. Klein. Cambridge: Cambridge University Press, 1999.

Shakespeare, William. *The Complete Works*. Edited by Stephen Orgel and A. R. Braunmuller. Harmondsworth: Penguin, 2002.

Sidney, Algernon. *Discourses Concerning Government*. Edited by Thomas G. West. Indianapolis: Liberty Fund, 1996.

Sprat, Thomas. *History of the Royal Society*. London, 1667.

Sr. Kenelme Digbyes Honour Maintained by a Most Couragious Combat. London, 1641.

Stanley, Thomas. *The History of Philosophy.* 4 vols. London, 1655–1660.

Sterne, Laurence. *The Life and Opinions of Tristram Shandy, Gentleman.* Edited by Melvyn New and Joan New. London: Penguin, 1997.

Stow, John. *A Suruay of London.* London, 1598.

Stubbe, Henry. *Legends, No Histories; or, a Specimen of some Animadversions upon The History of the Royal Society.* London, 1670.

———. *An Epistolary Discourse Concerning Phlebotomy.* London, 1671.

Swift, Jonathan. *A Discourse of the Contests and Dissensions Between the Nobles and the Commons in Athens and Rome.* London, 1701.

———. *A Proposal for Correcting, Improving, and Ascertaining the English Tongue.* London, 1712.

———. *T—l—d's Invitation to Dismal.* London, 1712.

———. *A Serious and Useful Scheme to Make an Hospital for Incurables.* London, 1733.

———. *The Prose Works.* 14 vols. Edited by Herbert Davis. Oxford: Blackwell, 1951–1968.

———. *The Poems.* 3 vols. Edited by Harold Williams. Oxford: Clarendon Press, 1958.

Temple, William. *An Introduction to the History of England.* London, 1695.

———. *The Works of Sir William Temple.* 2 vols. London, 1731.

Toland, John. *The Art of Governing by Partys.* London, 1701.

———. *Memorial of the State of England.* London, 1705.

———. *The Description of Epsom.* London, 1711.

———. *Reasons for Naturalizing the Jews in Great Britain and Ireland.* London, 1714.

———. *The State-Anatomy of Great Britain.* London, 1717.

———. *The Destiny of Rome.* London, 1718.

Tyrrell, James. *The General History of England.* 5 vols. London, 1704.

Twisse, William. *A Discovery of D. Jacksons Vanitie.* Amsterdam, 1631.

Wallis, John. "An Extract of Letters from Dr. John Wallis to the Publisher, 1672." *Philosophical Transactions* 7 (1672): 5160–5170.

White, John. *The Planter's Plea; or, The Grounds of Plantation Examined.* London, 1630.

White, Thomas. *Quaestio Theologica, quomodo, Secundum Principia Peripatetices Digbeanae.* Paris, 1652.

———. *The Grounds of Obedience and Government.* London, 1655.

———. *Peripateticall Institutions.* London, 1656.

———. *Devotion and Reason.* Paris, 1661.

Wilson, Thomas. *David's Zeal for Zion.* London, 1641.

Withers, George. *The Modern States-Man.* London, 1653.

SECONDARY SOURCES

Agamben, Giorgio. *Homo Sacer: Sovereign Power and Bare Life.* Translated by Daniel Heller-Roazen. Stanford, Calif.: Stanford University Press, 1998.

Albritton, Robert. "The Politics of Locke's Philosophy." *Political Studies* 24 (1976): 253–267.

Alexander, Peter. *Ideas, Qualities, and Corpuscles: Locke and Boyle on the External World.* Cambridge: Cambridge University Press, 1985.

Allison, Henry. "Locke's Theory of Personal Identity: A Re-examination." *Journal of the History of Ideas* 27 (1966): 41–58.

Anderson, Perry. *The Origins of Postmodernity.* London: Verso, 2002.

Anstey, Peter. *John Locke and Natural Philosophy.* Oxford: Oxford University Press, 2011.

Appleby, Joyce. *Economic Thought and Ideology in Seventeenth-Century England.* Princeton, N.J.: Princeton University Press, 1978.

Aravamudan, Srinivas. *Tropicopolitans: Colonialism and Agency, 1688–1804.* Durham, N.C.: Duke University Press, 1999.

Armitage, David. *The Ideological Origins of the British Empire.* Cambridge: Cambridge University Press, 2000.

Ashcraft, Richard. *Revolutionary Politics and Locke's Two Treatises of Government.* Princeton, N.J.: Princeton University Press, 1986.

———. *Locke's Two Treatises of Government.* London: Allen & Unwin, 1987.

———. "Latitudinarianism and Toleration: Myth Versus Political History." In *Philosophy, Science, and Religion in England, 1640–1700,* edited by Richard Kroll, Richard Ashcraft, and Perez Zarogin, 149–175. Cambridge: Cambridge University Press, 1992.

Ayers, Michael. *Locke: Epistemology and Ontology.* London: Routledge, 1991.

———. "Locke's Logical Atomism." In *Rationalism, Empiricism and Idealism: British Academy Lectures on the History of Philosophy,* edited by Anthony Kenny, 6–22. Oxford: Clarendon Press, 1986.

Backscheider, Paula. *Daniel Defoe: His Life.* Baltimore: Johns Hopkins University Press, 1989.

Bakhtin, Mikhail. *The Dialogic Imagination.* Translated by Caryl Emerson and Michael Holquist. Austin: University of Texas Press, 1981.

Baker, Herschel. *The Wars of Truth: Studies in the Decay of Christian Humanism in the Earlier Seventeenth Century.* Cambridge, Mass.: Harvard University Press, 1952.

Baker, J. N. L. "Nathanael Carpenter and English Geography in the Seventeenth Century." *Geographical Journal* 71:3 (1928): 261–271.

BBC News. "Lord Desai's Response to the Tory MP John Townend's Remarks." Accessed January 16, 2011. http://news.bbc.co.uk/2/hi/uk_news/politics/1304770.stm.

Bhabha, Homi. *The Location of Culture.* London: Routledge, 2004.

Bouwsma, William. *John Calvin: A Sixteenth-Century Portrait.* New York: Oxford University Press, 1988.

———. *The Waning of the Renaissance, 1550–1640.* New Haven, Conn.: Yale University Press, 2000.

Bronner, Stephen Eric. *Reclaiming the Enlightenment: Towards a Politics of Radical Engagement.* New York: Columbia University Press, 2004.

Buckle, Steven. *Natural Law and the Theory of Property: Grotius to Hume*. Oxford: Clarendon Press, 1991.

Burke, Peter. *Languages and Communities in Early Modern Europe*. Cambridge: Cambridge University Press, 2004.

Carey, Daniel. *Locke, Shaftesbury, and Hutcheson: Contesting Diversity in the Enlightenment and Beyond*. Cambridge: Cambridge University Press, 2006.

Carey, Daniel, and Lynn Festa, eds. *The Postcolonial Enlightenment: Eighteenth-Century Colonialism and Postcolonial Theory*. Oxford: Oxford University Press, 2009.

Chakrabarty, Dipesh. *Provincializing Europe: Postcolonial Thought and Historical Difference*. Princeton, N.J.: Princeton University Press, 2000.

Clancy, Thomas H. *Papist Pamphleteers: The Allen-Persons Party and the Political Thought of the Counter-Reformation in England, 1572–1615*. Chicago: Loyola University Press, 1964.

Clericuzio, Antonio. "From van Helmont to Boyle: A Study of the Transmission of Helmontian Chemical and Medical Theories in Seventeenth-Century England." *British Journal for the History of Science* 26 (1993): 303–334.

———. *Elements, Principles, and Corpuscles: A Study of Atomism and Chemistry in the Seventeenth Century*. Dordrecht: Kluwer Academic Publishers, 2000.

Colley, Linda. *Britons: Forging the Nation, 1707–1837*. Revised ed. New Haven, Conn.: Yale University Press, 2009.

Collinson, Patrick. *The Elizabethan Puritan Movement*. Berkeley: University of California Press, 1967.

Cranston, Maurice. *John Locke: A Biography*. London: Longmans, 1966.

Daniel, Stephen H. *John Toland: His Methods, Manners, and Mind*. Kingston and Montreal: McGill-Queens University Press, 1984.

Daston, Lorraine, and Katherine Park. "Unnatural Conceptions: The Study of Monsters in Sixteenth- and Seventeenth-Century France and England." *Past and Present* 92 (1981): 20–54.

———. *Wonders and the Order of Nature, 1150–1750*. New York: Zone Books, 1998.

Davidson, Arnold. "The Horror of Monsters." In *The Boundaries of Humanity: Animals, Humans, Machines*, edited by James Sheehan and Morton Sosna, 36–67. Berkeley: University of California Press, 1991.

Debus, Allen. *The Chemical Philosophy: Paracelsian Science and Medicine in the Sixteenth and Seventeenth Centuries*. 2 vols. New York: Science History Publications, 1977.

———. *The English Paracelsians*. New York: Watts, 1966.

Deutsch, Helen, and Felicity Nussbaum, eds. *Defects: Engendering the Modern Body*. Ann Arbor: University of Michigan Press, 2000.

Dewhurst, Kenneth. *John Locke: Physician and Philosopher*. London: The Wellcome Historical Medical Library, 1963.

Dijksterhuis, E. J. *The Mechanization of the World Picture*. Oxford: Clarendon Press, 1961.

Doody, Margaret Ann. *The Daring Muse: Augustan Poetry Reconsidered.* Cambridge: Cambridge University Press, 1985.

Dobbs, Betty Jo. "Studies in the Natural Philosophy of Sir Kenelm Digby." *Ambix* 18:1 (1971): 1–25.

Dunn, John. *The Political Thought of John Locke: An Historical Account of the Two Treatises of Government.* Cambridge: Cambridge University Press, 1969.

Eccleshall, Robert. *Order and Reason in Politics: Theories of Absolute and Limited Monarchy in Early Modern England.* Oxford: Oxford University Press, 1978.

Emerton, Norma. *The Scientific Reinterpretation of Form.* Ithaca, N.Y.: Cornell University Press, 1984.

Fairer, David. "'Where Fuming Trees Refresh the Thirsty Air': The World of Eco-Georgic." *Studies in Eighteenth-Century Culture* 40 (2011): 201–218.

Felski, Rita. *Uses of Literature.* Oxford: Blackwell, 2008.

Fincham, Kenneth, and Peter Lake. "The Ecclesiastical Policies of James I and Charles I." In *The Early Stuart Church, 1603–1642,* edited by Kenneth Fincham, 23–50. Stanford, Calif.: Stanford University Press, 1993.

Fink, Zera. *The Classical Republicans: An Essay in the Recovery of a Pattern of Thought in Seventeenth-Century England.* 2nd ed. Evanston, Ill.: Northwestern University Press, 1962.

Finnis, John. *Aquinas: Moral, Political, and Legal Theory.* Oxford: Oxford University Press, 1998.

Flew, Antony. "Locke and the Problem of Personal Identity." *Philosophy* 26 (1951): 53–68.

Foucault, Michel. *The History of Sexuality.* Vol. 1. Translated by Robert Hurley. New York: Vintage Books, 1990.

———. *Discipline and Punish: The Birth of the Prison.* Translated by Alan Sheridan. New York: Vintage Books, 1995.

Foxon, David. "Defoe: A Specimen of a Catalogue of English Verse, 1701–1750." *The Library,* 5th series, 20:4 (1965): 277–297.

Franklin, Julian. *John Locke and the Theory of Sovereignty: Mixed Monarchy and the Right of Resistance in the Political Thought of the English Revolution.* Cambridge: Cambridge University Press, 1978.

———. "Sovereignty and the Mixed Constitution: Bodin and His Critics." In *The Cambridge History of Political Thought, 1450–1700,* edited by J. H. Burns, 298–328. Cambridge: Cambridge University Press, 1991.

Gadamer, Hans-Georg. *Truth and Method.* 2nd ed. Translation revised by Joel Weinsheimer and Donald G. Marshall. New York: Crossroad, 1989.

Gasking, Elizabeth. *Investigations into Generation, 1651–1828* (Baltimore: Johns Hopkins University Press, 1967).

Giddens, Anthony. *The Consequences of Modernity.* Stanford, Calif.: Stanford University Press, 1992.

Gilbert, Scott F. "The Genome in Its Ecological Context: Philosophical Perspectives on Interspecies Epigenesis." *Annals of the New York Academy of Sciences* 981 (2002): 202–218.

Goodin, Susanna. "Locke and Leibniz and the Debate over Species." In *New Essays on the Rationalists,* edited by Rocco Gennaro and Charles Huenemann, 163–178. New York: Oxford University Press, 1999.

Gordon, Scott. *Controlling the State: Constitutionalism from Ancient Athens to Today.* Cambridge, Mass.: Harvard University Press, 1999.

Grant, Ruth. *John Locke's Liberalism.* Chicago: University of Chicago Press, 1987.

Greenblatt, Stephen. *Cultural Mobility: A Manifesto.* Cambridge: Cambridge University Press, 2010.

Greenleaf, W. H. *Order, Empiricism, and Politics: Two Traditions of Political Thought, 1500–1700.* London: Oxford University Press, 1964.

Gwyn, W. B. *The Meaning of the Separation of Powers: An Analysis of the Doctrine from Its Origin to the Adoption of the United States Constitution.* New Orleans: Tulane University Press, 1965.

Hagner, Michael. "Enlightened Monsters." In *The Sciences in Enlightened Europe,* edited by William Clark, Jan Golinski, and Simon Schaffer, 175–217. Chicago: University of Chicago Press, 1999.

Hale, Matthew. *The History of the Common Law of England.* 1713; reprint, Chicago: University of Chicago Press, 1971.

Hall, Marie Boas. "Boyle's Method of Work: Promoting His Corpuscular Philosophy." *Notes and Records of the Royal Society of London* 41:2 (1987): 111–143.

Hanafi, Zakiya. *The Monster in the Machine: Magic, Medicine, and the Marvelous in the Time of the Scientific Revolution.* Durham, N.C.: Duke University Press, 2000.

Haraway, Donna. *Simians, Cyborgs, and Women: The Reinvention of Nature.* New York: Routledge, 1991.

Harris, Jonathan Gil. *Foreign Bodies and the Body Politic: Discourses of Social Pathology in Early Modern England.* Cambridge: Cambridge University Press, 1998.

Harris, Victor. *All Coherence Gone.* Chicago: University of Chicago Press, 1949.

Henry, John. "Occult Qualities and the Experimental Philosophy: Active Principles in Pre-Newtonian Matter Theory." *History of Science* 24:4 (1986): 335–381.

———. *The Scientific Revolution and the Origins of Modern Science.* 2nd ed. Basingstoke: Palgrave, 2002.

Hicks, Philip. *Neoclassical Literature and English Culture.* Houndmills, Basingstoke: Macmillan, 1996.

Hill, Christopher. *Change and Continuity in Seventeenth-Century England.* Cambridge: Cambridge University Press, 1975.

———. *Puritanism and Revolution: Studies in Interpretation of the English Revolution in the Seventeenth Century.* 1958; reprint, New York: St. Martin's Press, 1997.

———. *Intellectual Origins of the English Revolution Revisited.* Oxford: Clarendon Press, 1997.

Hoerder, Dirk, Christiane Harzig, and Adrian Shubert, eds. *The Historical Practice of Diversity: Transcultural Interactions from the Early Modern Mediterranean to the Postcolonial World.* New York: Berghahn Books, 2003.

Hont, Istvan. "Free Trade and the Economic Limits to National Politics: Neo-Machiavellian Political Economy Reconsidered." In *The Economic Limits to Modern Politics*, edited by John Dunn, 41–120. Cambridge: Cambridge University Press, 1990.

Hunter, Michael. "Alchemy, Magic, and Moralism in the Thought of Robert Boyle." *British Journal for the History of Science* 23:4 (1990): 387–410.

———. *Robert Boyle, 1627–1691: Scrupulosity and Science*. Woodbridge: Boydell Press, 2000.

———. *Boyle: Between God and Science*. New Haven, Conn.: Yale University Press, 2009.

Israel, Jonathan, ed. *The Anglo-Dutch Moment: Essays on the Glorious Revolution and Its World Impact*. Cambridge: Cambridge University Press, 1991.

———. *Radical Enlightenment: Philosophy and the Making of Modernity, 1650–1750*. Oxford: Oxford University Press, 2001.

Jacob, James. *Robert Boyle and the English Revolution: A Study in Social and Intellectual Change*. New York: Burt Franklin, 1977.

———. *Henry Stubbe: Radical Protestantism and the Early Enlightenment*. Cambridge: Cambridge University Press, 1983.

Jacob, Margaret, and James Jacob. "The Anglican Origins of Modern Science: The Metaphysical Foundations of the Whig Constitution." *Isis* 71:2 (1980): 251–267.

Jones, Richard Foster. *Ancients and Moderns: A Study of the Rise of the Scientific Movement in Seventeenth-Century England*. 1936; reprint, St. Louis, Mo.: Washington University Press, 1963.

———. *Ancients and Moderns: A Study of the Background of the Battle of the Books*. St. Louis, Mo.: Washington University Studies, 1936.

———. *The Triumph of the English Language*. Stanford, Calif.: Stanford University Press, 1953.

Jordan, W. K. *Men of Substance: A Study of the Thought of Two English Revolutionaries, Henry Parker and Henry Robinson*. Chicago: University of Chicago Press, 1942.

Kaplan, Barbara Beigun. *Divulging of Useful Truths in Physick: The Medical Agenda of Robert Boyle*. Baltimore: Johns Hopkins University Press, 1993.

Kargan, Robert Hugh. *Atomism in England from Hariot to Newton*. Oxford: Clarendon Press, 1966.

Keller, Eve. *Generating Bodies and Gendered Selves: The Rhetoric of Reproduction in Early Modern England*. Seattle: University of Washington Press, 2007.

Kendall, R. T. *Calvin and English Calvinism to 1649*. Oxford: Oxford University Press, 1979.

Keynes, Geoffrey. *The Life of William Harvey*. Oxford: Clarendon Press, 1966.

Kidd, Colin. *British Identities Before Nationalism: Ethnicity and Nationhood in the Atlantic World, 1600–1800*. Cambridge: Cambridge University Press, 1999.

Kliger, Samuel. *The Goths in England: A Study in Seventeenth- and Eighteenth-Century Thought*. Cambridge, Mass.: Harvard University Press, 1952.

Kocher, Paul H. *Science and Religion in Elizabethan England*. San Marino, Calif.: The Huntington Library, 1953.

Kramer, Matthew. *John Locke and the Origins of Private Property*. Cambridge: Cambridge University Press, 1997.

Kramnick, Isaac. *Bolingbroke and His Circle: The Politics of Nostalgia in the Age of Walpole*. Ithaca, N.Y.: Cornell University Press, 1992.

Kroll, Richard. *The Material Word: Literate Culture in the Restoration and Early Eighteenth Century*. Baltimore: Johns Hopkins University Press, 1991.

Kuhn, Thomas. "Robert Boyle and Structural Chemistry." *Isis* 43:1 (1952): 12–36.

Latour, Bruno. *We Have Never Been Modern*. Translated by Catherine Porter. Cambridge, Mass.: Harvard University Press, 1995.

Longueville, Thomas. *The Life of Kenelm Digby*. London: Longmans, Green, and Co., 1896.

Low, Anthony. *The Georgic Revolution*. Princeton, N.J.: Princeton University Press, 1985.

McCann, Edwin. "Cartesian Selves and Lockean Substances." *The Monist* 69:3 (1986): 458–482.

MacDougall, Hugh A. *Racial Myth in English History: Trojans, Teutans, and Anglo-Saxons*. Hanover, N.H.: University Press of New England, 1982.

Mackie, J. L. *Problems from Locke*. Oxford: Clarendon Press, 1976.

Maier, Anneliese. *An der Grenze von Scholastik und Naturwissenschaft: Studien zur Naturphilosophie des 14. Jahrhunderts*. Essen: Essener Verlagsanstalt, 1943.

Markley, Robert. *Fallen Languages: Crises of Representation in Newtonian England, 1660–1740*. Ithaca, N.Y.: Cornell University Press, 1993.

Marshall, John. *John Locke: Resistance, Religion, and Responsibility*. Cambridge: Cambridge University Press, 1994.

McCormick, Ted. "Alchemy in the Political Arithmetic of Sir William Petty." *Studies in the History of Philosophy of Science* 37 (2006): 290–307.

McGuire, J. E. "Boyle's Conception of Nature." *Journal of the History of Ideas* 33:4 (1972): 523–542.

McKeon, Michael. "Introduction." In *Theory of the Novel: A Historical Approach*, edited by Michael McKeon, xiii–xviii. Baltimore: Johns Hopkins University Press, 2000.

Mendle, Michael. *Dangerous Positions: Mixed Government, the Estates of the Realm, and the Answer to the XIX Propositions*. University: University of Alabama Press, 1985.

———. *Henry Parker and the Civil War: The Political Thought of the Public's Privado*. Cambridge: Cambridge University Press, 1995.

Merchant, Carolyn. *The Death of Nature: Women, Ecology, and the Scientific Revolution*. San Francisco, Calif.: Harper and Row, 1980.

Milton, Anthony. *Catholic and Reformed: The Roman and Protestant Churches in English Protestant Thought, 1660–1640*. Cambridge: Cambridge University Press, 1995.

Milton, J. R. "Locke, Medicine, and the Mechanical Philosophy." *British Journal for the History of Philosophy* 9:2 (2001): 221–243.

Morrill, John. "The Sensible Revolution." In *The Anglo-Dutch Moment: Essays on the Glorious Revolution and Its World Impact*, edited by Jonathan Israel, 73–104. Cambridge: Cambridge University Press, 1991.

Munasinghe, Viranjini. "Nationalism in Hybrid Spaces: The Production of Impurity Out of Purity." *American Ethnologist* 29:3 (2002): 663–692.

Muthu, Sankar. *Enlightenment Against Empire.* Princeton, N.J.: Princeton University Press, 2003.

Needham, Joseph. *A History of Embryology.* Cambridge: Cambridge University Press, 1934.

Negri, Antonio. *The Savage Anomaly: The Power of Spinoza's Metaphysics and Politics.* Translated by Michael Hardt. Minneapolis: University of Minnesota Press, 1991.

Negri, Antonio, and Michael Hardt. *Empire.* Cambridge, Mass.: Harvard University Press, 2000.

Newman, William. *Atoms and Alchemy: Chymistry and the Experimental Origins of the Scientific Revolution.* Chicago: University of Chicago Press, 2006.

Nozick, Robert. *Anarchy, State, and Utopia.* New York: Basic Books, 1974.

Nussbaum, Felicity. *The Limits of the Human: Fictions of Anomaly, Race, and Gender in the Long Eighteenth Century.* Cambridge: Cambridge University Press, 2003.

Oakeley, Francis. "The Absolute and Ordained Power of God in Sixteenth- and Seventeenth-Century Theology." *Journal of the History of Ideas* 59:3 (1998): 437–461.

Okie, Laird. *Augustan Historical Writing: Histories of England in the English Enlightenment.* Lanham, Md.: University Press of America, 1991.

Olivecrona, Karl. "Locke's Theory of Appropriation." *Philosophical Quarterly* 24 (1974): 220–234.

Oster, Malcolm. "Virtue, Providence, and Political Neutralism: Boyle and Interregnum Politics." In *Robert Boyle Reconsidered,* edited by Michael Hunter, 19–36. Cambridge: Cambridge University Press, 1994.

Parfit, Derek. "Personal Identity." *Philosophical Review* 80 (1971): 3–27.

Pateman, Carol. *The Sexual Contract.* Stanford, Calif.: Stanford University Press, 1988.

Pegis, Anton C. "Molina and Human Liberty." In *Jesuit Thinkers of the Renaissance,* edited by Gerard Smith, 75–132. Milwaukee, Wisc.: Marquette University Press, 1939.

Peterson, R. T. *Sir Kenelm Digby: The Ornament of England, 1603–1665.* London: Jonathan Cape, 1965.

Pinto-Correia, Clara. *The Ovary of Eve: Egg and Sperm and Preformation.* Chicago: University of Chicago Press, 1997.

Pitts, Jennifer. *A Turn to Empire: The Rise of Imperial Liberalism in Britain and France.* Princeton, N.J.: Princeton University Press, 2005.

Pocock, J. G. A. *The Ancient Constitution and the Feudal Law.* 1957; reprint, Cambridge: Cambridge University Press, 1987.

Preston, Claire. *Thomas Browne and the Writing of Early Modern Science.* Cambridge: Cambridge University Press, 2005.

Principe, Lawrence M. "Newly Discovered Boyle Documents in the Royal Society Archive." *Notes and Records of the Royal Society of London* 49:1 (1995): 57–70.

Reinhartz, Dennis. *The Cartographer and the Literati: Herman Moll and His Intellectual Circle*. Lewiston, N.Y.: Edwin Mellen Press, 1997.

Resnick, David. "John Locke and the Problem of Naturalization." *Review of Politics* 49:3 (1987): 368–388.

Robbins, Caroline. *The Eighteenth-Century Commonwealthman*. Cambridge, Mass.: Harvard University Press, 1959.

Roberts, Marthe. *Origins of the Novel*. Translated by Sacha Rabinovitch. London: Harvester, 1980.

Rogers, John. *The Matter of Revolution: Science, Poetry, and Politics in the Age of Milton*. Ithaca, N.Y.: Cornell University Press, 1996.

Romanell, Patrick. *John Locke and Medicine: A New Key to Locke*. Buffalo: Prometheus Books, 1984.

Sarasohn, Lisa. *Gassendi's Ethics: Freedom in a Mechanistic Universe*. Ithaca, N.Y.: Cornell University Press, 1996.

Sargent, Rose-Mary. *The Diffident Naturalist: Robert Boyle and the Philosophy of Experiment*. Chicago: University of Chicago Press, 1995.

Schmidgen, Wolfram. *Eighteenth-Century Fiction and the Law of Property*. Cambridge: Cambridge University Press, 2002.

———. "Illegitimacy and Social Observation: The Bastard in the Eighteenth-Century Novel." *ELH* 69 (2002): 133–166.

———. "The Last Royal Bastard and the Multitude." *Journal of British Studies* 47:1 (2008): 53–76.

Schneider, Ulrich Johannes. "Über das Stottern in Gedanken: Gegen die Begriffsgeschichte." *Archiv für Begriffsgeschichte* 7 (2010): 125–132.

Schochet, Gordon J. "From Persecution to 'Toleration.'" In *Liberty Secured? Britain Before and After 1688*, edited by J. R. Jones, 122–157. Stanford, Calif.: Stanford University Press, 1992.

———. *Patriarchalism in Political Thought*. New York: Basic Books, 1975.

Seed, Patricia. *Ceremonies of Possession in Europe's Conquest of the New World*. Cambridge: Cambridge University Press, 1995.

Seidel, Michael. *Satiric Inheritance: Rabelais to Sterne*. Princeton, N.J.: Princeton University Press, 1979.

Seigel, Jerrold. *The Idea of the Self: Thought and Experience in Western Europe Since the Seventeenth Century*. Cambridge: Cambridge University Press, 2005.

Shanahan, Timothy. "God and Nature in the Thought of Robert Boyle." *Journal of the History of Philosophy* 26 (1988): 547–569.

Shapin, Steven, and Simon Schaffer. *Leviathan and the Air Pump: Hobbes, Boyle, and the Experimental Life*. Princeton, N.J.: Princeton University Press, 1985.

Shapiro, Alan. *Fits, Passions, and Paroxysms: Physics, Method, and Chemistry and Newton's Theories of Colored Bodies and Fits of Easy Reflection*. Cambridge: Cambridge University Press, 1993.

———. "The Evolving Structure of Newton's Theory of White Light and Color." *Isis* 71:2 (1980): 211–235.

Shapiro, Barbara. *Probability and Certainty in Seventeenth-Century England*. Princeton, N.J.: Princeton University Press, 1983.

Sheehan, James, and Morton Sosna, eds. *The Boundaries of Humanity: Humans, Animals, Machines*. Berkeley: University of California Press, 1991.

Simmons, A. John. *The Lockean Theory of Rights*. Princeton, N.J.: Princeton University Press, 1992.

Siskin, Clifford. *The Work of Writing: Literature and Social Change in Britain, 1700–1830*. Baltimore: Johns Hopkins University Press, 1998.

Siskin, Clifford, and William Warner, eds. *This Is Enlightenment*. Chicago: University of Chicago Press, 2010.

Skinner, Quentin. "History and Ideology in the English Revolution." *Historical Journal* 8:2 (1965): 151–178.

———. *The Foundations of Modern Political Thought*. 2 vols. Cambridge: Cambridge University Press, 1978.

———. *Hobbes and Republican Liberty*. Cambridge: Cambridge University Press, 2008.

Smith, R. J. *The Gothic Bequest: Medieval Institutions in British Thought, 1688–1863*. Cambridge: Cambridge University Press, 1987.

Sommerville, J. P. *Politics and Ideology in England, 1603–1640*. London: Longman, 1986.

Southgate, Beverley C. *Covetous of Truth: The Life and Work of Thomas White, 1593–1676*. Dordrecht: Kluwer, 1993.

Sreenivasan, Gopal. *The Limits of Lockean Rights in Property*. New York: Oxford University Press, 1995.

Stamos, David. *The Species Problem: Biological Species, Ontology, and the Metaphysics of Biology*. Lanham, Md.: Lexington Books, 2003.

Starnes, De Witt T., and Gertrude E. Noyes. *The English Dictionary from Cawdrey to Johnson*. Chapel Hill: University of North Carolina Press, 1946.

Statt, Daniel. "Daniel Defoe and Immigration." *Eighteenth-Century Studies* 24:3 (1991): 293–313.

———. *Foreigners and Englishmen: The Controversy over Immigration and Population, 1660–1760*. Newark: University of Delaware Press, 1995.

Stewart, M. A. "Locke's Mental Atomism and the Classification of Ideas." Part 1. *Locke Newsletter* (1979): 53–82.

———. "Locke's Mental Atomism and the Classification of Ideas." Part 2. *Locke Newsletter* (1980): 25–62.

Taylor, Charles. "Atomism." In *Powers, Possessions and Freedom*, edited by Alkis Kontos, 39–62. Toronto: University of Toronto Press, 1979.

———. *Sources of the Self: The Making of the Modern Identity*. Cambridge, Mass.: Harvard University Press, 1989.

Todd, Dennis. *Imagining Monsters: Miscreations of the Self in Eighteenth-Century England*. Chicago: University of Chicago Press, 1995.

Trevor-Roper, Hugh. *Catholics, Anglicans, and Puritans: Seventeenth-Century Essays*. Chicago: University of Chicago Press, 1988.

Tuck, Richard. *Philosophy and Government, 1572–1671*. Cambridge: Cambridge University Press, 1993.

Tully, James. *A Discourse on Property: John Locke and His Adversaries*. Cambridge: Cambridge University Press, 1980.

Turner, Victor. *The Ritual Process: Structure and Anti-Structure*. New York: de Gruyter, 1995.

Tutino, Stefania. *Thomas White and the Blackloists: Between Politics and Theology During the English Civil War*. Aldershot: Ashgate, 2008.

Tyacke, Nicholas. *Anti-Calvinists: The Rise of English Arminianism, c. 1590–1640*. Oxford: Clarendon Press, 1987.

Speybroeck, Linda van, Dani De Waele, and Gertrudis van de Vijver. "Theories in Early Embryology: Close Connections Between Epigenesis, Preformationism, and Self-Organization." *Annals of the New York Academy of Sciences* 981 (2002): 7–49.

Vickers, Brian, ed. *Occult and Scientific Mentalities in the Renaissance*. Cambridge: Cambridge University Press, 1984.

Vile, M. J. C. *Constitutionalism and the Separation of Powers*. Oxford: Clarendon Press, 1967.

Wahrman, Dror. *The Making of the Modern Self: Identity and Culture in Eighteenth-Century England*. New Haven, Conn.: Yale University Press, 2004.

Waldron, Jeremy. *The Right to Private Property*. Oxford: Clarendon Press, 1988.

———. *God, Locke, and Equality: Christian Foundations in Locke's Political Thought*. Cambridge: Cambridge University Press, 2002.

Walmsley, Jonathan. "Morbus—Locke's Early Essay on Disease." *Early Science and Medicine* 5:4 (2000): 366–393.

Wear, Andrew. *Knowledge and Practice in English Medicine, 1550–1680*. Cambridge: Cambridge University Press, 2000.

Webster, Charles. "Harvey's *De Generatione*: Its Origins and Relevance to the Theory of Circulation." *British Journal for the History of Science* 3:3 (1967): 262–274.

———. *The Great Instauration: Science, Medicine, and Reform, 1626–1660*. New York: Holmes and Meier, 1976.

———. *From Paracelsus to Newton: Magic and the Making of Modern Science*. Cambridge: Cambridge University Press, 1982.

Weinbrot, Howard. *Britannia's Issue: The Rise of British Literature from Dryden to Ossian*. Cambridge: Cambridge University Press, 1993.

Werbner, Pnina. "Introduction: The Dialectics of Cultural Hybridity." In *Debating Cultural Hybridity: Multi-Cultural Identities and the Politics of Anti-Racism*, edited by Pnina Werbner and Tariq Modood, 1–4. London: Zed Books, 2000.

Westfall, Richard. "The Development of Newton's Theory of Color." *Isis* 53:3 (1962): 339–358.

———. "The Foundations of Newton's Philosophy of Nature." *British Journal for the History of Science* 1:2 (1962): 171–182.

Weston, Corinne Comstock. *English Constitutional Theory and the House of Lords, 1556–1832.* London: Routledge, 1962.

Weston, Corinne Comstock, and Janelle Renfrow Greenberg. *Subjects and Sovereigns: The Grand Controversy over Legal Sovereignty in Stuart England.* Cambridge: Cambridge University Press, 1981.

Wheeler, Roxann. *The Complexion of Race: Categories of Difference in Eighteenth-Century Culture.* Philadelphia: University of Pennsylvania Press, 2000.

Wilding, Michael. *Dragon's Teeth: Literature in the English Revolution.* Oxford: Clarendon Press, 1987.

Willer, Stefan. "Metapher und Begriffsstutzigkeit." In *Begriffsgeschichte im Umbruch?* edited by Ernst Müller, 69–80. Hamburg: Felix Meiner Verlag, 2005.

Wilson, Kathleen. *The Island Race: Englishness, Empire, and Gender in the Eighteenth Century.* London: Routledge, 2003.

———, ed. *A New Imperial History: Culture, Identity, and Modernity in Britain and the Empire, 1660–1840.* Cambridge: Cambridge University Press, 2005.

Wilson, Mary Floyd. *English Ethnicity and Race in Early Modern Drama.* Cambridge: Cambridge University Press, 2003.

Wojcik, Jan W. "The Theological Context of Boyle's *Things Above Reason.*" In *Robert Boyle Reconsidered,* edited by Michael Hunter, 139–156. Cambridge: Cambridge University Press, 1994.

———. *Robert Boyle and the Limits of Reason.* Cambridge: Cambridge University Press, 1997.

Wood, Neal. *The Politics of Locke's Philosophy: A Social Study of "An Essay Concerning Human Understanding."* Berkeley: University of California Press, 1983.

Woolhouse, Roger. *Locke: A Biography.* Cambridge: Cambridge University Press, 2007.

Wooton, David. *Paolo Sarpi: Between Renaissance and Enlightenment.* Cambridge: Cambridge University Press, 1983.

Worden, Blair. "Classical Republicanism and the Puritan Revolution." In *History and Imagination,* edited by Hugh Lloyd-Jones, Valerie Pearl, and Blair Worden, 182–200. New York: Homes and Meier, 1981.

———. "Providence and Politics in Cromwellian England." *Past and Present* 109 (1985): 55–99.

———. "The Revolution of 1688–9 and the English Republican Tradition." In *The Anglo-Dutch Moment,* edited by Jonathan Israel, 241–280. Cambridge: Cambridge University Press, 1991.

INDEX

ACKNOWLEDGMENTS

Every book is a little utopia, a dream of animating the indifference of the material, a hope of turning the buried toward life. Without such dreams and hopes, this book would not have been written. Without the following friends, these dreams and hopes would not have survived: Saher Alam, Miriam Bailin, Scott Black, Ben Bönniger, Lara Bovilsky, David Brewer, Dillon Brown, Marshall Brown, Jim Chandler, Patricia DeMarco, Nancy Durbin, Matt Erlin, David Fairer, Wayne Fields, Christa Fischbach, Stephen Gregg, Tracy Hargreaves, Rob Henke, Vivien Jones, Melanie Kleinert, Marshall Klimasewiski, Ethan Knapp, Tom Krise, Jonathan Lamb, Joe Loewenstein, Deidre Lynch, Ruth Mack, Audrey Petty, Jessica Rosenfeld, Henning Schmidgen, Ebba Segerberg, Vince Sherry, Rob Swearingen, Lynne Tatlock, Helen Thompson, John Whale.

At a crucial period in the gestation of this book, the National Endowment for the Humanities provided a fellowship that allowed me to go on leave and study the early modern science of mixture. The Folger Shakespeare Library in Washington, D.C., awarded the fellowship in 2007 and provided a warm welcome, a wonderful work environment, and precious resources. The group of scholars that came together that year—Katherine Eggert, Hannibal Hamlin, Linda Peck, and Julia Rudolph—was unusually sociable and supportive. I look back fondly to our many conversations and longingly to the greatest privilege: the feeling of shared and unbridled intellectual adventure.

Closer to home, I would like to acknowledge the remarkable intellectual community at Washington University in St. Louis. It is no longer a secret that the degree of intellectual exchange across various departmental and institutional lines on our campus is extraordinary. I would like to thank, in particular, the members of the Eighteenth-Century Salon, the Early Modern Reading Group, and the Political Theory Workshop for providing crucial feedback on my work in progress. All of these groups include faculty and graduate students, and it is the contribution of the latter that I wish to salute: Matt Augustine, Joe Conway, Anna Deters, Nick Miller, Katie Parker, and Courtney Weiss Smith have been wonderful intellectual co-conspirators, in formal and less formal settings, at Blueberry Hill and elsewhere.

More far-flung audiences deserve thanks as well—in particular, the members of the Mellon Seminar at Vanderbilt University that Jonathan Lamb invited me to join in 2006 and 2007, the members of our Shandy-inspired, self-organized, and National Humanities Center–sponsored Eighteenth-Century Summer Institute in Chicago in 2007, those who attended the *Juxtapositions* lecture I gave at Buffalo in 2007, and those who responded to my work at the UCLA Center for Seventeenth- and Eighteenth-Century Studies conference "Letters Before the Law" in 2008. Shortly before completing final revisions to the manuscript, I received valuable advice from the Eighteenth-Century Seminar at the Newberry Library.

Special thanks for acts of personal and intellectual friendship go to David Fairer, whose durable enthusiasm for this project gave energy and confidence when they were flagging; Matt Erlin, who devoted his discerning eye to the entire manuscript and his attentive ear to many honest conversations; and Joe Loewenstein, who always inspires and who has freely given many intellectual and linguistic gifts. I am very grateful to Bruno Latour and Michael Hardt, who read chapters and offered encouraging comments. Two anonymous readers for the press helped me improve my argument, and while others were unsure what my book was about (including, during some intervals, myself), Jerry Singerman offered enthusiastic support and wise guidance from the moment he saw the proposal.

An earlier version of parts of Chapter 4 was published in *The Eighteenth Century: Theory and Interpretation*. I would like to thank the editor for the permission to include these parts here.

I owe less conventional thanks to Spoon and Britt Daniel. During the demanding academic year of 2009–2010, their explorations of detail and impact gave vivid pleasure. Finer feelings, indeed.